S0-EAH-559

Beijing Old and New

A Historical Guide to Places of Interest

by ZHOU SHACHEN

With Descriptions of Famous Sites Within
One Day's Journey of Beijing

NEW WORLD PRESS
Beijing, China

First Edition   1984
Second Printing   1987

ISBN 7-80005-040-8

Published by
NEW WORLD PRESS
24, Baiwanzhuang Road, Beijing, China

Distributed by
CHINA INTERNATIONAL BOOK TRADING CORPORATION
(GUOJI SHUDIAN)
P.O. BOx 399, Beijing, China

Printed in the People's Republic of China

Contents

A General Survey of Beijing

Beijing is one of the world's oldest and best known capital cities. Five hundred years ago, few cities on earth could rival it in terms of size and detailed planning. The rectangular web of streets which surrounds the Imperial Palace in the center of the city and the extensive transportation network which connects Beijing with the outlying provinces offer first-hand evidence of early high-level scientific city planning. Since its beginnings as a settlement in China's northern plains, Beijing has evolved through a complex series of stages to become the nation's political center. Beijing is a city with deep-rooted cultural traditions and a history of revolutionary struggle. Today it is leading China on the road to becoming a powerful modern socialist country.

The Edge of the North China Plain

The site of the city of Beijing has undergone several changes in the past several thousand years, but the spatial dimensions of the city itself have not varied to any great extent. The precise location of the present center of the city is 39°56′N, 116°20′E at an elevation of 44.38 meters above sea level. The northwestern section of the city rises gradually to no more than ten meters above the southeastern section.

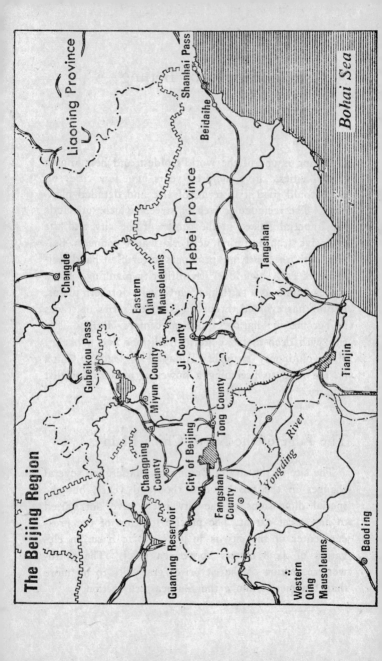

The Beijing Region

Liaoning Province

Hebei Province

Bohai Sea

Shanhai Pass

Beidaihe

Tangshan

Chengde

Eastern Qing Mausoleums

Gubeikou Pass

Miyun County

Ji County

Tong County

Tianjin

Changping County

City of Beijing

Guanting Reservoir

Yongding River

Fangshan County

Western Qing Mausoleums

Baoding

In its earliest days, the old city stood on the slight ridge of land gradually formed by alluvial deposits. In prehistoric times, the Yongding River in the west and the Chaobai River in the east flowed south through the mountains carrying large amounts of sand down-river to form a vast silted base, which became the edge of the North China Plain.

The extensive Yanshan Mountain range forms a sylvan screen to the northeast of the city. Not far to the northwest, the vast Mongolian plateau begins. The Gulf of Bohai lies 113 kilometers to the east. To the west is the long winding Taihang Mountain range, and to the south the vast North China Plain. The small gulf-shaped plain which surrounds Beijing has led geologists to call this area the "Beijing Gulf." In fact, Beijing is not the center of the "Beijing Gulf" but rather in its southwestern corner. Early writers described the city setting with the sea on one side and the mountains in the background as a "heavenly paradise" or a "city of the gods."

Beijing has a continental monsoon climate commonly found in the temperate zone. In winter, it is influenced by air currents coming out of Siberia and Mongolia in the northwest, while in summer it is dominated by warm, moist air currents from the southeast. A general change of wind direction takes place in March or April and again in September. Wind velocity in Beijing is comparatively low, averaging 2 m/s. The average annual rainfall of 630 millimeters may be regarded as a generous "heavenly endowment" for North China, which is otherwise predominantly dry and short of rain.

Beijing's average annual temperature is 11.8°C. The coldest month in the year is January, with an average of —4.7°C. The hottest month is July, when the temperature averages 26.1°C. Rapid temperature rises in the spring are sometimes accompanied by sandstorms. On windless days though, springtime in Beijing is wonderfully pleasant. Autumn, with its clear skies, is the briefest but finest season of all.

In geographical terms, the selection of the site of ancient Beijing was not fortuitous. The mountains surrounding Beijing in the north, east and west acted as boundaries with the outlying grazing lands. The people living in the Beijing basin maintained economic links with the nomadic tribes beyond the passes of Gubeikou in the north and Nankou in the west, and closer and more frequent commercial contacts with the people of the central plain region along the course of the Yellow River. The pivotal role played by Beijing in the trade among these different regions stimulated the rise of the ancient city of Ji.

A Long History of Civilization

The Beijing region was the home of the forebears of the Chinese nation. Some half a million years ago, Peking Man lived in Zhoukoudian (Chou-kou-tien) in the southwestern suburbs of Beijing. In that period, the climate of Beijing was warmer and more humid than it is today, and the many forests and lakes supported large numbers of living creatures. The fossil remains of Peking Man, his stone tools and the evidence of his use of fire, as well as the more modern

(16000 B.C.) tools, bone needles and articles of adornment belonging to Upper Cave Man are some of China's earliest cultural relics, and a permanent part of the cultural legacy of the world.

Some four to five thousand years ago, primitive agriculture and grazing was practiced to the southwest of Beijing. It is said that the legendary Yellow Emperor (Huang Di) fought battles against the tribal leader Chiyou in the "wilderness of the prefecture of Zhuo." Zhuolu, a town to the west of present-day Beijing, is perhaps the site of the earliest metropolis in the region. The legendary capital established by Huang Di's successor, Emperor Yao, was called Youdu (City of Quietude) and was the site of the historical city of Ji.

During the Warring States period, the Marquis of Yan annexed the territory of the Marquis of Ji and made the city of Ji the administrative center of the State of Yan. The site of this city lies to the north of Guang'anmen Gate in present-day Beijing near the White Cloud Temple (Baiyunguan).

In the early third century B.C., after the First Emperor of Qin (Qin Shi Huang) conquered six states and unified China, the city of Ji became the administrative center of the Guangyang Commandery, one of the 36 prefectures of the first centralized feudal empire in Chinese history. For ten centuries up through the end of the Tang dynasty, Ji remained a strategic trading and military center, and the object of frequent power struggles.

Two emperors — Emperor Yang of the Sui dynasty and Emperor Taizong of the Tang dynasty — left their traces here. When he was organizing military expeditions against Korea, Emperor Yang amassed his troops and supplies at Ji and made the city a supply center for the front. Emperor Taizong also stationed troops at Ji and carried out military training there. He is credited with building the Temple for Compassion for the Loyal (Minzhongsi) dedicated to the memory of the troops who died in battle. This temple was the precursor of the Temple of the Origin of the Dharma (Fayuansi) located outside the old walls of the city.

At the beginning of the Tang dynasty, Ji was little different from any other large feudal city. Several centuries later, however, when the Tang was nearing a state of collapse, the Qidans (Khitans) emerged from the upper reaches of the Liao River and moved south to occupy Ji and make it their second capital. They called the city Nanjing (Southern Capital) or Yanjing. Emperor Taizong of the Liao dynasty carried out reconstruction projects and built palaces which were used as strongholds from which the Qidans set out to conquer the central plains of China.

In the early 12th century, the Nüzhen (Jurchen) conquered the Liao and established the Jin dynasty. In 1153, Wan Yanliang transferred the Jin capital from Huiningfu in present-day Liaoning Province to Yanjing and renamed it Zhongdu (Central Capital) as a challenge to the Southern Song dynasty, which had its capital at Lin'an (present-day Hangzhou). Before the ascension of Wan Yanliang to the throne, the city of Yanjing had changed little from the Liao period.

The rebuilding of the new city began in 1151 with expansion to the east, west and south. Palaces were constructed on a scale similar to the Northern Song capital at Bianliang (modern Kaifeng), and many of the

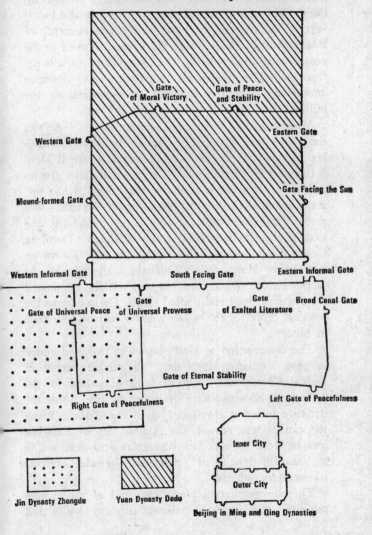

The Beijing City Limits in Successive Dynasties

Gate of Moral Victory

Gate of Peace and Stability

Western Gate

Eastern Gate

Mound-formed Gate

Gate Facing the Sun

Western Informal Gate

South Facing Gate

Eastern Informal Gate

Gate of Universal Peace

Gate of Universal Prowess

Gate of Exalted Literature

Broad Canal Gate

Gate of Eternal Stability

Right Gate of Peacefulness

Left Gate of Peacefulness

Jin Dynasty Zhongdu

Yuan Dynasty Dadu

Inner City

Outer City

Beijing in Ming and Qing Dynasties

actual building materials were transported from Bianliang. The new expanded city, with its splendid buildings in the style of the Song, had a circumference of
18 kilometers. The walls of the Imperial Palace in the
center measured roughly five kilometers in circumference. The registered population of Zhongdu
amounted to 225,592 households, or approximately one
million people.

Mongol armies occupied Zhongdu in 1215. At this
time, the city of Kaiping (in present-day Inner Mongolian Autonomous Region) served as the principal Mongol capital (Shangdu), while Yanjing was given provincial status. It was not until 1271 that Kublai Khan formally adopted the new dynasty's name — Yuan — and
made Yanjing the capital. Kublai rebuilt the city and
gave it the Chinese (Han) name of Dadu (Ta-tu) or
Great Capital, though in Mongol it was known as
Khanbalig (Marco Polo's Cambaluc), the City of the
Great Khan. When the Mongols finally eliminated
the Southern Song and unified China, Dadu became the
political center of the whole country for the first time
in history.

The construction of Dadu began in 1267 and ended
in 1293, extending throughout the entire period of
Kublai Khan's rule. The magnificent palaces of the
Jin capital Zhongdu were destroyed by fire during the
dynastic turnover from the Jin to the Yuan. When
the capital was rebuilt, the original site of Zhongdu
was replaced by a larger rectangular area centered in
a beautiful lake-filled region in the old capital's
northeastern suburbs.

The construction of Dadu consisted of three main
projects — the imperial palaces, the city walls and

moats, and the canal. The first stage was the construction of the palace buildings, the greater part of which were completed in 1274. The next stage was the construction of the mansions of the imperial princes, the offices of the government, the Taimiao (The Imperial Ancestral Temple) and Shejitan (The Altar of Land and Grain) to the east and west of the palace, and a system of streets to serve for ordinary residences. In 1293, the strategic Tonghui Canal, connecting the capital to the Grand Canal, was completed.

As the capital city of the Yuan dynasty, Dadu enjoyed great fame throughout the 13th century world. The envoys and traders from Europe, Asia and Africa who paid visits to China were astounded by the splendor and magnificence of Dadu. Marco Polo's description of the palaces of Cambaluc, as he called Khanbalig, is the most famous of all:

"You must know that it is the greatest palace that ever was. . . . The roof is very lofty, and the walls of the Palace are all covered with gold and silver. They are also adorned with representations of dragons, beasts and birds, knights and idols, and sundry other subjects. . . . The Hall of the Palace is so large that it could easily dine 6,000 people, and it is quite a marvel to see how many rooms there are besides. The building is altogether so vast, so rich and so beautiful, that no man on earth could design anything superior to it. The outside of the roof also is all colored with vermilion and yellow and green and blue and other hues, which are fixed with a varnish so fine and exquisite that they shine like crystal, and lend a resplendent luster to the Palace as seen for a great way around."

The new Dadu was a rectangular city more than 30 kilometers in circumference. In the later years of Kublai's rule, the city population consisted of 100 thousand households or roughly 500 thousand people. The city's layout was the result of uniform planning. The broader streets were 24 paces wide and the narrow ones measured half this width. The streets were laid out in a chessboard pattern which created an impression of relaxed orderliness. The designers interspersed imposing palaces with quiet gardens, and their achievements in stone and plaster sculpture and painting reached great heights. The names of two contemporary artisans have come down to us; the sculptors Yang Qiong and Liu Yuan. The latter was known for the plaster statues he created for temples. The Liulansu Lane at the northern end of Fuyou Street in present-day Beijing was named after Liu Yuan.

On August 2, 1368, Ming troops seized Dadu and renamed it Beiping (Northern Peace). Zhu Yuanzhang, the founding emperor of the Ming dynasty, however, made Nanjing his first capital. Beginning in 1406, the Ming Yongle emperor spent 15 years constructing walls some 12 meters high and 10 meters thick at their base around the city of Beiping. The construction of palace buildings and gardens began in 1417 and was completed in 1420. The following year, the Yongle emperor formally transferred the capital from Nanjing to Beiping and, for the first time, named the city Beijing (Northern Capital).

Extensive reconstruction work was carried out in Beijing during the first years of the Ming dynasty. The northern city walls were shifted some 2.5 kilometers to

the south. Evidence of great advances in the art of
city planning is the district known as the Inner (Tartar)
City. The Outer or Chinese City to the south was
built during the reign of the Jiajing emperor (1522-
1566), adding to the rectangular city a slightly wider
"base" at the south. (See chart on page 15.)

Following the founding of the Qing dynasty by the
Manchus in 1644, more attention was paid to the
building of suburban gardens, the most famous of
which were the Yuanmingyuan Gardens. Constructed
over the course of an entire century, the imposing
columned palaces and open-air pavilions blended with
the serenity of well-planned gardens to create a masterpiece of garden architecture unrivaled in the history
of China.

The plan of the old city of Beijing was first laid in
the Yuan dynasty. Yet only after undergoing extensive reconstruction during the subsequent Ming and
Qing dynasties did the city emerge as an architectural
masterpiece fit to serve as the capital of the Chinese
empire. Seen from above, a north-south axis bisects
the city with the Imperial Palace occupying a central
place. In Yuan times, this palace was known as
Danei (The Great Within). In the Ming, it was renamed the Forbidden City (Zijincheng) and more
recently it has come to be called the Palace Museum
(Gugong Bowuyuan). It too is designed with its
thousands of halls and gates arranged symmetrically
around a north-south axis. Its dimensions and luxuriance are a fitting symbol of the power and greatness
of traditional China.

After the collapse of the Qing dynasty in 1911, China fell prey to the depredation of the Northern War-

lords and Kuomintang reactionaries. Beijing suffered
the same fate as the rest of China, hobbling along like
an old camel without a sense of direction. The Chinese People's Liberation Army formally entered Beijing on January 31, 1949, beginning a new chapter in
the long history of the city. It was in Tian'anmen
Square in the heart of Beijing on October 1, 1949, that
Chairman Mao Zedong proclaimed the establishment
of the People's Republic of China, with Beijing as its
capital.

Scenes of Beauty

Beijing's recorded history began as early as 1000
B.C. The city has served as the capital of China for
more than 1,000 years. Numerous cultural antiquities
have come down to us due to the accumulated efforts
of generations of gifted artisans. Beijing's natural
surroundings provide a wonderful variety of scenic
spots. Thus the skills of man mingle with the beauties
of nature to give the city a panorama of scenes of interest almost beyond description. It is said that sightseeing in Beijing leaves one feeling stimulated and re-
freshed rather than tired out. Visitors feel an unwit-
ting reluctance to bid farewell to the city's famed
pavilions, towers, gardens and palaces.

The city is a museum of history. The palaces of the
Ming and Qing emperors present magnificent exterior
views and house countless artistic treasures. The rectangular Forbidden City is surrounded by high walls,
with tall towers situated above its gates. The four

corners of the Forbidden City walls are topped with skillfully designed watch-towers.

Whether walking on the streets or sightseeing within the palace, visitors are ineluctably attracted by the memorial pillars, pagodas, memorial archways (*pailou*), ancient temples, bronze and stone lions, stone sculptures and *bixi*, reptile-like creatures that resemble the tortoise.

Buildings bearing the characteristics of different historical periods are found everywhere. Jade Islet (Qiongdao) in Beihai Park is designed after the imaginary paradise of Penglai, a seaborne abode of the immortals. Scenes of beauty from southern China, such as the Forest of (Stone) Lions in Suzhou, can be found in the Summer Palace. Besides the monumental architecture of the Temple of Heaven and the fine old Lama Temple (Yonghegong), there is a host of other Buddhist and Daoist temples, mosques and churches.

Of all the great wonders in the Beijing area, the Great Wall ranks first. Winding for a thousand miles through the ridges and valleys of the mountains, it is said to be the only man-made object in the world that can be viewed from the moon. The magnificent battlements and beacon towers at Badaling are easily accessible from Beijing. In the words of a poet, "Mountain pass after mountain pass secrete in their folds the white clouds, while the ridges wind their way like a dark blue stream to the sky."

The Beijing area is noted for its landscapes. The famous Baihuashan and Lingshan mountains are seven to eight hundred meters higher than Mount Tai or Taishan, the most famous of China's Five Great Peaks. Mount Shangfangshan has been known since ancient

Famous Sites in the City of Beijing

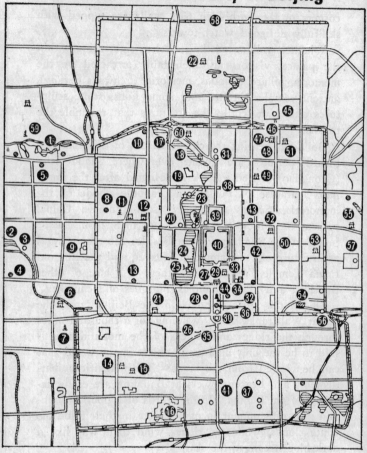

1. Beijing Zoo
2. Yuyuan Lake Park
3. Angler's Terrace
4. Military Museum of the Chinese People's Revolution
5. Beijing Planetarium
6. White Cloud Temple
7. Temple of Heavenly Peace
8. Lu Xun's Former Residence

times for its caves and stone engravings. There are also the roses of Mount Miaofengshan, the pine trees of Mount Cuiweishan and the beautiful hills and waters of the Summer Palace. For hundreds of years the names of the Three Front Lakes (Qiansanhai) — Nan-

9. Altar of the Moon
10. Xu Beihong Memorial Hall
11. Miaoying Monastery White Dagoba
12. Temple of Great Charity
13. Cultural Palace of the Nationalities
14. Ox Street Mosque
15. Temple of the Origin of the Dharma
16. Joyous Pavilion Park
17. Reservoir Lake
18. Shicha Lake
19. Prince Gong's Mansion
20. Beijing Library
21. Southern Cathedral
22. Yellow Temple
23. Beihai Park
24. Central Lake
25. South Lake
26. Antiques Street
27. Zhongshan Park
28. The Great Hall of the People
29. Gate of Heavenly Peace
30. South Facing Gate
31. Drum Tower and Bell Tower
32. Monument to the People's Heroes
33. Working People's Cultural Palace
34. Imperial Historical Archives
35. Dazhalan Street
36. Chairman Mao Zedong Memorial Hall
37. Temple of Heaven
38. Iron Lion Lane
39. Prospect Hill Park
40. Forbidden City
41. Beijing Museum of Natural History
42. Wangfujing Street
43. China Art Gallery
44. Museum of Chinese History and Museum of Chinese Revolution
45. Altar of Earth
46. Confucian Temple
47. Imperial College
48. Capital Library
49. Memorial to Prime Minister Wen
50. Lantern Market Street
51. Lamasary of Harmony and Peace
52. Dongsi Mosque
53. Temple of Wisdom Attained
54. Beijing Railway Station
55. Temple of the God of Mount Tai
56. Ancient Observatory
57. Altar of the Sun
58. Relics of Yuan Dynasty City Walls
59. Five Pagoda Temple
60. Soong Ching Ling's Former Residence

hai (South Lake), Zhonghai (Central Lake) and Beihai (North Lake) — were associated with their beautiful ripples. Witness the following lines: "An emerald green tower floats among the treetops; a miniature palace rises from the ripples in the lotus ponds."

In the gentle ripples of the Golden River (Jinshuihe) before Tian'anmen Gate and the moat surrounding the Forbidden City, the reflections of red walls and yellow tiles can be seen. The Three Rear Lakes (Housanhai) — the Shichahai, Houhai and Jishuitan — which stretch northwest from Beihai Park, are pleasant places to relax throughout the year. Jade Spring in Jade Spring Mountain (Yuquanshan) is widely known as the "first spring in China." Otherwise known as the Fishing Terrace (Diaoyutai), Yuyuantan is said to have been the favorite fishing spot of the hermit Wang Yu some 800 years ago. It served the recreational needs of the emperors of the Jin dynasty. In addition, we must list the Guanting, Miyun and Ming Tombs reservoirs, all built after the founding of the People's Republic, as places of great beauty.

The caves once occupied by Peking Man, the spacious tombs of thirteen Ming emperors and the "Eight Great Sights of Yanjing," famous since the Jin dynasty, enable us to trace the evolution of civilization within a short distance of Beijing.

But we should never forget that many of these monumental antiquities were created by the emperors of China to flaunt the "Mandate of Heaven," a claim that Heaven had conferred upon the emperors the right to absolute dictatorship. The supreme authority of the emperors and the sanctity of their persons were inviolable. What remains for our enjoyment today is an outstanding collection of works of art bearing the vestiges of their feudal origins.

Beijing in the Modern World

Since the founding of the People's Republic in 1949, great changes have taken place in Beijing. The city walls were demolished to facilitate transportation and to allow for general expansion. By 1982, the population of Beijing exceeded ten million and the total area of the municipality was increased to over 17,800 square kilometers. The number of administrative districts has also been augmented. At present, the city of Beijing is divided into ten districts: East City, West City, Chongwen, Xuanwu, Chaoyang, Fengtai, Haidian, Shijingshan, Mentougou and Yanshan. Beijing municipality is comprised of the following nine counties: Tongxian, Shunyi, Changping, Daxing, Fangshan, Pinggu, Huairou, Miyun and Yanqing, in addition to the urban districts listed above.

Beijing is now the political and cultural capital of China as well as a center of international activity and an important socialist industrial base. It is a city of friendship; its citizens extend their hospitality to state guests and casual visitors alike. It has joined the ranks of the great cities of the modern world.

The Beijing of the future is developing on the basis of the symmetrical layout of the old city with its clearly demarcated north-south axis. Yet the work of renovation and expansion is not confined by the restrictions of the past. The plan for Beijing's development combines the enduring qualities of the past with future needs to form an organic whole. The plan makes great leeway for future development and avoids the hazards of blind urban sprawl.

General principles have been laid down to effect coordination between the city and the countryside to facilitate the supply of vegetables and non-staple foods, and between industry and agriculture for protection of the environment. There is also a uniform plan to make maximum use of surface and underground space. In the near future, we shall witness the emergence of a modern capital for socialist China which both retains its past dignity and incorporates the techniques of modern urban construction.

The overall city plan covers an area of 1,000 square kilometers, from Dingfuzhuang in the east to Shijing-shan in the west and from Qinghe in the north to Nan-yuan in the south. The area of the city proper measures 300 square kilometers, of which the main urban district occupies 220 square kilometers. A traf-fic network consisting of four beltways and 28 radial roads, as well as underground and suburban railways, links up the city center with the rest of the city and the city itself with the surrounding towns. The growing road system follows the basic plan of the old city with its chessboard pattern, and the newly constructed beltways and expanding radial system have been design-ed to incorporate the old roads in a rational way.

Tian'anmen will continue to serve as the center of the city, and the north-south and east-west axes of the city will be further developed. Construction on 38-kilometer-long Chang'an Boulevard will concentrate on offices concerned with political, economic, Communist Party and foreign affairs. The area encompassing the palaces and city gates has been designated as a landmark district, while an increasing number of other important cultural relics, revolutionary landmarks and former residences of noblemen and princes are being renovated and opened to the public.

The landmark district, encompassing Zhongnanhai, Beihai, Jishuitan and Shichahai, will provide a landscaped background for the Imperial Palace and the moat. Small decorative buildings, fountains and tree-lined walkways will link the parks mentioned above with Jingshan Park, Zhongshan Park and the Workers' Cultural Palace. The mansions of Prince Gong and the Prince Regent will also be included in the project. When the work is completed, the city of Beijing, preserved in its entirety and yet born anew, will be more magnificent than at any point in its glorious past.

Chapter 1
Principal Sites Around Tian'anmen

Beijing's Central Axis and Tian'anmen Square

The focal point of the north-south axis of the city of Beijing is the central archway of Tian'anmen Gate. The imaginary axis line, 7.8 kilometers long, begins in the south at the Yongdingmen Gate (no longer extant) in the former outer city wall; proceeding north, it passes in turn through the Zhengyangmen Gate (South-Facing Gate, popularly known as Qianmen or Front Gate), Tian'anmen Gate and Duanmen Gate (which stand before the Imperial Palace), and the Wumen Gate, the southernmost entrance to the Palace proper; from there, it continues north through the five main ceremonial halls of the Imperial Palace and leaves the Palace through its northernmost gate, Shenwumen (Gate of Divine Prowess); it then passes through the Longevity Pavilion (Wanshouting) atop Prospect Hill (Jingshan) and ends at the Drum and Bell Towers.

The north-south axis splits the city of Beijing into halves, each of which was provided in Ming times with symmetrically arranged pairs of gates. Although the gates were torn down to make way for modern roadways, their names still remain as designations for districts of the city: for example, Dongzhimen and Xizhimen, Fuchengmen and Chaoyangmen, and Xuanwumen and Chongwenmen. It is curious, however, that the central axis upon which the monuments of Beijing are built lies approximately 200 meters east of the true axis of symmetry as calculated from the distance between the city walls.

With the exception of the Imperial Palace, nearly all the structures built in and around Tian'anmen Square date from after the founding of the People's Republic of China in 1949. During the Ming (1368-1644) and Qing (1644-1911) dynasties, gates with three openings each stood at the southern, eastern and western extremes of a narrow plaza which ended at the north with Tian'anmen Gate. The gate to the east of this area was called the Left Chang'anmen Gate (Chang'an meaning eternal peace); that to the west was called the Right Chang'anmen Gate; and that to the south was called the Great Ming Gate during the Ming dynasty, the Great Qing Gate during that dynasty, and finally the China Gate (Zhonghuamen) after the founding of the Republic of China in 1912. The area defined by these gates was entirely surrounded by red-painted walls, and with a widened section at its northern end formed a large T-shaped enclosure to which the common people were denied entrance.

During the Ming dynasty, a roofed corridor called the "Thousand *Bu* Corridor" was built within this plaza. *Bu* is both a word meaning "footstep" and a measure of distance equal to approximately five feet.

During the Ming and Qing dynasties, the principal organs of the Chinese government established their of-

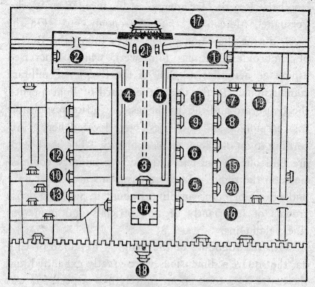

Gate of Heavenly Peace
in the Qing Dynasty

1. Left Gate of Eternal Peace
2. Right Gate of Eternal Peace
3. Great Qing Gate
4. Thousand *Bu* Corridor
5. Board of Ceremonies
6. Board of Finance
7. Board of War
8. Board of Works
9. Board of Personnel
10. Board of Punishments
11. Board of Imperial Family Affairs
12. Censorate
13. Supreme Court
14. Chessboard Street
15. Board of Meteorology and Astronomy
16. Glutinous Rice Lane
17. Forbidden City
18. South Facing Gate
19. Imperial Academy
20. Imperial Hospital
21. Gate of Heavenly Peace

fices to the east and west of this area. To the east
stood the Boards of Ceremonies, Finance, War, Works,
Personnel, Meteorology and Astronomy, etc. On the
west, during the Ming period, were found the Bureau
of Embroidered Robes (Jinyiwei), which supervised
espionage activities as well as the five chief military
commissions. In the Qing, the Board of Punishments,
the Censorate and the Taichangsi (an office responsible
for ceremonies and sacrifices) were located here. According to an old book of local history, "The six boards
are laid out on the left and the five military commissions on the right." In those days, this area must have
had an air of otherworldliness about it, with its dense
crowds of luxuriantly dressed officials and numerous
fine palanquins.

With the founding of the People's Republic of China, the square's dimensions were greatly expanded and
the entire area took on an entirely new aspect. It was
here on October 1, 1949 that Mao Zedong, speaking
before a crowd of 300,000, proclaimed the formal
establishment of the People's Republic, and with his
own hands raised for the first time the Chinese national
flag with its red field and five stars. From that day
on, a large portrait of Mao Zedong has hung over the
central archway of Tian'anmen Gate, with large
plaques with raised lettering on each side: to the east,
the message reads, "Long Live the People's Republic of
China" and to the west, "Long Live the Unity of the
Peoples of the World." High above Mao Zedong's
portrait in the eaves of the gate tower hangs China's
national emblem.

Tian'anmen — the Gate of
Heavenly Peace

Tian'anmen Gate was the southern and principal gate of the Imperial Palace during the Ming and Qing dynasties. To enter the Palace Museum through its present gate — the Meridian Gate (Wumen) — it is necessary to first pass through Tian'anmen.

Tian'anmen is one of the finest monumental gates in the world, and is extraordinary in terms of the thickness of its walls and the height of its imposing tower. The immediate vicinity of the gate contains some examples of uniquely Chinese forms of decoration — ornamental columns (huabiao), stone lions and white marble bridges.

Early in the Ming dynasty, a wooden memorial gate with upturned eaves capped with yellow glazed tiles was built at the present site of Tian'anmen. This structure, with its ten columns and nine openings, was known as the Gate That Bears Heaven (Chengtianmen). After being destroyed by fire, it was rebuilt in 1465 during the reign of the Ming Emperor Xianzong. However, the old wooden structure was replaced by a large wooden gate tower with ten columns and nine bays.

At the end of the Ming dynasty, the peasant leader Li Zicheng defeated the Ming forces and entered Beijing. In the upheaval which took place when Li was driven out of the city by the Qing troops, many buildings within the Ming palace were destroyed. The Gate That Bears Heaven burned, leaving only the foundation of its walls.

In 1651, under the Qing Shunzhi emperor, the gate tower was rebuilt in the style of the original tower and renamed Tian'anmen — the Gate of Heavenly Peace. The Gate today retains the basic character of the early Qing gate.

The base of Tian'anmen, pierced with five arched gateways and set on a foundation of white marble, stands ten meters high. It is built of huge bricks, each weighing approximately 24 kilograms. On top of this massive structure stands a palace-like gate tower with its roof top 33.7 meters above the ground. A low wall surrounding the gate tower in turn encircles a white marble balustrade which frames the gate tower on its four sides. The roof is covered with the same imperial yellow glazed tiles found on every building within the Imperial Palace.

On the main and sloping ridges of the roof are a menagerie of decorative animals with protracted mouths which are purported to protect the palace and its inhabitants from danger. Prominent among these are ten carved dragon heads placed at the ends of the main roof ridge and at each of the eight corners of the double roof.

Immediately in front of the southern entrance to Tian'anmen, seven arched bridges, shaped like curving jade belts, cross the Golden River (Jinshuihe). The easternmost bridge in front of the Workers' Cultural Palace and the westernmost bridge in front of the Zhongshan Park were rebuilt in 1690 under the Qing Kangxi emperor. The central bridge is slightly wider than the rest and forms part of the Imperial Way — the path over which only the emperor could pass — and is also known as the "Imperial Way Bridge." The five

View of the Palace Museum (Forbidden City) from Coal Hill

A bronze lion in
the Palace Museum

The Hall of Supreme Harmony
(Palace Museum)

A Close-up of the Dragon and Phoenix Stone before
the Hall of Preserving Harmony (Palace Museum)

The Gate of Heavenly Peace (Tiananmen)

Nine Dragon Wall in Beihai Park

The glazed tile ridge
with carved animals

The Monument to the People's Heroes

The Great Hall of the People

Chairman Mao Zedong Memorial Hall

central bridges stand before the five arched gateways
of the Gate's base and are provided with two low carved white marble balustrades. The balustrades on the
central bridge are adorned with coiling dragons while
those on the surrounding four bridges are carved with
patterns of lotus flowers.

One of the more unusual features of Tian'anmen is
a pair of 10-meter-high white marble ornamental columns (*huabiao*) topped by a "dish for collecting dew."
A carved stone animal known as a "heaven-gazing
hou" (a small, lion-like legendary creature) squats inside each dish. The purpose of these dishes was to
catch the "jade dew" imbibed by the emperor to ensure
long life. According to local legend, the "heaven-
gazing *hou*" kept watch on the emperor's activities
while he was away from the Palace, anxiously awaited
his early return and hoped that he would not overin-
dulge in pleasure seeking. If the emperor did not return in good time, the creatures would warn him,
"Your Majesty, you mustn't spend so much time enjoying yourself. Hurry back and attend to state affairs!
Awaiting your return, we've nearly worn our eyes out!"
Thus, the pair of "heaven-gazing *hou*" have another
name — "Watching for the Monarch's Return," and
the ornamental stone columns are known as the
"Watching Columns."

Beneath the ornamental columns stands a pair of
finely carved stone lions in attitudes of perfect submis-
siveness. The lion to the west has one paw on an embroidered ball, with its head turned slightly to the east
and its eyes gazing westward. The lioness to the east
is playing with a cub, with her head turned to the
west and her eyes gazing eastward. That the bold and

powerful king of the beasts should be reduced to an obedient watchdog in the presence of the emperor is a clear manifestation of the Son of Heaven's supreme authority.

In the Ming and Qing periods, Tian'anmen was off limits to commoners and served as the main entrance to the Imperial Palace. Several hundred meters in front of the Gate stood the "Great Ming Gate" and between the two ran the Imperial Way. The Thousand *Bu* Corridor reserved solely for the use of officials and nobles stood on either side of the Imperial Way.

The Great Ming Gate remained closed most of the year and was opened only on the following ceremonial occasions:

(1) At the winter solstice, when the emperor offered sacrifices to heaven at the Temple of Heaven in the south of the city.

(2) At the summer solstice, when he sacrificed to the earth at the Altar of Earth in the north of the city.

(3) In the second month of the lunar calendar, when he proceeded to the Altar of the God of Agriculture (Xiannongtan) to plow several furrows in the sacred field.

(4) In early spring, when he sacrificed to the God of Grain.

The emperor's exit from the palace was a major undertaking. Beginning at Tian'anmen, the roads along the emperor's route were sprinkled with water to settle the dust while a layer of yellow earth was spread over them to ensure a proper appearance, as well as to avert traffic accidents. Thousands of officials and soldiers lined the road to guard the emperor's progress. At the appointed time, the five gateways of Tian'anmen were opened simultaneously and the emperor, clad in robes embroidered with dragons and wearing a golden crown, passed through the central gateway seated in his grand sedan chair. Civil and military officials led the procession and brought up the rear as well. With imperial banners fluttering and the ceremonial guard armed with a forest of flags and weapons, it was a truly awe-inspiring sight.

In old China, the most exciting celebration at Tian'anmen was that which followed the triennial imperial examinations. The candidates who won the top three places lined up to be summoned to an imperial audience. To the east of Tian'anmen, an "imperial dragon canopy" was erected and, with the top candidate in the lead, the entire body of new officials presented themselves before the official written list of successful candidates. Beneath the canopy, the prefect of Beijing presented the top scholar with a golden emblem for his hat and draped his shoulders with a banner of red silk. The successful candidates were then received at the city yamen where they were treated to a celebratory feast.

The most horrifying events which took place before Tian'anmen were the imperial trials. A group of accused men who had already been subjected to severe torture were led one by one to kneel before the magistrate's bench, which was placed on the western side of the Gate. The magistrate, appointed by the emperor to determine the prisoner's guilt, would ask the accused several random questions and pen a red check by the man's name to indicate that the death sentence had been granted, in which case execution would take place immediately. If by a stroke of luck a defendant's name were not checked off, he would receive a year's reprieve. In this case, the man's relatives, who had been waiting for the verdict at the western side of the Gate, would rush forward and drape a string of sweet and sour hawthorns around the accused man's neck to congratulate him on his good fortune.

In imperial times, Tian'anmen's most important function was to serve as the scene of imperial proclamations for grand state celebrations such as the enthronement of an emperor or an emperor's marriage. A proclamation platform was set up above the central gateway. Imperial edicts, attached to the mouth of a carved wooden Golden Phoenix (in Ming times, they were tied with colored rope to a dragon head on the end of a pole), were lowered onto a "cloud plate" held by officials from the Board of Ceremonies who stood in front of the gate tower. After being placed in the Imperial Pavilion nearby, the edicts were sent to the Board of Ceremonies itself where they were copied onto imperial yellow paper by special scribes and dispatched to all parts of the empire. Such documents became known as the Imperial Proclamations of the Golden Phoenix.

Ironically, the imperial edict announcing the abdication of the last Qing emperor, Puyi, on December 25, 1911, was issued by Empress Dowager Longyu in the traditional fashion. No finer mockery of the "Divinely Appointed Son of Heaven" can be imagined.

Tian'anmen has also been the scene of acts of national insult and injury. In 1900, the ornamental columns in front of the Gate were damaged by the cannons of the Eight-Power Allied Forces. On July 7, 1937, Japanese troops staged the Marco Polo Bridge Incident and soon after occupied Beijing. When they nailed a sign calling for the establishment of a "New East Asian Order" onto the walls of Tian'anmen, those Chinese who were unwilling to be enslaved by a foreign power felt as if the nails had been driven into their own hearts. During those years of humiliation, Tian'anmen fell into disrepair, the paint peeling off its red walls, its window lattices broken and gaping, its colorful decorations streaked and dulled, a profusion of weeds sprouting up wherever they could gain a foothold.

Tian'anmen has also been the scene of important revolutionary movements. On the afternoon of May 4, 1919, several thousand students from Beijing University and 13 other institutions met at the Gate to demonstrate against the signing of the Treaty of Versailles by the Chinese representatives, and to protest against the Northern Warlord government's traitorous policies. This marked the start of the May 4th Movement, which set the stage for the founding of the Communist Party of China.

On the morning of March 18, 1926, workers, students and other local residents streamed towards Tian'anmen to take part in another protest demonstration, this one directed against an ultimatum issued to Duan Qirui's warlord government by the envoys of eight nations — Great Britain, the United States, Japan, France, Italy, Holland, Belgium and Germany.

On December 9, 1935, Beijing students marched to Tian'anmen to demonstrate their opposition to the Japanese imperialists' progressive invasion of northern

China and to the Kuomintang's policy of non-resistance. Over ten thousand people participated, calling for an end to the civil war and the formation of a united front against the foreign invaders. And from 1945 to 1949, Tian'anmen was even more frequently the meeting place for members of progressive student movements.

It was only after the founding of the People's Republic in 1949 that Tian'anmen regained its former grandeur following a complete renovation. Tian'anmen Square has also changed radically. With a total area of 40 hectares, it is now one of the largest public squares in the world.

Monument to the People's Heroes

The Monument to the People's Heroes, erected by resolution of the First Chinese People's Political Consultative Conference, was the first large-scale memorial built in New China.

Facing Tian'anmen (Gate of Heavenly Peace), its northern facade is dominated by a gilded inscription, "Eternal Glory to the People's Heroes," in the hand of Mao Zedong, and its southern facade by a longer inscription composed by Mao Zedong and in the calligraphy of Zhou Enlai which reads:

"Eternal glory to the people's heroes who laid down their lives in the people's war of liberation and the people's revolution in the past three years. Eternal glory to the people's heroes who laid down their lives in the people's war of liberation and the people's revolution in the past 30 years. Eternal glory to the people's heroes who from 1840 laid down their lives in the many struggles against internal and external enemies, for national independence and the freedom and well-being of the people."

The laying of the cornerstone of the Monument took place on September 30, 1949. Present at the occasion, in addition to the deputies to the First People's Political Consultative Conference, were Mao Zedong, Zhou Enlai, Zhu De and numerous other veteran revolutionaries.

The construction began on August 1, 1952, and was completed in May of 1958. The largest memorial of its kind ever built in China, it rises 37.94 meters from the ground and is as tall as a ten-story building. The 17,000 separate pieces of marble and granite employed in its construction weigh over ten thousand metric tons, and the quality of the materials used gives the Monument an estimated life of 800 to 1,000 years. The white marble and granite was quarried in Fangshan on the outskirts of Beijing and Tai'an County in Shandong Province, and the huge slabs of mauve granite in the shaft are from Fushan near the city of Qingdao.

The base of the Monument covers an area of 3,000 square meters. The shaft rests on a double platform, the lower of which is fringed with balustrades. Steps lead up to it on four sides. On the upper platform is a double plinth from which the shaft rises. The upper plinth is decorated with eight bas-reliefs of peonies, lotuses and chrysanthemums and other flowers which symbolize the virtues of nobility, purity and chastity — a fitting expression of the veneration in which the martyrs are held by the people.

The shaft is decorated near its summit on its east and west facades with ornaments made up of a red star within a semicircle of pines, cypresses and flags.

It is surmounted by a hipped roof with upswept clouds above and drapery below. Liu Kaiqu, the well-known sculptor in charge of design for the project, attempted to merge Chinese tradition with the spirit of our times.'

The lower plinth is decorated with ten two-meter-high marble bas-reliefs of lifelike figures depicting the Chinese revolutionary movement over the course of the past hundred years.

The reliefs begin chronologically on the east side of the Monument with "Burning the Opium," which occurred on June 3, 1839, when chests of opium were destroyed by the Chinese populace at Humen. Torrents of dark smoke roll up before an angry crowd and in the background, rows of cannons and a harborful of battleships are making ready for war.

The second relief shows the 1851 Jintian Uprising, a crucial event in the Taiping Revolution. A swarm of heroes of the Han and Zhuang nationalities swoop downhill wielding spears, swords, mattocks and homemade guns under a sky filled with fluttering flags.

The south side begins with the Wuchang Uprising, one of the key events leading up to the Revolution of 1911. In the middle of the night, rebellious soldiers and civilians storm the mansion of the local Imperial Viceroy. The mansion's signboard is knocked down; the Qing dragon flag is trampled upon; flames leap out of the mansion and light up the sky, symbolizing the deadly blow inflicted upon the last feudal dynasty in Chinese history.

The May 4th Movement (1919) is depicted in the next panel. Standing before a crowd of patriotic students demonstrating at Tian'anmen, a young man delivers a speech demanding "national sovereignty as a defense against the foreign powers and punishment for all traitors." The angry crowd responds with indignation to the humiliation China is being subjected to at the hands of foreign powers.

The panel devoted to the May 30th Movement (1925) is a representation of the undaunted struggles against imperialism by people from all walks of life under the leadership of the working class. Here tens of thousands of workers, students and urban residents fight their way through the barriers of sandbags and barbed wire protecting the British Concession in Shanghai.

The west side of the shaft depicts the Nanchang Uprising, a military action directed against the Kuomintang which took place on August 1, 1927. The panel shows a company commander signaling the start of the uprising with a wave of his hand. A soldier holds up a lantern, and the action begins; a flag unfurls, horses neigh and people carry ammunition to the soldiers. Next to this is the panel entitled "Guerrilla War Against the Japanese Invasion" (1937-45). In the distance, bands of guerrillas thread their way through forests and fields of tall crops to battle the enemy. Peasant supporters of both sexes make ready with spades; an aged woman delivers a gun to her son; a group of young men wait for their officer's orders.

Of the ten panels, "Crossing the River" is the largest. A bugler gives the call to battle; an officer fires a volley of signal shots. Crossing the Yangtze River, the soldiers of the People's Liberation Army land on the south bank and rush towards Nanjing, then the stronghold of the Kuomintang. In the background, battleships plow through the waves. This bas-relief is flanked by two complimentary panels, "Supporting the Front Lines" and "Welcoming the People's Liberation Army" (1949).

The Great Hall of the People

Situated on the west side of Tian'anmen Square, with a total floor space of over 171,000 square meters, the Great Hall of the People is one of the truly grand modern structures in Beijing. With its green and yellow glazed-tile roof, its magnificent portico and colonnades, and the large Chinese national emblem hanging over its main entrance, it is a sight both majestic and dignified.

The flight of granite steps, though only ten meters in height, acts to reduce the almost overwhelming immensity of the structure. Rows of pines and cypresses planted on each side of its central portico set the Great Hall off from Tian'anmen Square and also serve to soften the severity of its geometric design and placement.

Entering through the great bronze doors, the visitor will first pass through a spacious lobby which leads to the Central Hall. The predominant colors in the Hall are pastel yellow and creamy white, which blend harmoniously with the pink marble floor and white marble columns. The Hall is lit by a set of five crystal chandeliers designed in the form of traditional Chinese palace lanterns.

The Central Hall is an ideal point for orienting oneself to the overall layout of the Great Hall: the Auditorium lies to the west, the Banquet Hall to the north and the offices of the Standing Committee of the National People's Congress are reached through a long corridor to the south.

The interior decorations for the Hall were chosen from a wide range of possibilities. In the Banquet Hall, for instance, traditional Chinese palace lanterns give way to hanging chandeliers, recessed lamps and crystal wall lamps. The ceiling panels are decorated in gilded molded plaster with modern designs derived from the recessed ceilings found in traditional palaces and temples.

The Auditorium covers an area of 3,000 square meters and was designed to present no visual obstructions. At the highest point in the immense arched ceiling is a red star set in the center of a golden sunflower which in turn is surrounded by a galaxy of 500 ceiling lamps. The Auditorium is equipped with 12-channel simultaneous interpretation equipment for every one of the 9,700 seats. Behind the Auditorium is a quiet courtyard covering an area of 6,000 square meters. From here one may pass through an archway to the office building of the Standing Committee of the National People's Congress.

The construction of the Great Hall of the People, including the installation of sound equipment, air conditioners and television transmitters, was completed in ten months in 1959.

Chairman Mao Zedong Memorial Hall

The Chairman Mao Zedong Memorial Hall stands on the former site of the Zhonghuamen Gate at the southern end of Tian'anmen Square. The small open area to the south of the Hall was popularly known as Chessboard Street in the Ming dynasty when it was a busy hub of commerce.

Situated directly between the Monument to the People's Heroes and the Zhengyangmen Gate, the Hall occupies a prominent position in the square, relieving the isolation of the Zhengyangmen and acting as a counterbalance to Tian'anmen standing opposite.

The Memorial Hall stands in the center of a large square platform of red Sichuan granite and is surrounded by two balustrades of white marble carved with evergreen motifs. The Hall's design and the symmetry of its four facades strengthen the effect of its "centrality" and enhance its overall severity and solemnity.

The Memorial Hall is enclosed by an expanse of pines, cypresses, willows and hawthorns. The northern and southern entrances are fronted by large groups of sculptures which, taken together with the carvings on the Monument to the People's Heroes, offer an artistic rendering of the epic of the last hundred years of Chinese history.

The awesome appearance of the mausoleum derives in part from its peristyle and the 12 octagonal columns with granite facing from Fujian Province which line each of its four sides. The two flights of steps leading up to the glass-paneled main doors were designed to reduce the overwhelming effect of the palatial building.

The Hall has two stories. Only the first, which consists of a North Hall, a Hall of Mourning, a South Hall, and four ante-rooms, is open to the public.

The interior of the North Hall is dominated by a

white marble statue of Chairman Mao seated in an armchair. On the wall behind the statue is an immense tapestry, 24 meters in length, portraying a vast panorama of China's mountains and rivers. Note too the four square columns of creamy red marble supporting 110 lamps in the form of sunflowers, the traditional decorated ceiling and the red carpet covering the marble floor.

One enters next the Hall of Mourning, the heart of the mausoleum. In the center of the Hall, surrounded by fresh flowers, is a black bier displaying on its sides the emblems of the People's Republic of China, the People's Liberation Army and the Chinese Communist Party, and the dates of Chairman Mao's birth and death: 1893-1976. The late Chairman, wearing his accustomed gray suit and draped with the bright red flag of the Communist Party, lies in a crystal casket. In the background are two rows of potted pines. The rare and durable Phoebe nanmu wood used in the carved doors and paneling of this hall had been obtained in advance from a particular peak on Hainan Island under the supervision of Zhou Enlai.

Before leaving the Memorial Hall, the visitor must pass through the South Hall, with its floor of red granite from northeastern China. Here the predominant feature is the white marble north wall carved with Mao Zedong's poem *Reply to Comrade Guo Moruo* in the late Chairman's own calligraphy.

Across the small square to the south of the Memorial Hall stands the newly refurbished Zhengyangmen Gate, which separates this dignified edifice from the Qianmen area, one of Beijing's busiest commercial districts.

The Palace Museum

The Palace Museum is the former palace of the emperors of the Ming and Qing dynasties, and as such is also known as the Forbidden City (Zijincheng). There are four entrance gates: the Meridian Gate (Wumen) to the south, the Gate of Divine Prowess (Shenwumen) to the north, the Eastern Flowery Gate (Donghuamen) to the east and the Western Flowery Gate (Xihuamen) to the west. The palace occupies 720,000 square meters of land in the heart of Beijing. It is the largest and best preserved group of ancient buildings in China today, with a total of more than 9,000 rooms covering an area of about 150,000 square meters. Surrounding it is a wall more than ten meters high and a moat more than 52 meters wide. The perimeter of the entire palace is six kilometers.

The palace grounds are divided into two main sections, the Front Palace (Qianchao) to the south and the Inner Palace (Neiting) to the north. In the center of the Front Palace stand the "Three Great Halls" — the Hall of Supreme Harmony (Taihedian), the Hall of Complete Harmony (Zhonghedian) and the Hall of Preserving Harmony (Baohedian) — the Hall of Literary Glory (Wenhuadian) and the Hall of Military Prowess (Wuyingdian). Here the emperors performed grand ceremonies and held audience with their officials. The Inner Palace which includes the Palace of Heavenly Purity (Qianqinggong), the Hall of Prosperity (Jiaotaidian) and the Hall of Earthly Peace (Kunninggong), together with the Imperial Garden and various halls to the east and west, was the emperor's domestic quarters and the area of the palace where the empress, concubines and children of the emperor lived, amused themselves and worshipped the gods. In addition, this section contained storerooms, libraries and a hall of historical archives. Preparatory work for the construction of the Imperial Palace began as early as 1407, while the actual construction was started in 1417 under the Ming Yongle emperor and completed three years later. Thus, the overall design of the palace buildings as they stand today is precisely that inherited from the Ming dynasty.

A visit to the Palace Museum begins at its southern main entrance — the Meridian Gate (Wumen). In the past, passage through the central opening was restricted to the emperor, while civil and military officials as well as imperial clansmen used the two side openings. The emperor would pass through the Meridian Gate on his way to offer sacrifices to the gods or to his ancestors. Bells were sounded if he was heading for the Temple of Heaven or the Altar of Earth, and drums were beaten if his destination was the Imperial Ancestral Temple.

The Meridian Gate opens on to a large square crossed by the Golden River (Jinshuihe), which in turn is spanned by five white marble bridges known as the Golden River Bridges. The brick-walled banks of the river are lined with a curving white marble balustrade which appears like a fine belt of jade. Crossing the bridges and ascending a flight of steps, one arrives at the main palace gate, the Gate of Supreme Harmony (Taihemen), which leads on to a huge courtyard of more than 30,000 square meters. Here a sea of flagstones surrounded by low buildings and gates gives an impression of great vastness. To the east and west of

the courtyard are the Hall of Manifest Benevolence
(Tirenge) and the Hall of Enhanced Righteousness
(Hongyige), while the splendid Hall of Supreme
Harmony (Taihedian) stands prominently in the cen-
ter. Directly north of the Hall of Supreme Harmony
on terraces of the same height are the Hall of Complete
Harmony (Zhonghedian) and the Hall of Preserving
Harmony (Baohedian). Together these three are
commonly known as the "Three Great Halls" (Sanda-
dian) and are the major components of the Front
Palace.

During the Ming and Qing dynasties, only the most
important ceremonies were held in the Hall of Supreme
Harmony; for example, the enthronement of an emperor, the celebration of the first day of the New Year,
the winter solstice, the Spring Festival (which lasted
from the first day to the fifteenth day of the first
lunar month of the year), the emperor's birthday, the
announcement of the names of successful candidates in
the imperial examinations and the proclamation of important imperial directives.

The imposing appearance of the "Three Great Halls"
derives from the broad, stately terraces on which they
stand. The I-shaped terraces are composed of three
layers of white marble, each layer bounded by a low
balustrade. The pillars are ornamented at the top with
carved cloud patterns, dragons and phoenixes and the
panels between the pillars are adorned with vases of
lotus leaves. At the base of the pillars is a small channel for water drainage and beneath each pillar a dragon's
head with a hole in its mouth which serves both prac-
tical and ornamental functions. If you visit the Palace on
a rainy day you will witness the magnificent sight of

1,142 dragons on the three terraces simultaneously spurting rain water from their mouths.

At the center of the north and south ends of each of the terraces are three flights of steps, the middle flights decorated in their centers with slabs of exquisitely carved marble. This was part of the Imperial Way which corresponded with the north-south axis of the city. The staircase to the north of the Hall of Preserving Harmony is the most spectacular of them all. The large marble panels in the middle staircase are framed with a border of swirling flowers, while the lower section of each panel is composed of ocean waves. In the center, a sea of curled clouds set off groups of nine (the imperial number) coiling dragons (the emperor's personal symbol) that rise out of their midst, all in high relief. These stone carvings are considered to be some of the finest in China.

The construction of the Hall of Supreme Harmony was initiated in 1420 under the Ming Yongle emperor. The extant structure was rebuilt by the Qing Kangxi emperor in 1695. The Hall is 35 meters high and occupies an area of 2,377 square meters. It is the main hall of the Palace and the tallest building in the entire palace complex. In the exact center of the Hall stands a wooden platform about two meters high, a fitting representation of imperial power. On this platform, set between two golden pillars decorated with coiling dragons, is a golden lacquerware throne carved with innumerable dragons. Directly above the throne, a mirrored sphere hangs from an umbrella-shaped niche filled with yet more golden dragons.

In the Hall's veranda is a display of musical instruments; on one side a set of bronze bells and on the other a set of jade musical stones. In addition, there are mouth organs, vertically and horizontally blown bamboo flutes, and a *qin*, a zither-like instrument without bridges. Every time the emperor approached his throne, the bronze bells and the musical stones were sounded, resulting in a wonderfully harmonious clatter that was known as *shao* music. Outside the Hall, fragrant smoke would rise from incense burners cast in the shape of heaters, tripods (*ding*) and cranes. Within the Hall, civilian and military officials would kneel on the platform in an order determined by their rank, a true microcosm of feudal society. Though incense fumes no longer rise about the Hall of Supreme Harmony, everything remains arranged as if the "Son of Heaven" had just departed.

Heading northwards, the next building along the Imperial Way is the Hall of Complete Harmony which was constructed under the Ming Yongle emperor in 1420 in the form of a square pavilion. Here the emperor would rest before attending to the business of state in the Hall of Supreme Harmony. Each year, on the day before going to the Temple of Heaven or the Altar of Earth to offer sacrifices, he would come here to review the text of the sacrificial prayers. Ceremonies for receiving tribute were also rehearsed here. Also, on the day before conferring titles of honor on the Empress Dowager and before all major ritual events, the emperor would come here to read memorials to the throne and congratulatory documents.

To the north of the Hall of Complete Harmony stands the Hall of Preserving Harmony which, like its immediate southern neighbor, was built in 1420. During the Qing dynasty, the emperors held annual feasts here on New Year's Eve and on the fifteenth day of the first lunar month attended by the nobility of the various national minorities as well as important civil and military court officials. Beginning with the reign of the Qing Yongzheng emperor (1723-35), the final imperial examination was held here rather than at the Hall of Supreme Harmony.

Beyond the broad rectangular courtyard that lies behind the "Three Great Halls" stands the Ming dynasty Gate of Heavenly Purity (Qianqingmen), the main entrance to the "Inner Palace." Before the gate a pair of golden lions and ten golden vats are arranged. Here the Qing emperors would sometimes hold court while seated on a throne placed before the gate. The northern half of the Imperial Palace, the "Inner Palace," begins here with a dizzying succession of exquisite courtyards, halls, towers and pavilions. On the north-south axis of the Palace lie the Palace of Heavenly Purity (Qianqinggong), the Hall of Prosperity (Jiaotaidian), the Hall of Earthly Peace (Kunninggong) — collectively known as the "Three Rear Palaces" (Housangong) — and the Imperial Garden (Yuhuayuan). From the Ming up through the time of the Qing Kangxi emperor, the emperors lived in the Palace of Heavenly Purity and the empresses in the Hall of Earthly Peace. Later, the Palace of Heavenly Purity was converted for holding audiences with courtiers and foreign diplomats, while the Hall of Earthly Peace was used for offering sacrifices to the gods. At present, the padouk wood cabinets, lacquerware stove stands, crane-shaped candle holders and the cloisonne braziers and incense burners are all arranged as they were in the old days.

The Hall of Prosperity is a small ceremonial hall.

During the reign of the Qianlong emperor (1736-96), the 25 major imperial seals were kept here. These are here on display along with a chiming clock and a classical style water clock (clepsydra) made in 1745.

To the east and west of the "Three Rear Halls" lie the Hall of Solemnity (Duanningdian), where the emperor's clothing was stored; the Hall of Great Diligence (Maoqindian), where books, writing brushes and ink were kept; the Upper Study (Shangshufang), where the imperial princes met with their tutors; and the South Study (Nanshufang), where members of the Imperial Academy currently attending the emperor carried on their work. There are four auspiciously named gates on each side of the "Three Rear Halls"; to the east, the Gate of Solar Perfection (Rijingmen), the Gate of Imperial Glory (Longguangmen), the Gate of Beautiful Harmony (Jinghemen) and the Gate of Basic Transformation (Jihuamen); to the west, the Gate of Lunar Glory (Yuehuamen), the Gate of the Splendor of the Phoenix (Fengcaimen), the Gate of Intense Happiness (Longfumen) and the Gate of Proper Criteria (Duanzemen). These gates lead to the six eastern palaces and the six western palaces, to be discussed below.

The Imperial Garden (Yuhuayuan) lies to the north of the Hall of Earthly Peace (Kunninggong), with the Hall of Imperial Peace (Qin'andian) at its northernmost point. This building is in typical Ming style and differs from the other buildings in that its roof is flat. With a glazed tile ridge lining the four edges of the roof and its carved white marble balustrade, the Hall of Imperial Peace epitomizes classical beauty and elegance. Inside stands a statue of the Daoist Xuanwu. The garden's ancient pines and cypresses, artificial hills and pools, and its smaller temples and pavilions are all fine relics of the Ming and Qing dynasties. At the northern end of the garden atop the Mountain of Accumulated Refinement (Duixiushan) stands the Imperial Viewing Pavilion (Yujingting). Each year the imperial family would climb up to this pavilion on the Double Ninth Festival on the ninth day of the ninth lunar month. East of the Mountain of Accumulated Refinement stands the Hall of Literary Elegance (Chizaotang) where a library of rare books was kept. A set of rare classical books entitled *Selections from the Four Branches of Literature (Siku Huiyao)*, a revision of the *Complete Library of the Four Branches of Literature (Siku Quanshu)*, compiled during the Qianlong reign, still survives in good condition — the only copy to be found in China.

The principal buildings to the east of the "Three Rear Halls" are the Hall of Ancestral Worship (Fengxiandian), the Hall of Abstinence (Zhaigong) and the six eastern palaces. The above are collectively known as the "Inner Eastern Road" (Neidonglu), and now house an exhibition of Chinese art. The Hall of Ancestral Worship was once the Imperial Family Temple and, as the name suggests, the Hall of Abstinence was the place where the emperor came each year to fast (which meant eating no wine or meat) before offering the solemn sacrifices to Heaven and Earth. The Hall of Great Benevolence (Jingrengong) was originally the living quarters of the empress of the Shunzhi emperor (reigned 1644-62) and the Kangxi emperor's birthplace. During the Ming dynasty, the Hall of Heav-

enly Favor (Chengqiangong) was the living quarters
of the empresses and the imperial concubines. The Hall
of Eternal Harmony (Yonghegong) was in the Ming
times the living quarters of the highest ranking concubines and during the Qing that of the empresses and
the concubines. The Hall of Sunlight (Jingyanggong)
was from Ming times a repository for books. To its
rear was the Imperial Study, used by the emperor as
a reading room. During the Qianlong reign, a copy of
the *Book of Songs* (*Shi Jing*) in the hand of Gaozong
(emperor of the Southern Song, reigned 1127-62) and illustrated by Ma Hezhi was preserved here. The Qianlong
emperor wrote the words "Hall for the Study of Poetry" (Xueshitang) on a wooden board and had it
placed inside this room. The Palace of Concentrated
Purity (Zhongcuigong), built in the Ming dynasty, was
the living quarters of the crown prince.

Beyond the "Inner Eastern Road" to the east is another group of buildings commonly known as the "Outer Eastern Road" (Waidonglu), which includes the
Nine-Dragon Wall (Jiulongbi) and the Qianlong
Garden. The main entrance to this section of the palace is the Gate of Ultimate Greatness (Huangjimen),
which leads directly to a second gate, the Gate of Peaceful Longevity (Ningshoumen). Beyond this are the
Hall of Ultimate Greatness (Huangjidian) and the
Palace of Peaceful Longevity (Ningshougong), both
of which house a collection of fine paintings. Be-
hind the Palace of Peaceful Longevity lie the Hall of
Character Cultivation (Yangxingdian), the Hall of
Delighted Longevity (Leshoutang) and the Hall of
Peace and Rest (Yihexuan), known together as the

"Treasure Houses" (Zhenbaoguan) because of their display of priceless antiques.

This section of the Forbidden City has an interesting history. The construction of the Hall of Ultimate Greatness was ordered in 1689 by the Kangxi emperor and was originally called the Palace of Peaceful Longevity (Ningshougong). When Kangxi's grandson, the Qianlong emperor, rebuilt the palace in 1772, he renamed it the Hall of Ultimate Greatness. At this time, Qianlong formulated a plan to rule for 60 years after which he would abdicate in favor of his son. Twenty years before his planned abdication, he set about preparing suitable living quarters for his retirement. Calculating that he would be 85 at the time and worried that he might not live that long, Qianlong began burning incense and praying to Heaven to grant him long life. He also chose propitious names for the various buildings that would give sustenance to his hopes: the Hall of Delight and Longevity, the Hall of Peace and Rest, the Hall of Character Cultivation, etc. In 1795, a healthy 85-year-old Qianlong realized his life-long ambition. He abdicated in favor of his son, the Jiaqing emperor, but in the name of counselor to the throne retained all of his former authority. He died three years later.

Among this group of buildings is a reminder of the darker side of Palace life — the well where the Pearl Concubine (Zhenfei) was drowned. A concubine of the Guangxu emperor, this ill-fated woman supported him as he strove for reform and political power, and soon became his favorite. By evoking the jealousy and hatred of the Empress Dowager Cixi, she suffered brutal treatment and was placed under house arrest and

denied access to the emperor. In 1900, when the Eight-
Power Allied Forces invaded Beijing, the Empress
Dowager fled with Guangxu to Xi'an, leaving orders
with the head eunuch Cui Yugui to dispose of the Pearl
Concubine by throwing her down the well.

The six palaces known as the "Western Road" (Xi-
lu) can be reached either through a gate west of the
Gate of Heavenly Purity or through the western gate
of the Imperial Garden. Among the buildings in this
section, the Palace of Concentrated Beauty (Chuxiu-
gong) was twice the home of Empress Dowager Cixi.
Standing behind it, the Hall of Beautiful Vistas (Li-
jingxuan) now houses an exhibition of Qing dynasty
works of art. The Hall of Double Glory (Chonghua-
dian), where Qianlong lived as a prince, was the
site of an annual tea party held during the first lunar
month. There in the company of the grand secretaries,
palace ministers and members of the Imperial Academy,
Qianlong would drink tea, write poetry and engage in
general merry-making.

In the Palace of Establishing Happiness (Jianfu-
gong), Qianlong spent his leisure time admiring flowers. The Hall of Temporal Benevolence (Fuchen-
dian), which dates from the Qianlong period, was
where princes, dukes and ministers held ceremonial
feasts at the New Year. The Longevity Hall (Chang-
shougong) was built in the Ming period and served
as the temporary resting place of the body of Qianlong's empress before her burial. In 1884 when the Empress Dowager Cixi lived here, it was frequently the
scene of operatic performances.

The Queen Consort's Palace (Yikungong) was
first built in the Ming dynasty and rebuilt in 1655 by

the Qing Shunzhi emperor. In 1802, the Jiaqing emperor
decided to connect this building to the Palace of Concentrated Beauty and replaced the Gate of Concentrated Beauty with a new building, the Hall of Manifest
Harmony (Tihegong). It was here that Cixi selected
Empress Longyu and the concubines Jin and Zhen for
the Guangxu emperor. Nowadays, the Palace of
Concentrated Beauty, the Queen Consort's Palace and
the Palace of Everlasting Life (Yongshougong) house
displays of historical artifacts.

A place deserving special mention is the Hall of
Mental Cultivation (Yangxindian), which lies to the
south of these three palaces. It was here beginning in
1840 that the Qing dynasty surrendered to foreign demands in a shameless act of national betrayal. After
1861, Cixi "ruled the country from behind a screen"
in this hall, encouraging Zeng Guofan, Li Hongzhang
and Zuo Zongtang to collude with the foreign imperi-
alist powers to suppress the Taiping Rebellion.

In politics, Cixi was a cruel and ruthless despot, but
in her personal life she wallowed in luxury. In the
years before her death, she personally received over 200
million taels of silver annually in taxes. She dined on
rare delicacies such as bear's paws, deer's sinews,
shark's fins and sea cucumbers served on dishes of
gold, silver and jade. Records dated 1894 list over 1,500
items of gold, silver and jade tableware stored in the
Palace of Peaceful Longevity where the Empress Dowager dined. This imperial pantry contained 180 kilograms of gold and 328 kilograms of silver. On an ordinary day, she would be served about 100 dishes at each
meal, and an evening meal might include at least a
half dozen varieties of swallow's nest.

Besides being something of a glutton, Cixi was a notorious fashion-plate. At one instance in 1894, she ordered 135 outfits at a cost of 38,000 taels of silver. One of these, a pale magenta gown embroidered with designs of fairies and immortals to be worn on her birthday, required the labor of four to five hundred people and cost 360 taels of silver. She strove by all possible means to retain her youth and for this purpose had a room set aside for the manufacture of longevity potions containing such precious materials as powdered pearls. She loved to attend the opera, to gamble and to play with her dogs. In short, her life was one extended extravaganza of waste.

Beyond the "Western Road" of the Forbidden City lies the "Outer Western Road" (Waixilu) comprised of a group of large-scale Buddhist temples. These include the Rain Flower Pavilion (Yuhuage), the Hall of Flowers (Yinghuadian) and the Palace of Benevolent Peace (Cininggong), the Palace of Longevity and Health (Shoukanggong), the Palace of Peace and Longevity (Shou'angong) and the Garden of Benevolent Peace (Cining Huayuan) where the empress dowagers retired to be cared for in their old age. During the Ming and Qing dynasties, the Palace of Benevolent Peace served as the living quarters of the emperor's mother. Princesses would also hold their marriage ceremonies here.

Chapter 2
Tales of Streets and Alleys

Beijing's Alleys

How many hutongs* are there altogether in Beijing? Old local residents have a saying: "There are 360 large hutongs and as many small hutongs as there are hairs on an ox." Yet despite these numbers, the hutongs are laid out on a chessboard pattern which was established at least as early as the Ming dynasty. In those days the capital was divided into the eastern, western, northern, southern and central districts, with a total of 33 neighborhoods, which were subdivided into hutongs.

Division into neighborhoods began with the Tang dynasty (618-907) when the city, then named Youzhou, was divided into 28 walled residential districts guarded at the gates by sentries. A curfew was imposed at night. During the Liao dynasty (907-1125), Youzhou was renamed Xijunfu and the city was divided into 26 residential districts, while in the days of the Jin dynasty (1115-1234) Xijunfu became Zhongdu (the Central Capital) and was divided into more than 60 residential areas. Under the Yuan (1206-1368), the city was renamed Dadu (Great Capital) and divided into 50 districts, in-

---

* Hutong, the local designation for lanes or alleys, derives from the Mongol language.

cluding the Jintaifang (Golden Terrace District) and
the Wendefang (Literature and Morality District).

The 33 residential districts mentioned above were
established under the Ming Hongwu (reigned 1368-98)
and Jianwen (reigned 1399-1402) emperors, and increased in number to 40 after the time of the Yongle emperor (reigned 1403-24). Some of these divisions still
exist today. The subdistrict office of Baizhifang in the
Xuanwu District, for example, administers an area little
different from the Ming dynasty Southern District's
Baizhifang. The Qing rulers made use of the already
existing city structure and divided the capital into five
districts, reducing the number of residential districts
to ten. During the last years of the Qing, the old residential district system was abolished and Beijing was
divided into ten outer districts and 12 inner districts.
Nowadays the city is divided into four districts — the
East City and West City Districts and the Chongwen
and Xuanwu Districts — each subdivided into numerous
subdistricts.

At present, Beijing has about 4,550 hutongs, the broad-
est over four meters wide and the smallest — the eastern part of Dongfu'an Hutong, a mere 70 cm across —
just wide enough for a single person to traverse.
Although the city has changed a great deal over the
last 500 years, the hutongs to a large degree still remain as they were during the Ming and Qing times.

Beijing's best known hutongs fall into three categories. Many were the former sites of imperial government offices. Lumicang Hutong, in the neighborhood
of today's Nanxiao Street, is the site of the former nine
large imperial granaries of the late Ming and early
Qing periods. Each year, the emperor transported large

amounts of grain from Zhejiang Province to the capital
and stored it in the Lumicang (Salary Rice Granary),
the New South and North Granaries, the Water Transport Granary, the South Gate Granary, the New
Wealth Granary, the Old Great Granary, the Peace
Granary and the Prosperous Peace Granary. Later,
these names were all adopted by the lanes in which
the granaries stood. Off Xi'anmennei Street runs the Xi-
shiku (Western General Warehouse) Alley, once called
Houku Dajie (Back Warehouse Street) because it was
the site of ten warehouses serving the imperial palaces
and gardens. The storehouses include the Jiaziku,
Chengyunku Guangyingku and Guangjiku.

Dongchang (Eastern Prosperity) Hutong, originally
called Dongchang (Eastern Yard) Hutong and situated
to the south of the China Art Gallery, gained its name
during the Yongle period when the alley contained the
offices of the newly created eunuch administration or
"Dongchang." The Dongchang had a notorious reputation as an official entity whose employees trumped up
charges against the loyal and good and terrorized innocent people. It was here that the infamous eunuchs
Liu Jin and Wei Zhongxian had numerous people, including members of the imperial family, high officials
and nobles, put to death.

A second group of hutongs derive their names from
the officials or nobles who resided therein. After the
Ming Yongle emperor established Beijing as
the capital of China, most of his officials moved to
Beijing from Nanjing and the alleys in which
they lived took on their names. Yongkang Hutong in
the northern section of the city was originally named

Marquis Yongkang Lane after the Yongkang Marquis, Xu Zhong. Sanbulao (Three-Never-Old) Hutong north of the Temple to Protect the Nation (Huguosi) in the West City District was originally named Sanbao Laodie (Father Sanbao) Alley after the "Sanbao" court eunuch, Zheng He, who lived there. Sanbulao is a later corruption of the original name and Laodie is an old term of respect for an elder person.

In the East City District lies the Red Star Hutong, once named His Excellency Wuliang (Immeasurable) Alley. This is a corruption of the name of the Ming Hongwu emperor's general Wu Liang (written differently from *wuliang*, immeasurable). In the neighborhood of Xisi (Western Four Archways) Street there are three alleys named the Front, Middle and Rear Maojiawan Hutongs, which are said to have once been the home of the Ming dynasty scholar Mao Wenjian.

The third group of hutongs derive their names from old markets and trading centers. These include Xianyukou (Fresh Fish Market), Luomashi (Horse and Mule Market), Gangwashi (Pottery Market), Yangshi (Goat Market), Zhushi (Pig Market), Mishi (Rice Market), Meishi (Coal Market) and Zhubaoshi (Jewelry Market). Other hutongs are named after historical sites and ancient relics. One example of this is the Qilinbei (Unicorn Stela) Hutong north of Eastern Di'anmen Street, which derives its name from a Ming dynasty stela that once stood at its entrance.

Every one of Beijing's four thousand hutongs has its own anecdotes and legends. Standing in the Maor (Hat) Alley is the Xianyougong (Illustrious Blessing Hall) which contains a slab of stone, the top (or "hat") of which is carved with a beautiful branch of plum blos-

soms with a crescent moon at its tip. The painting came
to be known as the "plum branch and the moon" and
gave rise to a popular story about a "plum blossom
girl" who painted plum blossoms.

Beijing's Residential Courtyards

Beijing's hutongs are lined with row upon row of
residential courtyards — a traditional Chinese architectural form used extensively since the 12th century. The
courtyard plan offers strong defensive capabilities and
met the requirements of the patriarchal clans of traditional Chinese society. Most of the courtyards extant
today were built in the Qing dynasty and still constitute the most common form of housing for Beijing
residents. The scale, design and decoration of the
courtyards followed a strict code in which numerous
details were differentiated according to rank. Generally speaking, the courtyards can be divided into
those of princes, dukes, officials and common citizens.
According to a recent study by Chen Yougu, we can
determine the status of the original owner of a courtyard by its structure:

"The princes' mansions of the Ming dynasty were
the largest, being divided into front and rear sections,
each section containing three main buildings along a
central axis. In addition, small halls lined the sides
of the courtyards, the entire layout modeled after the
Imperial Palace. In the time of the Ming Hongzhi
emperor (reigned 1488-1505), the scale of the buildings
was reduced and the middle halls of the front and rear
sections were replaced by corridors. Under the Qing,

the dimensions of the princes' mansions were fixed as
follows: the main entrance, 5 *jian*;* the main hall, 7
jian; the rear hall, 5 *jian*; and 2 major sleeping quarters, each 5 *jian*. Under the Ming, a top ranking duke's
front, middle and rear halls were permitted to extend
to 7 *jian*, and he was allowed a 3-*jian* front gate decorated with gold-lacquered animal faces with tin rings.
Officials of the first to fifth ranks could have
major and minor halls of 7 *jian*, but on their gates, officials of the first and second ranks were permitted
green animal faces with tin rings, while officials of the
third, fourth and fifth ranks were permitted plain
black-painted rings. Officials of the sixth and seventh
ranks had major and minor halls of 3 *jian* and a single
main gate painted black with iron rings. Ordinary
citizens were not permitted to have rooms of more
than 3 *jian* in size — although they were not limited in
terms of the number of rooms they could build.
Nobles with the rank of duke were forbidden to construct a decorated gabled (*xieshan*) roof, or below to
have double eaves, decorative caisson ceilings, red-
painted gates and windows, or to build secondary halls
that exceeded the limits set down for the main halls.
Although the Qing period saw many changes in these
rules, the system laid down by the Ming remained
basically intact."

The normal arrangement of a "four-square" courtyard (*siheyuan*) consists of a south-facing main hall
(*zhengfang*), a north-facing southern hall (*nanfang*) and
two halls along the east and west sides. The four halls
surround a rectangular courtyard longer on its north-

---

* A *jian* or bay was the non-specific area within 4 pillars; one
jian was approximately 15 square meters.

south axis. Sometimes due to lack of space, the courtyard only had buildings on three sides, in which case
the southern hall was replaced by a wall.

In the three- or four-hall courtyards that house most
of Beijing's residents, the courtyard itself is the main
center of activity. Besides being the source of light,
ventilation and the means of access to one's residence,
it is also used for resting or performing household
chores. Large or middle sized residences were made
up of two or more connected courtyards built along a
single axis, with auxiliary wings added along the sides.
Such "high class housing" was built on a large scale
with buildings of particularly fine quality, and often
included a flower garden. Today, scores of these
formerly privately owned mansions and 12 princes'
mansions still stand. The princes' mansions will be introduced below.

Beijing's Princes' Mansions

Beginning from as early as 1421 under the Ming
Yongle emperor, countless princes' mansions were
built in Beijing, though here only the mansions of the
eight great families of the early Qing period and four
great mansions built after the time of the Tongzhi emperor (reigned 1862-74) will be briefly described. The
mansions of Princes Chun and Gong will be introduced
in greater detail.

With the exception of Prince Qing's Mansion, bestowed upon Yi Kuang,* the princes' mansions are all

---

* A powerful conservative Manchu official active during the late
Qing and early republican periods.

built on the same basic model and constructed from
the finest materials, including carved bricks and
timber, paintings and carved stones.

Although some freedom was allowed in the construction of the auxiliary wing sections of the mansions,
the buildings around the central axis were all built according to set specifications. Each mansion has a main
gate 3 *jian* wide with a raised entrance way, and smaller gates to the east and west. Before the main gate
there are stone lions and horses, lantern poles and
hitching posts. Immediately inside the entrance to the
sides are two 3-*jian* halls, beyond which is a 3- or
5-*jian* Silver Peace Hall. From here a paved path
leads to the second gate. Inside the second gate there
are again 3-*jian* halls to the east and west and in the
eastern part of the courtyard a "Column to the Ancestors." The entrails of a pig were placed in a vessel on the top of this column when sacrifices were being
carried out. Directly north from here lies the 5-*jian*
Spirit Hall.

In the northeast corner of the central courtyard of
each mansion stands the family temple. To the west
of the mansion stands a Clinic of Good Fortune, where
the servants — women, eunuchs and guards — were
sent when seriously ill, though they were not permitted
to hold their funerals here — this privilege being reserved for concubines and their offspring.

The Qing dynasty mansions are found in the following locations in Beijing:

1. Prince Li's Mansion is in Jiangfang Hutong,
Dongxie Street, to the south of Xi'anmen. Just after
the founding of the People's Republic, the Ministry of
Interior Affairs had its office here.

2. Prince Rui's Mansion was built in the early Qing dynasty on the present site of the Nanchizi Primary School. Under the Ming, the Hongqing Palace was situated here, and in 1650, under the Shunzhi emperor, the mansion was pulled down and rebuilt as the Magala Temple. Qianlong renamed it the Pudu Temple in 1776, and in 1778, a new mansion was built for Chun Ying, the fifth generation descendant of Dorgun.* The mansion was the Datong Middle School before the founding of the People's Republic, and became the Beijing No. 24 Middle School after 1949. It is now divided into two schools, the Foreign Ministry Road (Waijiaobujie) Middle School and the No. 24 Middle School.

3. Prince Yu's Mansion in the Third Western Lane at Dongdan is now the site of the Capital Hospital (formerly the Peiping Union Medical College).

4. Prince Su's Mansion was formerly situated in Dongjiaomin Lane, but after the signing of the Treaty of 1901 the area became legation property and was the site of the British Army barracks. The mansion was moved to the northern end of Nanchuanban Lane in Beixinqiao, but the new construction did not follow the pattern of the other princes' mansions.

5. Prince Zheng's Mansion is situated in Erlong (Two Dragon) Road in Xidan. Formerly the China University, it is now part of the Ministry of Education offices.

6. Prince Zhuang's Mansion is located in Xitaipingcang in Ping'anli.

---

* Dorgun (1612-50), a Manchu prince who routed Li Zicheng's troops from Beijing and acted as regent for the Shunzhi emperor.

7.   The Shuncheng Prince's (*junwang*) Mansion is on Peace Bridge Road (Taiping Dajie) in the West City District and now serves as the offices of the Chinese People's Political Consultative Conference. In 1924, the mansion became the property of Zhang Zuolin.

8.   The Keqin Prince's (*junwang*) Mansion on New Culture Road in Xuanwumennei is now the New Culture Road Second Primary School. Although the mansion is not large, it is exquisitely constructed. The main halls of the front and central courtyards are five *jian* in size, while the main hall in the rear courtyard is seven. Eastern and western wings neatly line the sides of the courtyards.

The eight princes listed above were the Eight Great Families of the early Qing. According to Qing convention, a son inherited a title one rank below that of his father. Thus, a prince of the first rank's (*qinwang*) son would become a *junwang* and the latter's son would become a *beile* — the rank below *junwang*. The only exception to this rule were the nobles who had given special service such as the eight "Iron Capped" noblemen who had helped to establish Qing rule.

The four princes' mansions introduced below were bestowed upon their owners at a later date than the mansions listed above. The oldest of these was conferred upon Prince Yi, the 13th son of the Kangxi emperor.

Prince Yi's Mansion in Chaonei Road is nowadays the offices of the Science Press. In the early part of the Tongzhi period (1862-74) the Yi family was stripped of its rank and moved to Beijige Hutong in Dongdan. Nowadays the buildings at Dongdan are the dormitories of the Chinese Youth Art Theater.

In 1872, the Tongzhi emperor granted the right of permanent princeship to the Gongzhong Prince Yi Xin and in 1875, the Guangxu emperor bestowed the same right on Prince Chun, Yi Huan. In 1908, Prince Yi Kuang was given the same honor and moved into the mansion on Dingfu Street.

Prince Chun owned two mansions, one in Taiping Hu (Peace Lake) in the West·City District and one on the north bank of Houhai (Rear Lake). The mansions remained the property of the family for over 60 years and were occupied by three generations. The first Prince Chun, Yi Huan, was the seventh son of the Daoguang emperor (reigned 1821-50). When his brother ascended the throne as the Xianfeng emperor, Yi Huan was given the title of Prince Chun (*junwang*), but as a son of the former emperor he continued to live in the Imperial Palace. In March 1859 Yi Huan left the Palace for a new residence at Taiping Hu and in July of 1864 was given the title of Prince of the First Rank (*qinwang*). In September, 1872, he was promoted and given the title Prince Chun (Chun Qinwang). In 1875, Yi Huan's second son, Zai Tian, took the throne as the Guangxu emperor and conferred permanent princeship on his family. The residence is particularly famous for its fine gardens. In 1913 and 1914 the mansion became Zhonghua University and later Republic (Minguo) University. Nowadays it is the Central Conservatory of Music.

In accordance with Qing dynasty regulations, because the Guangxu emperor was born in the Huaiyin Study in Prince Chun's Mansion at Taiping Hu, when he ascended the throne, the property could no longer serve as a residence and had to be returned to the emperor. The rest of the Yi family moved to a new mansion on the north bank of Houhai. In 1891, Yi Huan died of illness and was awarded the posthumous title of "Xian" (Sagacious). The Guangxu emperor gave him the special title "The Emperor's Own Deceased Father, Sagacious Prince Chun." In November 1908, Yi Huan's grandson Puyi, in the name of the "Successor to Tongzhi and Guangxu," took the throne as the Xuantong emperor and changed Yi Huan's honorary title to "Sagacious Prince Chun, Deceased Ancestor of the Emperor." After Yi Huan's death, his son Zai Feng inherited his title and became the second generation Prince Chun. After Guangxu's death, Zai Feng's son Puyi took the throne at the age of three with his father as acting regent, and the family mansion was renamed "Mansion of the Regent Prince" or Beifu (Northern Mansion), as it stood to the north of the old residence at Taiping Hu.

The residence of Prince Chun was originally the home of Prince Cheng, and before it passed into the hands of Prince Shun, Yu Su, a noble of the sixth rank (*beizi*) lived here. In 1924, when Puyi was forced out of the Imperial Palace, he first returned here before moving to Tianjin. To the north of the mansion is one of Beijing's largest gardens. In recent years, the garden was the home of Soong Ching Ling, late Vice-Chairwoman of the People's Republic. The mansion now houses offices of the Ministry of Health.

Prince Gong's Mansion was first built in Iron Lion Alley in the eastern section of Di'anmen East Street, but the present Gong Mansion is at 17 Qianhaixi Street on the east bank of Shicha Lake. This mansion is the most exquisitely decorated and best preserved of the princes' mansions in Beijing, and besides the residence there is also a large garden.

The mansion is composed of three complexes of buildings — central, eastern and western — the first of these conforming to the standard mansion of a prince. Here, however, the central Spirit Hall has been destroyed. The rear hall is a two-story structure more than 180 meters wide, which is said to be 99.5 *jian* in size. An unusual wooden artificial hill forms the flight of stairs which gives access to the building. The buildings to the east are constructed in typical Ming style. A Chinese wisteria plant which is over 200 years old is still growing in front of it.

The main courtyard of the western complex includes the Xijin Studio (Xijinzhai) as its main hall and is entered via a gate with the name of "Courtyard of Heavenly Fragrance" carved above it. Surrounding the courtyard is a series of elegant rooms separated by Phoebe nanmu partitions. In the center of the courtyard are two rare midget crabapple trees nearly 300 years old.

The garden to the north of the rear hall was designed on a large scale without the constraints imposed on the mansion's formal buildings. The front section of the garden contains an artificial hill made from piled stones, an ancient wall, the Liubei Pavilion, the Peak That Has Flown In and the Green Cloud Mountain Range.

The back section of the garden has a multi-leveled artificial hill built of Taihu stones. The bottom level has tunnels leading through it and contains a stone with the character *fu* (happiness) written on it in the calligraphy of the Kangxi emperor. On the second level are two pools where fine lotuses bloom in late summer and early autumn. A small pavilion with a terrace stands on the hilltop and is considered an ideal place for appreciating the moon. A fishing pond stands in front of the hill. The eastern courtyard of the garden is surrounded by a low wall and contains a luxuriance of flowers and trees. Screened by the artificial hill is the Futing (Hall of Happiness) built in such a way that sunlight falls on it from dawn to dusk. This building is said to be the only one of its kind in Beijing.

According to recent research by literary scholars, it was at Prince Gong's Mansion that Cao Xueqin, author of the *Dream of Red Mansions* (*Hongloumeng*), lived the life he was to write about in his famous novel. Researchers believe that the mansion and the large garden strongly resemble the Rongguo Mansion and Daguan (Great Vistas) Garden, since certain features of the garden described by Cao, including the layout of the buildings, tally with the layout of the mansion. There is still much controversy over the question, but as former Premier Zhou Enlai pointed out, the problem will not be easily resolved and whatever the outcome, the garden should be preserved as a memorial to Cao Xueqin.

Beijing's princes' mansions and large-scale private houses were often built with walled flower gardens laid out either behind or to the sides of the main buildings. Today a few such mansions dating from the Ming dynasty are still standing, such as the house and garden at 1 Great Peace Lane (Taiping Hutong). These gardens are ingeniously constructed with complementary buildings and terraces, well spaced vegeta-

tion and hill paths that wind their way around cool
and tranquil grottoes. They are an exquisite combination of classical Chinese architecture and tasteful
landscaping.

Chang'an Boulevard

Chang'an (Eternal Peace) Boulevard is the central
section of a 38-kilometer-long road which forms the
east-west axis of Beijing, linking the downtown area
with the suburbs. With its midpoint at Tian'anmen
Square, the road stretches without a single twist or
turn from Eight-*Li* Village (Balizhuang) in Tongxian
County in the east to Stone View Hill (Shijingshan)
in the west.

On the northern side of the boulevard, east of
Tian'anmen Square, stands the Beijing Hotel. The
central building, refurbished in 1982, is the oldest of the
three and is built on the site of the Qing dynasty Beijing Military Garrison Headquarters. The building
was demolished sometime after 1900 and in 1917 the
present seven-story structure was built with financing
from the Sino-French Bank of Industry and Commerce. Known as the Grand Hotel de Pekin, it was
under foreign management and served a chiefly foreign
clientele. The hotel remained in French hands until
1940 when, with the outbreak of World War II, the
majority of the stock was bought by Japanese interests.
The Japanese took over the management of the hotel
and in 1941 its name was changed to the Japan Club
(Riben Julebu).

The western section of the hotel was completed for National Day (October 1) in 1954. This light maroon seven-story edifice stands on the site of the Qing dynasty Board of Minority People's Affairs (Lifanbu). When the Qing rulers concluded a series of humiliating treaties with the foreign powers in China in the 19th century, the postal and customs services were taken over by the British and the Lifanbu was demolished and replaced by the general headquarters of the Beijing Postal Service.

The third and newest section of the hotel is the large apricot-colored building at the southern entrance of Wangfujing Street. It first began to receive guests on the eve of National Day (October 1) in 1974, the 25th anniversary of the founding of the People's Republic of China.

Past Wangfujing Street to the east on the northern side of Chang'an Boulevard there is a high terrace with rockeries composed of large pieces of stone from Taihu Lake in Jiangsu Province. Under the shade of sorbaria and a variety of flowering plums, visitors can rest on garden benches or on the low terrace wall. Next to the northern edge of the terrace was an alley called Dongdantoutiao, which was razed by the Eight-Power Allied Forces in 1900. After 1949, the rubble was removed and a children's cinema, a youth art theater, the Maritime Bureau and the Dongdan Post Office were erected. On the opposite side of the road, the Ministry of Foreign Trade now replaces what were once residences, shops and imperial government offices.

Further to the east on the south side of the boulevard lies Dongdan Park, with its rockeries, fine trees and flowers, as well as facilities for volleyball, basketball and other sports. The area where this park stands was once a densely populated residential area, but after the Eight-Power Allied Forces entered Beijing, the houses here were demolished to make way for a large square known as the Polo Grounds. For more than half a century this square remained out of bounds for Chinese children.

The western section of Chang'an Boulevard, which begins at the Great Hall of the People, was widened in 1950 by the demolition of three archways and their attached walls across the road. On the northern side of the road is the Beijing No. 28 Middle School, once a Qing dynasty bureau (Shengpingshu) which managed operatic performances for the imperial family. Further to the west is the New China Gate (Xinhuamen), the southern gate of Zhongnanhai (Central and South Lakes), the offices of the Central Committee of the Chinese Communist Party and the State Council of the People's Republic of China. The New China Gate was originally named the Precious Moon Tower (Baoyuelou) or the Tower for Gazing Towards Home (Wangxianglou). Tradition has it that the Qianlong emperor built it so that his Fragrant Concubine (Xiangfei), who hailed from Central Asia, could gaze towards her homeland during bouts of homesickness. (See Zhongnanhai, page 127.) When Yuan Shikai became President of the Republic, he gave the gate its present name. Continuing west, we come to the towering form of the telegraph office, and diagonally opposite this, the Hongbinlou Restaurant and the Capital Cinema. Chang'an Boulevard ends at Xidan, a busy commercial area.

The Chang'an Boulevard of today is both wide and magnificent, but in the past it was nothing more than a dirt road. Over 500 years ago, the Ming Yongle emperor began the reconstruction of Beijing and built a road in front of Chengtianmen (Gate That Bears Heaven) on the site of the Yuan dynasty southern city wall. At that time, because the road passed directly in front of the Imperial Palace and the walls of the Imperial City, it was known as Tianjie (Heaven Street). Yongle rebuilt the southern wall of the Imperial City further south, on a line with the Zhengyangmen Gate, and on either side of the Gate That Bears Heaven built gates called the Left Gate of Eternal Peace (to the east) and the Right Gate of Eternal Peace (to the west). From that time on, the section of the road leading east from the Left Gate to Dongdan was called East Chang'an Boulevard and that leading west from the Right Gate was called West Chang'an Boulevard. But, because the square in front of the Gate That Bears Heaven was off limits to commoners, it was prohibited to traverse East and West Cheng'an Boulevards. Only the top three scholars in the triennial imperial examinations, after receiving their titles in the Jindian (Golden Hall), could ride out of Tian'anmen (Gate of Heavenly Peace) and along this length of road.

During the Qing dynasty, the name of the Left Gate of Eternal Peace became the East Gate of Eternal Peace (Dongchang'anmen) and the Right Gate of Eternal Peace became the West Gate of Eternal Peace (Xichang'anmen), but the gates themselves remained unchanged. With the establishment of the Republic in 1912, the eastern and western sections of Chang'an

Boulevard were finally opened to the public, but at
that time, the flagstone road was merely seven meters
wide. During the Northern Warlord period the
flagstones were replaced with asphalt, but the widest
point on the road was still only 25 meters. It
was then that trolley cars ran on the road for the first
time.

In 1952, local authorities decided that the East and
West Gates of Eternal Peace were a serious hindrance
to traffic and pulled them down. In 1954, the memorial archways on Chang'an Boulevard were moved
to Taoranting Park. After 1959, with the rapid development of the city, an increasing number of high-rise
buildings appeared on the boulevard and it was widened to its present dimensions.

Dongjiaomin Lane (Former Legation
   Quarter)

Dongjiaomin (East Intercourse with the People)
Lane was first known as Dongjiangmi (East Glutinous Rice) Lane and in recent history as Legation
Street. In 1416, the Ming Yongle emperor decreed
that the district where the street now stands should be
set aside as an area for raising animals and growing
crops, and consequently it became a haven of serene
beauty. In the Ming and Qing times a number of government offices and princes' mansions were located
here.

When the Eight-Power Allied Forces occupied Beijing in 1900, they took a fancy to the beauty of this

district. In concluding the Xinchou Treaty of 1900, they forced the Qing government to agree to turn the district into a legation quarter where each country could station its own troops and where Chinese people would not be permitted to live. In accordance with the treaty, the area became the sole preserve of foreigners and, somewhat ironically, its name was changed from Glutinous Rice Lane to Intercourse with the People Lane.

The barracks of the British troops stood at the northern entrance to the quarter, close to Tian'anmen, while American troops guarded the western entrance, where there was a military supplies depot. Sentries were posted at all the entrances to prevent Chinese from "trespassing," and the surrounding walls were pierced with embrasures large and small for cannon. From the eastern entrance north, a large number of Chinese houses were demolished to create a military parade ground, and each country began constructing its own legation and residences.

Dongjiaomin Lane is now lined with Chinese government offices and multi-story apartment buildings. At the eastern end of the Lane stand the Xinqiao Hotel and the Tongren Hospital. At the westernmost extreme are Tian'anmen Square and the Zhengyangmen. Strolling on this quiet and peaceful street, the hustle and bustle of the city seems far away, and it is difficult to believe that you are in the very heart of Beijing.

Wangfujing Street

Wangfujing Street runs on a north-south axis through downtown Beijing, its southernmost point ending at the central section of East Chang'an Boulevard. In 1417, the Ming Yongle emperor built ten mansions for the highest ranking hereditary princes and other nobility in this vicinity. The road was then known as Princes' Mansions Street (Wangfujie), but later "well" (*jing*) was added to its name to commemorate the famous well in the street.

The well is thought to have been located directly south of the large Beijing Department Store. This may be assumed correct as there are two nearby lanes named Large Sweet Water Well Lane and Small Sweet Water Well Lane. In imperial days it was forbidden to dig wells at random in the vicinity of the Imperial Palace for it was feared that this would destroy the *fengshui** of the emperor's palace. Since Princes' Mansion Street contained a sweet water well, local residents all went there to draw water and it soon became as famous as the princes' mansions themselves. Not surprisingly then, "well" was simply added to the name of the street.

During the late Qing dynasty, Wangfujing Street was still only a narrow mud-paved alley with a few shops on it, but at the turn of the 20th century it began to develop rapidly. Dongjiaomin Lane's location in the neighborhood of the southern extremity of the street and the large number of government offices in the

---

* *Fengshui*, literally "wind and water," was the Chinese system of geomancy. The positioning of a building or tomb in relation to the natural landscape was believed to influence the fortunes of the occupants. In the case of Wangfujing Street, digging a well without careful *fengshui* planning might bring ruin to the royal family.

eastern part of the city attracted trade to the area. After the fall of the Qing dynasty in 1911, warlords began to move into Beijing, and increasing numbers of bureaucrats, politicians and landlords, both active and retired, collected in the eastern part of the city. For example, Li Yuanhong's private garden (Li was a president of the Northern Warlord government) was not far from the northern end of Wangfujing Street. Eventually, shops selling antiques, clocks, furs and Western-style clothes and goods sprung up in profusion to satisfy the demands of the wealthy residents of the area. In 1928, the street was paved with asphalt, another sign of its ever-increasing prosperity and importance.

Today Wangfujing Street features a children's emporium, an arts and crafts store, the Xinhua Bookstore, the Foreign Languages Bookshop, the Blue Sky Fashion Store, the Pulande Laundry and Dyeing Shop, the China Photo Studio, the Puwufang Game Store, just to mention a few. Some of the old shops are still doing business; for instance, the Hengdeli Watch Shop, the Shengxifu Hat Shop and the Tongshenghe Shoe Store.

The old Eastern Peace Bazaar (Dong'an Shichang), now renamed the East Wind Bazaar (Dongfeng Shichang), has a history of over 70 years and was originally the grounds where the soldiers of the Qing dynasty Eight-Banner troops practiced martial arts. Nowadays, the shelves at the bazaar are stocked with Beijing's famous local products, such as exquisitely carved ivory, cloisonne, laquerware, silk and paper flowers, silver filigree, gauze palace lanterns and miniature glass animals. Students, collectors and antiquarians often visit the second-hand book stalls at the market in search of old classics or out-of-print books.

Next to the bazaar is the Donglaishun Restaurant, famous for its mutton hot pot (*shuan yangrou*). Opened in 1903, it is a favorite dining place for members of the national minorities and other travelers visiting Beijing.

Every day, the East Wind Bazaar is visited by tens of thousands of shoppers. But perhaps the busiest shop on Wangfujing Street is the Beijing Department Store (Baihuo Dalou), which opened for business in 1955. In this single six-story building, close to 100,000 customers are served every day. However, it is only one of the almost 100 shops found in the 500-meter-long street where the hustle and bustle is unrivaled in all of Beijing.

Lantern Market Street

Lantern Market Street (Dengshikoudajie) is an ordinary little thoroughfare leading east off the southern section of Wangfu Street. Apart from the All-China Women's Association and the Chinese Child Welfare Committee, the majority of the buildings in the street are residential buildings serving various organizations or private homes. There are few shops. Nevertheless, as early as the Ming dynasty, this was the most fashionable place in Beijing to buy lanterns, and explains how the street earned its name. In the past, many poems were written to describe the splendor of the lantern market:

Why do so many people go to the Lantern Market?
A galaxy of brilliant pearly lights draws the
*   crowds near.*
By day, Chang'an Boulevard too is dazzling to the
*   eye,*
Due not to the lanterns but to the splendor of the
*   bazaar.*

                          (Fan Wenguang, *The Lantern Market*)

At that time, the market offered a wide variety of
goods ranging from precious furs from the borderlands
and antiques to clothing and articles for everyday use.
Also on display were exotic flowers, rare plants and
miniature trees and rockery. In the evening, the surrounding buildings and the street itself were festooned
with multicolored lanterns and ice lanterns which were
entirely transparent. Made by sprinkling water in particular patterns, the technique of their manufacture is
now a lost art.

The lantern market held once each year was attended not only by officials and ordinary citizens. Women
— traditionally confined to the home — were also permitted to join in the fun.

China's lantern markets have a long history. Beijing's
earliest markets were held in Lantern Market Street,
but later moved to the Langfang (Corridor House)
outside the Zhengyangmen Gate. For a short time,
markets were also held in Ministry of Works Road
(Gongbujie) in front of Tian'anmen. Although these
markets were extremely popular one hundred years
ago, the tradition began dying out after the invasion
of the Eight-Power Allied Forces in 900 and little
of it survives today.

The Dazhalan Market

During the Ming and Qing dynasties, Beijing was frequently placed under curfew at night. Barriers (*zhalan*) were erected at both ends of streets and alleys in the city and closed as soon as the curfew came into effect, thus making through passage impossible. According to the authoritative *Imperially Commissioned Record of the Major Events of the Great Qing Dynasty*, there were more than 1,090 barriers erected in the Inner City area as well as 196 inside the Imperial (Manchu) City. Dazhalan was just one of these 1,200-odd structures, and although the barrier itself is gone, its name has remained.

Dazhalan, literally the "Great Fence," was from very early times the site of a busy market. In the years of the Ming Yongle emperor (reigned 1403-24), it was already crowded with shops, and as trading in the city gradually became concentrated around the Zhengyangmen area, Dazhalan developed into a popular market. In 1900, when the Eight-Power Allied Forces attacked Beijing, Dazhalan was reduced to a heap of rubble, although it was quickly rebuilt as it basically stands today.

Dazhalan Street is 270 meters long and nine meters wide, with 37 shops and service establishments ranged along its sidewalks. Many of the speciality shops still bear their old names; for example, the Tongrentang Traditional Medicine Shop, which has continuously manufactured pills, powders and ointment since 1669; the old Juyuan Hat Shop, now called the Dongsheng

Hat Shop, opened in 1811 and specialized in producing officials' hats and satin boots for the nobility; and the famous Ruifuxiang Satin, Silk and Fur Shop, which opened in 1893. Also notable among the older shops here are the Neiliansheng Shoemaker's and the Nanyufeng Tobacco Shop, both more than 100 years old. The Xinrong General Store, although only a small shop, also has a history of 80 years.

These old shops enjoy a high reputation among local residents and their continued prosperity for almost four centuries can be traced not only to their favorable location in a busy market, but also to the fact that each of these famous old establishments has worked hard to develop their own individual specialities and have continued to sell genuine goods at fair prices. The Tongrentang, for example, formerly supplied dried medicinal herbs to the imperial court and was later appointed to make up prescriptions for the emperor. During the reign of the Guangxu emperor (1875-1908), the Empress Dowager Cixi ordered the shop to produce all the medicines used by the imperial court. During the Qing dynasty, the Neiliansheng Shoemaker's ensured their success by keeping careful records of the boot sizes and preferred styles of all the military and civil officials who shopped there. Thus if an official wished to have a pair of boots made, he merely sent a note to the shop and a pair of perfectly fitting boots would be made to order. After the fall of the Qing dynasty, the market for officials' footwear disappeared, but the shop's owners quickly adapted to the requirements of their new customers by making cotton shoes out of the layered cloth soles previously used to make the court boots. Soon business was just as brisk as before.

Another reason why Dazhalan became a busy market was because of the great number of public amusement places concentrated here. In former times, there were five large theaters, the Qingleyuan (Celebrating Happiness Playhouse), Sanqingyuan (Three Celebrations Playhouse), Guangdelou (Extensive Virtue Playhouse), Guangheyuan (Extensive Harmony Playhouse) and the Tongleyuan (Common Happiness Playhouse). Because the Qing rulers had made a law prohibiting "uproarious noises in the Inner City areas close to the Palace," the gentry and rich merchants who lived there would make the trip through Qianmen (Front Gate; or Zhengyangmen) in the evenings to see plays and operas.

After 1949, state-run enterprises were established here one after another and the opening of two department stores, women's clothing shop and children's shop, enabled the Dazhalan commercial sector to supply an even wider range of consumer goods. Nowadays, Dazhalan bustles with crowds from morning to night. On an average day 100,000 customers are served in the local shops and on holidays this figure more than doubles.

The Bridge of Heaven (Tianqiao)

Bridge of Heaven Street is a long, wide tree-'ined avenue with arterial roads radiating off in all directions. The bridge from which the area takes its name no longer stands, but was once located in the region of the Tianqiao Department Store. This bridge was built of white marble with carved balustrades and spanned the famous Dragon Beard Ditch (Longxugou). Because the bridge was on the road leading from the Forbidden City to the Temple of Heaven, the Ming and Qing emperors had to cross it on their way to offer sacrifices to Heaven, from which the bridge took its name.

The history of this bridge began more than 600 years ago when in the Yuan dynasty a high stone bridge was built across a river here. To the west of the bridge stood the wall surrounding the Altar to the God of Agriculture and in the middle of an expanse of paddy fields stood a pavilion. Near this large pavilion was a smaller thatched pavilion known as the Pavilion in the Midst of the Water (Shuixinting). During the reign of the Qianlong emperor, the river which had been filled in during the Ming dynasty was redredged and rows of willows were planted along its banks. The river itself was planted with red lotuses in an effort to create a landscape reminiscent of the southern Chinese countryside. As the number of visitors to the district increased, so did the number of shops that served them, and before long the area to the north of the bridge became known for its wineshops and teahouses. Under the Guangxu emperor, the river was again filled in when the road running between Zhengyangmen and Yongdingmen (Gate of Eternal Stability) was built. At this time, the bridge was demolished leaving only the stone balusters, and these too were removed when the road was widened. From then on the name of the bridge was all that remained.

Only after the 1911 Revolution did the Tianqiao area develop into a market. In 1913, the Northern Warlord government demolished the Lotus Lane Market outside Zhengyangmen and small retailers established seven alleys lined with new shops on the vacant ground around the site of the former Bridge of Heaven. There were shops specializing in imported goods and watches, establishments of astrologers and fortune-tellers, story-tellers and variety shows, second-hand clothing shops and teahouses where men would practice martial arts. Small theaters proliferated and the most famous of them, such as the Dangui (Orange Osmanthus), Tianle (Heavenly Happiness) and Xiaotaoyuan (Small Peach Garden) remained open for several decades. One popular attraction at the Bridge of Heaven was the "Eight Great Strange Performers," whose colorful stage names were: Cloud Flyer (Yunlifei), Zhang with His Tube, Big Soldier Huang, Spotted Bear, Little Pigtail Wang, Big Tin Teapot, the Sponge, and Big Gold Teeth.

Yunlifei, whose family name was Bai, was the father of the famous cross-talk (*xiangsheng*) performer Bai Quanfu. In his youth, he and Tan Xinpei performed in the Peking Opera with the Four Happinesses Society (Sixibanshe) troupe where he distinguished himself as an acrobat. When he became too old for acrobatics, he switched to story-telling and could narrate the entire *Journey to the West* (*Xiyouji*) from memory. Each time he came to an episode about the exploits of the Monkey King, he would launch into a display of martial arts. The appreciative crowds gave him the nickname "Cloud Flyer" in recognition of his superb skill. Bao San, the most famous wrestler at the Bridge of Heaven, who became an official referee after the founding of the People's Republic, and the famous

modern Pingju Opera artist Xin Fengxia, also performed here.

An old poem goes, "The wineshop banner and the
drums in the theaters at the Bridge of Heaven make
many a traveler forget his home." During the "cultural revolution," however, the plays and operas, variety shows and wrestling — all uniquely Chinese — were
banished and disappeared without a trace. Nowadays,
these old art forms are being revived and several teahouses are already back in business.

Iron Lion Lane

The section of Di'anmen (Gate of Earthly Peace)
Road that stretches east beyond the former walls of
the Imperial City was known by two different names;
for a short time after the Anti-Japanese War it was
known as Zhang Zizhong Road (after a northern army
general who was killed in fighting against the Japanese
invaders); but before this it was called Iron Lion Lane
(Tieshizi Hutong).

Iron Lion Lane was named after a pair of iron lions
which once stood outside the gate of one of the important mansions in the street — the former residence of
Tian Wan, the father of one of the concubines of the
Ming Chongzhen emperor. The iron lions remained
outside this gate for over 300 years until 1926 when
they were moved to the Drum Tower (Gulou). During
those 300 years, the mansion itself changed owners
several times. In the Ming dynasty, the Tian family
home was known as the Garden of Heavenly Spring
(Tianchunyuan). Later, under the Qing Kangxi em-

peror, it became the residence of Marquis Zhang Yong,
who had aided in suppressing anti-Qing rebellions. In
the Daoguang period of the Qing (1821-50), a man
named Zhu Xi bought the Garden of Heavenly Spring
for an extremely high price, and following extensive
renovations, renamed it the Garden of Increasing Antiquity (Zengjiuyuan). His contribution was the eight
major vistas which still exist today.

To the north of the eastern end of Iron Lion Lane
are two mansions that once served as the homes of
Qing dynasty princes. After the founding of the Republic in 1912, the Northern Warlord government's
Ministry of the Navy and Ministry of the Army had
their headquarters here. On March 12, 1925, Sun Yat-
sen died in these headquarters and three days later was
moved to the Temple of Azure Clouds (Biyunsi) in
the Fragrant Hills (Xiangshan). Yuan Shikai briefly had
his presidential office in the Ministry of the Army before transferring it to Zhongnanhai (the Central and
South Lakes).

In 1924, following the so-called Zhifeng War (between the Zhili — present Hebei Province — and Feng-
tian — present Shenyang, Liaoning Province — warlords), the Ministry of the Navy became Duan Qirui's
"interim government" office, and on March 18, 1926,
42 petitioning students were shot and killed outside
its gate in what became known as the March 18 Student
Movement. During the Anti-Japanese War (1937-45),
the building served as the headquarters of the Japanese
army. Nowadays, it has become a subsection of the
Chinese People's University, while the former Army
Ministry is now a public guest house.

Formerly, Iron Lion Lane was closed off at its east end and its western section much narrower than it is today. In 1954, when the east-west arterial roadway was being built, the lane was widened to form part of the 3.5-kilometer road that now stretches from Ping'anli in the west to Shitiao Street in the east. When Zhang Zizhong Road was rebuilt, all the widening was done on its southern side, leaving the ancient princes' residences undisturbed. The only difference now is that the pair of stone lions guarding the gate of the Chinese People's University stand slightly further north than their iron predecessors. They appear to preside over less territory than any other of Beijing's ornamental lions, but this is only because they have been placed extremely close to the university gate.

Liulichang Street — Antiques Street

Liulichang is known throughout China and the world for its association with traditional ancient books, calligraphy, paintings, rubbings, inkstones and ink. The street, which is only 750 meters in length, is located south of Hepingmen (Peace Gate) within walking distance of the Hepingmen Quanjude Peking Duck Restaurant.

In Ming and Qing times, Liulichang was a favorite haunt for scholars, painters and calligraphers who gathered there to write, compile and purchase books, as well as to paint pictures and compose poetry. By the Kangxi period (1661-1722), Liulichang had become a flourishing cultural center and was described as having "homes and buildings lined up like fish scales." During the Qianlong period (1736-96), the street was even more prosperous. One could find there "rooms filled to the roofbeams with all kinds of books," "a street filled with treasures and trinkets," and the "quintessence of all the markets in the capital concentrated in one street." When the Qianlong emperor decided to revise the *Complete Library of the Four Branches of Literature* he ordered scholars from all over the country to come to Beijing to work on the project. Interest in textual criticism was great at this time and Liulichang became a center for research in that field. The street then contained more than 30 bookshops and for visiting scholars, a book-buying trip to Liulichang was one of the pleasures of a stay in Beijing.

The Liulichang of the Qianlong period was described in some detail by a certain Li Wenzao in his notes on Liulichang booksellers: "To the south of the kiln is a bridge which separates the tile works into two sections. To the east of the bridge, the street is narrow and for the most part the shops there sell spectacles, metal flues for household use, and various daily necessities. To the west of the bridge, the road is wider, and besides the regular bookshops, there are shops selling antiques and other curios, shops specializing in calligraphy books, scroll mounters, professional scribes, engravers of name seals and wooden blocks for painting, as well as shops where stone tablets are inscribed. Here also are shops offering the articles needed by a scholar participating in the imperial examinations — brushes, paper, ink bottles, paperweights. . . ." This description of

Liulichang remained accurate up till the end of the
Qing dynasty. In his book *Postscript to the Bookshops
of Liulichang*, the bibliographer Miao Quansun (1844-
1919) listed bookshops the names of which had remained
unchanged from the Qianlong period up through the
early 20th century. Bookshops established more recently were also recorded, of which one, the Hanwenzhai,
was still in business during the 1950s.

At the end of the Qing dynasty, the Superior-Level
Normal School, the Five-Cities (in the Ming, Beijing
was divided into five city districts) School and the
headquarters of the Telephone Company were built on
the site of the glazed tile works and in 1927 when the
Peace Gate (Hepingmen) was opened up in the city
wall, the bridge was demolished and Nanxinhua Road
was built, dividing Liulichang into distinct eastern and
western sections. The eastern section became known
as a center for antiques and curios, while the western
section was famous for its books. The Shanghai Commercial Press, the China Publishing House and the You-
zheng Press, which published books of Chinese calligraphy, all established branches here.

In 1950, the People's Government passed laws to
prohibit the export of valuable antiques and books and
to ensure their preservation. At the same time, all important historical artifacts, paintings, calligraphy and
other works of art that were scattered among the Liulichang shops were bought up by the Palace Museum
and the Museum of Chinese History. Such rare books
as Song and Yuan woodblock editions, fine editions of
Ming and Qing classics, old hand-copied texts, manuscripts of famous writers, hand-annotated texts and
publications related to the history of the Chinese revolu-

An old memorial archway on West Changan Boulevard (1950s)

A "quadrangle" courtyard (1950s)

A memorial archway in old Beijing (ca. 1910)

View of the old Universal Prowess Gate (Xuanwumen)

A street scene near the Gate of Moral Victory (ca. 1910)

A modern street

View of Andingmen Street (ca. 1910)

Old and new (from Ancient Astronomical Observatory)

Boijing Library

Sanyuan Clover Leaf Expressway

tion were bought by the Beijing Library, Beijing University and Beijing Normal University.

At the time of the founding of the People's Republic in 1949, Liulichang still had over 170 shops. In 1956, following the transition to joint state-private ownership, many of the small shops were amalgamated into larger enterprises, yet despite this, their special characteristics were preserved. The Baoguzhai (Studio of Precious Antiquity) dealt in paintings and calligraphy, the Qingyuntang (Happy Cloud Studio) sold rubbings, collotypes, inkslabs and name seals, and the Yunguzhai (Studio of Charming Antiquity) sold pottery, bronzes, jade and porcelain from various dynasties, as well as fine handicrafts from the Ming and Qing dynasties. The Cuizhenzhai (Studio of Collected Treasures) specialized in ancient inscriptions, porcelain and pottery and the Moyuange (Affinity for Ink Pavilion) specialized in the calligraphy and paintings of famous modern artists. The Jiguge (Draw from Antiquity Pavilion) produced ceramic figurines and horses designed on ancient models as well as colored rubbings, while the Suiyaxuan (Gallery of Profound Refinement), built on the old site of Haiwangcun (Village of the Sea King), dealt in books on history, literature and philosophy as well as important modern works on archeology and medicine. The list also includes Hukaiwen, Daiyuexuan and Yidege, all of which dealt exclusively in Chinese writing brushes, ink and other writing implements, as well as a variety of arts and crafts. Today, inside the large courtyard of the China Bookshop, the China Art Gallery sells works of famous Chinese artists and calligraphers — hand scrolls, hanging scrolls, albums and fans.

Liulichang also contains shops for paper, scroll-mounting, book binding and the carving of stone tablets and name seals. The most famous of these is Rongbaozhai (Studio of Glorious Treasures) which has a history of over 200 years. Here internationally renowned reproductions of Chinese paintings are made using the traditional technique of woodblock color printing. It was the craftsmen of Rongbaozhai who reproduced in six volumes the collection of *Beiping Woodcut Stationery with Illustrated Poems* edited by Lu Xun and Zheng Zhenduo in 1933.

Liulichang's history can be traced back to the Tang dynasty (618-907) when its present site was part of the prefecture of Ji. Under the Liao (907-1125) it was known as Haiwangcun (Village of the Sea King) and the kiln for producing glazed tiles was first built in the Yuan dynasty (1206-1368). When the Ming rulers began erecting their palaces in Beijing, the factory was greatly enlarged and became one of the five kilns under the direct control of the Board of Works. The majority of the glazed structural components of the Ming halls and palaces were produced in these factories and it is from this that the street derives its name.

In 1979, the State Council approved a recommendation to restore and expand Liulichang. Plans include the restoration of the original shops and the broadening of the road into a 15-meter-wide pedestrian mall that will offer easy access to all parts of the district. On the site of an old temple, a museum containing historical materials related to Liulichang will be constructed. It will house galleries displaying classical paintings, calligraphy and other antiquities.

The City Walls and Gates

In the long history of Beijing, the earliest city walls were built in Zhongdu, capital of the Jin dynasty (1115-1234). At that time more than a million civilians and soldiers toiled for three years to expand the old Liao dynasty capital, taking Bianliang (now Kaifeng), capital of the Northern Song dynasty, as a model. According to Ming dynasty survey records, the Jin dynasty city walls had a perimeter of about 18 kilometers.

The Jin capital was destroyed by the Mongol rulers of the Yuan dynasty. The sumptuous palaces within the walls were set ablaze and the fires continued to burn for more than one month. In 1264, the Yuan rulers abandoned the site of the former Jin capital and constructed a new city known as Dadu, centered on the Jin emperors' auxiliary palaces. The new city walls had a perimeter of 30 kilometers and were 21.6 meters wide at the base and 16.7 meters wide at the top. This was the embryonic form of present-day Beijing.

In 1368, Zhu Yuanzhang, who had become the first Ming emperor, attacked and captured the Yuan capital Dadu and established his new capital at Nanjing. His son Zhu Di, as prince of Yan (the area of northern Hebei Province, including Beijing), garrisoned Beijing. In 1403 Zhu Di renamed Beiping (Northern Peace) Beijing (Northern Capital) and in 1421 officially made it the capital of China. This was the first time the city was known as Beijing. In the middle period of the Ming dynasty, plans were made for a new encircling wall outside the old walls. Work was begun on the southern city wall, but because of a lack of finances the project was abandoned and the work ceased with the completion of the eastern and western corner towers. This resulted in an overall truncated pyramidal shape for the inner and outer cities.

Since 1949, economic construction and development has necessitated the gradual demolition of the city walls. Twenty-eight radiant roads connect the city center and suburban scenic areas, factories and schools. Nowadays, the old city walls remain only in name, and on their ruins row after row of multi-story buildings have already been built.

Many of the city gates are still standing, however, and are wonderful reminders of the past. Not counting the Gate of Peace (Hepingmen), the Gate of Rejuvenation (Fuxingmen) and the Gate of National Foundation (Jianguomen), the city of Beijing at one time had 20 gates. Today, the four gates of the Forbidden City — the Meridian Gate (Wumen), the Gate of Divine Prowess (Shenwumen) and the East and West Flowery Gates (Donghuamen and Xihuamen) still retain their original form. Of the gates once belonging to the old inner walls, however, only the southern gate, the Zhengyangmen, remains intact.

Originally, the outer side of each city gate was fronted by fortifications, all of which were removed along with the gates themselves. These fortifications, an essential part of the overall city plan, took the form of secondary gate towers built just outside the gates. They were connected to the main city wall by semi-circular curtain-walls. Because of their resemblance to an earthenware jar, they were known as "urn walls" (wencheng). In fact, Beijing also has square "urn walls," for example, outside Xizhimen.

The main function of the "urn walls" was to strengthen the defense capabilities of the garrison troops protecting the city. Atop the "urn walls" were tall "urn towers" with openings widening outwards affording archers protection while allowing them to shoot freely. In the event of a surprise attack, the main gates would be closed quickly to prevent the enemy from entering the city. When the defense prepared for an engagement with the enemy, they first concentrated their forces within the "urn walls." If the enemy took the "urn walls," they became an easy target for the garrison troops deployed on the main city gate. Within the "urn walls" there were usually one or two temples, where in the old days people prayed to the gods to protect the city.

The Three Front Gates of the Former City Walls

"Nine inside, seven outside, four in the Imperial City" is a phrase used by Beijing residents since Ming times as an aid to remembering the number of gates in the walls of their city. More explicitly, it means that there are four gates in the walls of the Imperial City, seven gates in the Outer City walls and nine gates in the Inner City walls. The Three Front Gates (Qiansanmen) refer to the central gates in the southern wall of the Inner City: the principal Zhengyangmen, known in the Yuan dynasty as the Beautiful Main Gate (Lizhengmen); the eastern Gate of Exalted Literature (Chongwenmen), known earlier as the Gate of Civilization (Wenmingmen); and the western Gate of Universal

Prowess (Xuanwumen) known under the Yuan as the
Allegiance Gate (Shunchengmen).

Nowadays, the sites of the three gates are linked
up by the newly constructed southern section of the
Second Ring Road, which runs parallel to Chang'an
Boulevard, from Dongbianmen (Eastern Informal
Gate) and Chongwenmen in the east, past Zhengyangmen and Xuanwumen to Xibianmen (Western Informal Gate) in the west. This road was formerly
called Nanchenggen (Southern City Wall) Road and
because the Imperial City, like the emperor's throne,
faced south, the gates were called the Three Front Gates.
. On the southern side of this stretch of road, 38 multi-
story apartment buildings, each over 12 stories high,
have been built in a straight line along the base
of the old city wall. The wall itself was dismantled in
the 1950s. The Qiansanmen apartment blocks, completed at the end of 1978, reflect the drive to modernize
the city of Beijing. With a total floor space of 350,000
square meters, they provide accommodations for an estimated 5,000 families or over 20,000 people. Among
the other high-rise buildings along this new road are
two public guest houses, the Quanjude Peking Duck
Restaurant and the offices of the Communist Youth
League. Five planned shopping areas, with a total of
150 different shops and services, will cater to the needs
of local residents.

The buildings were constructed with the modern
technique of bonding interior walls molded on-site
to prefabricated exterior walls, thereby providing a
strong overall structure and good protection against
earthquakes. Eliminating the use of bricks also reduces
the need for intensive manual labor. In laying the foun-

dations, a combination of techniques was used, including that of poured concrete piles, which lowered the cost and generally facilitated the construction procedure. As a result, the outer shells of the entire complex were erected in less than two years. The interior designers have made use of light-weight materials for interior partitions and have experimented with a wide variety of decorative schemes. Modern installations include elevators, light-weight plastic plumbing and extensive waterproofing.

The individual apartments in the Qiansanmen blocks have been built on a variety of models, the basic unit being a two-room apartment with a total area of about 55 square meters. All units are equipped with central heating, gas for cooking and running water. The buildings are designed to withstand earthquakes measuring up to 8 on the Richter scale and each block is equipped with fire prevention and smoke dispersal equipment.

Beautification of this broad stretch of roadway has already begun. Chinese pines, lacebark pines, cypresses and snow pines stand alongside persimmon trees and Chinese ginkos. Planted among these trees are a number of flowering plants, including peaches, weeping forsythias, roses, roses of Sharon and crape myrtle.

Beijing's Memorial Archways

The memorial archways of old Beijing were tall-roofed gateways that towered over the city's streets. At first they were erected as memorials to chastity or filial piety displayed by particular individuals, but later they lost this significance and were used commonly to decorate the streets leading into the city as well as the entrances to temples, parks, officials' residences and tombs.

Memorial archways were first built in Beijing in the Yuan dynasty (1206-1368). When the capital was rebuilt in the time of the Ming Yongle emperor (reigned 1403-24), every major road was embellished with a number of these archways. Historical records show that there were once as many as 57 in the city, the most famous being the Dongdan (Eastern Single) Archway, the Xisi (Western Four) Archways, the Eastern and Western Chang'an Boulevard Archways, the Qianmen Archways, the Dongjiaomin Lane Archway of Disseminating Literature and the Chongwenmen (Gate of Exalted Literature) Road Stone Archway. In 1914, a Maintain Moderation (Lüzhong) Memorial Archway was built in Public Security Street and a Remain in Peace (Daohe) Archway was built in Judiciary Street to the east and west respectively of Tian'anmen Gate.

The Dongsi Archways were built at a crossroads known in the Yuan dynasty as Crossroads Street. Archways were erected over each of the four roads, the northern and southern archways bearing the inscription "Great City Street." In the Ming and Qing dynasties the north-south road running through these two gates was still called Great City Street and the four gates became known as Dongsi (Eastern Four). The eastern gateway was inscribed with the words "Perform Benevolent Deeds" and the western gateway with "Perform Righteous Deeds." In 1699, a house in the neighborhood caught fire and as the fire spread all four gateways were destroyed. Later, however, they were rebuilt in the same style.

The white marble archway over Chongwenmen Road was built at the end of Xizongbu Alley to commemorate the death of the German Minister Baron von Kettler, who was killed at the time of the Yi He Tuan Movement (known in the West as the "Boxer Rebellion") in 1900. With the signing of a treaty in 1901, Qing authorities agreed to construct an archway over the spot where the shooting occurred and it became a symbol of China's humiliation. The archway was demolished in 1911 following Germany's defeat in World War I.

Archways differ widely in construction. The number of openings could vary between one and five, while the high-ridged roofs with their upturned eaves above the archways might number as many as nine or ten. They were constructed entirely of wood, stone, or glazed tiles, or of combinations of wood and stone, wood and brick, etc. The supporting columns were designed in two distinct forms, some of which extend beyond the roofs overhead while some others do not.

The Dongdan Archway was destroyed in 1900 when the Eight-Power Allied Forces attacked Beijing, and the Xidan Archway met the same fate when trolley cars were installed in Beijing. All the other archways mentioned above were still standing in 1949. As the population of the capital grew and the pace of reconstruction increased, these centuries-old structures became a hindrance to traffic. In 1954 many of them were taken down as part of a project to widen the city roads and ensure traffic safety. Several archways were

removed to Taoranting (Joyous Pavilion) Park where
they are now on display.

At the present time, the only memorial archways
to be found within the confines of the former city walls
are a pair with a single opening and three roofs situated on Chengxian Road near the Guozijian (former
Imperial College). Outside the city near the Chaoyangmen (Facing the Sun Gate), a glazed tile archway
with three openings and seven roofs still stands, while
on the road leading to the Summer Palace there is a
second one made of wood. Many other memorial
archways, such as those built in tombs, parks, palaces
and temples, are carefully preserved as examples of
traditional Chinese architecture.

Street Markets and Temple Fairs

Temple fairs are a Beijing custom that dates back
to the Liao dynasty (907-1125). In the Yuan dynasty
(1206-1368), the bustling temple fair in Chenghuang-
miao (Temple of the City God) Street — present-day
Chengfang Street — became particularly famous. During the Ming dynasty (1368-1644), temple fairs gradually
became widespread, and under the Qing (1644-1911),
their numbers increased even further. After the 1911
Revolution, however, large permanent markets were
established and temple fairs gradually disappeared.

Temple fairs were said to have their origins in the
ancient "*she* sacrifice." A *she* was a place where sacrifices to the local god of earth were offered up. Altars of
the Gods of Earth and Grain were also known as
Earth Temples and it is from gatherings that took place

at these temples that temple fairs derived their name.

In Beijing, temple fairs were held in turn at the Earth Temple (Tudimiao), the Flower Market (Huashi), the White Pagoda Temple (Baitasi), the Protect the Nation Temple (Huguosi) and the Temple of Intense Happiness (Longfusi), with one fair taking place every ten days. Besides this, the famous annual Changdian (Factory Grounds) Fair was held during the first fifteen days of the first lunar month and the annual Peach of Immortality Palace (Pantaogong) Fair was held from the third day of the third lunar month inside the Dongbianmen (Eastern Informal) Gate. The fairs mentioned above took place regularly for over 300 years.

The Beijing Dongsi People's Bazaar, established more than 30 years ago, stands on the site of the old Temple of Intense Happiness (Longfusi). The temple, built during the reign of the Ming Jingtai emperor in 1452, could boast of having the largest pair of temple gates in Beijing. The temple was made up of five courtyards, each with a large central hall connected by long galleries. The five large halls were named the Hall of the Four Heavenly Kings, the Hall of Balustrades, the Hall of Ten Thousand Virtues, the Pilu (Vairocana) Hall and the Hall of the Great Law. In 1900, a large part of the temple was destroyed when the Eight-Power Allied Forces invaded Beijing.

Visitors to the temple fairs included both city folk and peasants from the outlying regions. Customers could buy a variety of locally made products such as "Gold Elephant Zhang's" double-edged combs, "Iron Knife Liu's" fruit knives and "Sanheju" wigs, as well as second-hand clothes, jewelry and cloth, bamboo and wicker products, flowers, birds, fish and insects. Nowadays, the Dongsi People's Bazaar, with an area of over 4,500 square meters, offers over 17,000 different articles and is one of the biggest shopping centers in Beijing.

The Changdian Fair was from its inception one of the city's busiest fairs and a favorite outing place for Beijing residents during the lunar New Year (Spring Festival). Changdian itself was a small street with only ten or so houses on it, but each year at the Spring Festival it, along with the adjacent Liulichang Street, Xinhua Road, the Lü Dongbin Hall (Luzudian), the Jade Emperor Pavilion (Yuhuangge) and the Shatu (Sandy Soil) Gardens, became a large market. In pre-Ming times, this area was a tiny village in a sparsely populated tract of countryside known from the Liao dynasty as the Village of the King of the Sea. By the time of the Ming Jiajing emperor (reigned 1521-66) when the city of Beijing was undergoing expansion, this area was already flourishing, and when the site was chosen in 1553 for the imperial Glazed Tile Works, its name became Liulichang Changdian (Glazed Tile Works Grounds). In the Qing dynasty, the tile works was moved to a site near the Western Hills, but the streets named Liulichang and Changdian remained and the area developed into a public market.

The Changdian Fair, held in the first lunar month, drew people from all parts of the city to buy and sell wares that included paintings and calligraphy, antiques, articles for daily use, children's toys, food products and seasonal fruit and vegetables. In addition, entertainment was provided in the form of acrobatics, conjuring, operas, etc.

After the founding of the Republic of China in 1912, the Changdian Fair continued to be held with the trade in antiques increasing markedly. With the downfall of the Qing dynasty, former residents of the Imperial Palace, as well as princes, nobles and the descendants of deposed officials whose wealth and position were declining came here to sell off their hoarded treasures. They found keen buyers among the emerging class of wealthy warlords, bureaucrats and politicians who were eager to pose as lovers of culture. Many foreigners also showed great interest in Chinese antiques and so the trade in this line flourished.

According to rough statistics available on the 1931 Spring Festival Market at Changdian, of a total of about 1,000 stalls, some 300 dealt in antiques and jade, over 200 in toys and novelties and over 100 in food products. In addition, there were over 100 stalls selling daily necessities and 200 that sold miscellaneous goods. Businessmen from overseas also realized the potential of the Changdian Fair as a market for their products and each year supplied a large volume of goods. By 1935, of the 100 stalls at the fair dealing in toys and novelties, 80 were selling Japanese goods.

After 1949, the Changdian Fair continued to operate each year at the Spring Festival. The 1963 market was the largest since the founding of the People's Republic with over 750 stalls attracting over four million visitors. Unfortunately, the fairs were discontinued in the late 1960s.

Chapter 3
Public Parks and Private Gardens

Zhongshan Park

Zhongshan Park is located to the west of Tian'an-men (Gate of Heavenly Peace) in the heart of the Inner City. It is the site of the former Altar of Land and Grain.

Entering through the main southern entrance, one comes to a large vestibular pavilion with long corridors running off from its eastern and western sides. In front of the pavilion stands a white marble memorial archway erected by the Qing Government to commemorate the German envoy Baron von Kettler, who was killed during the Yi He Tuan Movement ("Boxer Rebellion") in 1900. This archway originally stood outside the western entrance to the Xizongbu Alley, but after Germany's defeat in World War I it was removed to the Zhongshan Park and inscribed with the words "Triumph of Righteousness" (Gongli Zhansheng). After 1949 it was reinscribed in Guo Moruo's handwriting with "Defend the Peace" (Baowei Heping).

The path that runs through the archway is lined with umbrella-like scholartrees and verdant pines. On the eastern side of the path stands a strange and beautiful specimen of Lake Taihu stone known as "a slice of dark clouds," which was moved here from the Yuanmingyuan Gardens. The inscription carved on

it was composed by the Qianlong emperor. Further
on, this path is crossed by one running east-west. To
the east lies the peony pond, to the south wisteria
arbor, and to the north a grove of cypresses with trees
said to have been planted in the Liao dynasty (907-
1125). Seven of the trees are so large that it takes three
or four persons with arms outstretched to encircle the
trunk. One of the cypresses on the eastern side is particularly unusual, because a scholartree has grown out
from its trunk. This intertwined pair of trees is called
"the embrace of the scholartree and the cypress."

On the southern side of this east-west pathway lies
a greenhouse with fresh flowers on display all year
round. Included in the display are 39 varieties of
tulips presented to the park in 1977 by the Princess of
Holland. The eight "Orchid Pavilion" stelae, standing
inside a hall nearby, are engraved in the hand of the
Qianlong emperor with the text of a famous preface
to a collection of poems entitled "The Orchid Pavilion." The Pavilion Where the Rites Are Practiced
(Xilitang) was moved to the Zhongshan Park from the
Honglu Court, an office which during the Ming and
Qing dynasties was responsible for holding official
ceremonies. In imperial times all officials coming to
the capital to be received by the emperor for the first
time went first to the Honglu Court to learn the
proper protocol.

To the south of this path there is also a display of
rare goldfish in a multitude of colors, shapes and sizes.
Further south, one comes to one of the quietest spots
in the park, an area containing the Lotus Pool, Waterside Pavilion, Pavilion of Four Contentments and the
Pavilion to Welcome the Sunshine.

On the north side of the path is the Altar of Land and Grain. Here the landscape is particularly charming, with the lofty Concert Hall to the east and the Health Education Hall to the west. The area is planted with numerous fruit trees, hebaceous peonies and green lawns. A wide path through the center of the lawns leads to the Altar.

To the east of the Altar is another tranquil part of the park containing the Pavilion of the Pines and Cypresses and a tall rockery. Winding footpaths lead to secluded nooks and wend their way to the cross-shaped Touhu Pavilion, which takes its name from an old game which consisted of throwing arrows into a pot. South of this building lies the Kiosk for Meeting New Friends (Laijinyuxuan) where refreshments are sold.

To the west of the Altar of Land and Grain is the liveliest part of the park. Here among a forest of cypress trees stand artificial hills, thatched pavilions, a teahouse, a restaurant, a children's playground and an amusement park.

To the north of the Altar past the Zhongshan Hall is another copse of cypress trees, among which is a stone table built of hollow bricks dating from the Han dynasty. The classically elegant designs on the old bricks are still quite distinct. The southern bank of the Imperial Palace moat begins at the northern edge of the cypress copse. The moat (Tongzihe or Tube River) is also known as the Imperial River (Yuhe) and is used for ice skating in the winter and boating during the summer and autumn.

Over a thousand years ago the site of Zhongshan Park was the Temple of National Prosperity (Xingguo-

si) which stood in the northeastern suburbs of Yanjing, the Liao dynasty capital. Under the Yuan dynasty, the name of the temple was changed to the
Temple of Longevity and National Prosperity. Although no traces of the old buildings remain, the ancient cypresses planted inside the temple serve as a reminder of those days. In 1421, the Ming Yongle emperor built the Altar of Land and Grain symmetrically
opposite the Imperial Ancestral Temple (Taimiao),
which stands to the east of Tian'anmen. In 1914, the
Altar was renamed Central Park and opened to the
public on October 10. In 1928, the park was renamed
Zhongshan Park in tribute to the memory of Sun Yat-
sen.

After the founding of New China, the People's Government renovated the park's buildings, added new
facilities and planted many trees and flowers, transforming the park into a tranquil and attractive scenic
area.

Working People's Cultural Palace

The Working People's Cultural Palace lies to the
east of Tian'anmen, symmetrically opposite Zhongshan
Park. The large park stretches from a line parallel with
Tian'anmen in the south northwards to the Forbidden
City moat, and from the East Thousand *Bu* Corridor
before the Imperial Palace in the west to the eastern
palace walls — fully one half the width of the Forbidden
City. The park was originally built in 1420 as a large-
scale temple.

The central part of the park consists of three magnificent halls, each with its own auxiliary halls. The front hall, the largest of the three, has a double-eaved roof and rests on a three-layer stone base. Before it to the south is a spacious courtyard with long corridors enclosing it on each side. At the southern end of the courtyard is a compound containing a pavilion and several exquisite stone bridges spanning the Golden River (Jinshuihe). A forest of ancient cypress trees surrounds this group of buildings which, with their strong yet simple style, form a single integrated whole with the Imperial Palace.

In the past, the temple was known as the Imperial Ancestral Temple (Taimiao) and served as a repository for the memorial tablets of the emperors' ancestors. During the Ming and Qing dynasties, on occasions such as an emperor's ascending the throne, a triumphant return from battle or the presentation of prisoners of war, the emperor would first come here to offer sacrifices to his ancestors.

At other times, the huge temple stood empty except for the few bailiffs who guarded the doors and a great flock of gray cranes. The temple remained in this state for the better part of more than five hundred years until International Labor Day in 1951, when it became the Beijing Working People's Cultural Palace. On its main southern gate hangs an inscription of its name written in Mao Zedong's calligraphy.

Later, the other traditional buildings inside the palace were converted into a library, an exhibition hall, a theater and a stadium. Flower beds were laid out among the pines and cypresses to mark the rebirth of this ancient shrine.

Temple of Heaven (Tiantan Park)

The Temple of Heaven, situated in southeastern Beijing, is the largest extant sacrificial temple in China. During the Ming and Qing periods it was the site of imperial sacrifices to Heaven. It was here that the emperor conducted the elaborate and most exalted sacrifices addressed to "the Supreme Ruler of the Universe."

Construction of the Temple of Heaven was begun in the year 1406 during the reign of the Yongle emperor and took 14 years to complete. It was later expanded under the Qianlong (1736-96) and Jiaqing (1796-1820) emperors. The area of the Temple of Heaven is more than twice that of the Imperial Palace, occupying 2,668 hectares, or about 6,670 acres. The walls are 1,700 meters from east to west and 1,600 meters from north to south. The three main structures used in the sacrifices are circular in plan, corresponding to the supposed shape of Heaven. The glazed tile roofs of the temples are deep blue and the platforms constructed of slabs of white marble. Each of the three platforms consists of three tiers, making a total of nine tiers — nine in Chinese cosmology representing Heaven. In fact, the number and layout of every single slab used in the platforms is determined according to cosmological principles.

Originally the Temple of Heaven had only one main gate which faced west, but after it was made a public park in 1949, entrances were opened on the northern, southern and eastern sides as well. The Bridge of Cinnabar Steps (Danbiqiao) connects the main architectural structures of the Temple of Heaven — the Hall

Temple of Heaven

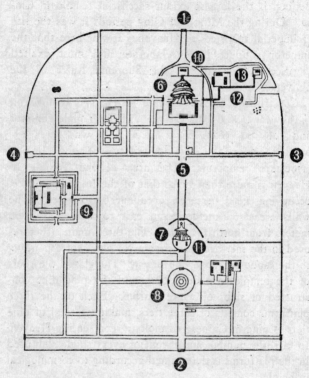

1. Northern Heavenly Gate
2. Southern Heavenly Gate
3. Eastern Heavenly Gate
4. Western Heavenly Gate
5. Bridge of Cinnabar Steps
6. Hall of Prayer for a Good Year
7. Hall of the Imperial Heavenly Vault
8. Altar of Heaven
9. Hall of Abstinence
10. Hall of Imperial Heaven
11. Echo Wall
12. Seventy-two Corridors
13. Sacrificial Chamber

of Prayer for a Good Year (Qiniandian) to the north and the Hall of the Imperial Heavenly Vault (Huangqiongyu) and the Altar of Heaven (Huanqiu) to the south. Though a bridge in name, it is actually a stone walkway 2.5 meters high extending 360 meters from north to south.

The section of wall enclosing the southern end of the temple grounds is square, while that in the northern end is semi-circular, based on the ancient notion that the Earth is square and Heaven round. Old cypress trees surround the buildings and create an appropriately spiritual atmosphere. The Temple of Heaven has two walls, dividing the area into inner and outer sections. The inner section contains the important sacrificial structures, while the outer section is occupied by several auxiliary buildings.

On the day before the sacrifices were to be conducted, the emperor came to the temple to perform a number of preliminary rituals. He spent the night fasting in the Hall of Abstinence, directly east of the Bridge of Cinnabar Steps. This hall is square in shape, surrounded by a moat and a high wall. Its facilities consist of a main hall, sleeping quarters, watch room and bell tower. There is also a small stone pavilion containing a bronze statue. The statue holds a plaque inscribed with "Rules of the Fast" to remind the emperor of his task. Legend holds that the statue is modeled after a Tang dynasty official who was once bold enough to point out the emperor's faults.

The Temple of Heaven also had an office of divine music to train musicians for the rituals as well as a sacrifice chamber, where animals were prepared for sacrifice.

At the north end of the Bridge of Cinnabar Steps one passes through the Gate of Prayer for a Good Year into a large square courtyard, in the center of which is a circular marble platform of three tiers with steps leading up on four sides. Each tier is bounded by an ornately carved white stone railing which from a distance looks like fine lace. Both the railings and the large flat slabs separating each of the staircases are carved with dragons, phoenixes and cloud scrolls depicting the ascent of the dragon and the phoenix. In the center of the platform stands what is perhaps one of the finest examples of Chinese wooden architecture, the Hall of Prayer for a Good Year. It was first built in 1420 and rebuilt according to the original plan as recently as 1890, after it was struck by lightning.

The circular Hall of Prayer for a Good Year has a three-tiered roof of sky-blue glazed tiles which become smaller as they near the peak. The peak itself, some 38 meters from the ground, is crowned with a spherical gilt ornament. The hall's roof, 30 meters in diameter, is supported exclusively with pillars and brackets without a single nail. Of its 28 pillars, the four central ones — the so-called Dragon Well Pillars — are 19.2 meters high. The other pillars, of Phoebe nanmu wood, are arranged according to the 12 months and the 12 time periods into which the day is divided. Each pillar is an enormous single tree trunk.

Set in the center of the flagstone floor is a round veined marble stone with a "found" pattern of a dragon and a phoenix. The hall has no actual walls, only frame doors all around. Twice a year the emperor would come here to perform the most sanctified ritual of the empire. On the fifteenth day of the first lunar month, he sacrificed here to ensure an abundant grain harvest. And at the winter solstice, he expressed his gratitude for the blessings received from Heaven.

The Hall of the Imperial Heavenly Vault (Huangqiongyu) at the southern end of the Bridge of Cinnabar Steps served as the storehouse for the spirit tablet of the Supreme Ruler of the Universe (Huangtian Shangdi). When the ceremonies were conducted, the tablet was moved to the Altar of Heaven, located directly to the south of the Hall of the Imperial Heavenly Vault. During the sacrifices, worship was offered to the Supreme Ruler of the Universe, to the spirits of the sun, moon, stars, clouds, rain, wind and thunder, as well as to the emperor's ancestors. During times of drought, prayers for rain were also offered here. The Hall of the Imperial Heavenly Vault stands 19.5 meters tall and is 15.6 meters in diameter. It was first built in 1530 and restored in 1752. The interior retains its original splendid decoration. Surrounding the hall is a circular wall constructed of tightly fitted bricks. A gate opens to the south, leading to the Altar of Heaven.

The Altar of Heaven is constructed of three tiers of green and white marble, the circumference of each tier being fitted with a white marble balustrade. The surface of the platform, the stairs and the railings are made up of stone slabs in multiples of nine. This is drawn from the ancient Chinese belief that nine was the numerical epitome of *yang*, the positive force, and symbolized Heaven. The top platform is 33.3 meters in diameter and has a circular stone in the center, which was considered the most sacred spot in the Chinese empire. The first ring of stones around it consists of nine slabs, the second ring of 18, the third of

27 and so forth until we reach the ninth and outermost row which consists of 81 slabs. Like the top level, the central and lower levels are each made up of nine concentric rings of stones, the slabs again being laid out in multiples of nine. Each tier has four approaches — one from each of the four directions — and the staircases at these points each have nine steps. To the southeast of the altar stands a glazed tile stove used for burning offerings of silk, and to the southwest is a "signal lantern platform." When lit before dawn on winter days, these fires must have added a particular eeriness to the scene.

The construction of the Altar of Heaven was begun in 1530. It was rebuilt once in 1749. The form of the structure was determined by its function. Because the sacrifices were made to Heaven, it was thought best to leave the structure open to the sky. Because Heaven is symbolized by a circle, the platform is round. It is surrounded by two sets of walls; the outer square wall symbolizing Earth and the inner round wall symbolizing Heaven.

A person standing in the center of the altar who speaks softly will hear the echo of his own voice. Others on the platform will not hear it because the sound echoes off the surrounding balustrade and returns directly to the center of the circle. In addition, if one stands on the first flagstone at the bottom of the staircase which leads up to the southern entrance door of the Hall of the Imperial Heavenly Vault and claps or shouts loudly, a single echo is produced; standing on the second flagstone, a double echo is produced; and on the third flagstone, a triple echo can be heard. Also, in the same courtyard, if two people stand at the east leads onto West Di'anmen Street.   The front gate, known as the Gate of Received Light (Chengguang-men), leads directly to the triple arched Bridge of Ever-lasting Peace (Yong'anqiao), built in 1332. Linking the Circular Wall with Qionghua Islet, the bridge has me-morial gateways at each end. The southern gateway is named Accumulated Emerald (Jicui) and the northern is named Piled-up Clouds (Duiyun). Beyond the north-ern gateway, 30 stone steps rise to the Temple of Eternal Peace (Yong'ansi). Inside the temple gate is the Hall of the Wheel of the Law (Falundian), with pavilions on either side of it and a terrace to its north laid with curiously shaped stones to form a tunnel and six caves. The second cave from the east is inscribed with the words, "Kunlun" (the Cosmic Mountain). The caves connect with the tunnel which leads directly to the White Dagoba Hill.

The White Dagoba is the aesthetic highpoint of Bei-hai Park. Below it on the southern slope of the hill is the Hall of Beneficent Causation (Shanyindian), where the view takes in the waters of Zhongnanhai

1. Jade Islet
2. White Dagoba
3. Little Western Heaven
4. Hall for Gazing at the Water
5. Tranquil Heart Study
6. Bridge of Everlasting Peace
7. Temple of Eternal Peace
8. Hall of Ripples
9. Mountain Climbing Bridge
10. Hall of Great Compas-sion and Truth
11. Hall of Correct En-lightenment
12. Jade Islet in Shady Springtime
13. Spring Rain Forest Pool
14. Painted Pleasure Boat
15. Altar to the Goddess of Silkworms
16. Hall of Heavenly Kings
17. Nine-Dragon Wall
18. Iron Screen
19. Five Dragon Pavilions
20. Botanical Gardens
21. Circular Wall
22. Hall of Received Light
23. Jade Urn Pavilion
24. Front Gate
25. Back Gate

(Central and South Lakes), the golden roofs of the Forbidden City and the tree-shaded buildings in nearby city streets.

Coming to the northern face of the hill, one notices that the neat layout of the southern side has given way to greater naturalness and intricacy, for this area of the park is a maze of pavilions and corridors leading around and between deep rocky crags. At the water's edge, a 300-meter semi-circular corridor follows the shoreline from the Tower Beside the Waters (Yiqinglou) in the east to the Pavilion of Sharing Coolness (Fenliangge) in the west. To the north in the central part of the corridor are the Hall of Ripples (Yilantang), which can also be reached by tunnel from the hilltop, and the Studio of the Peaceful Path (Daoningzhai). The corridor complex provides views of the eastern, northern and western sections of the park.

By crossing the Mountain Climbing Bridge (Zhishanqiao) to the east and passing through the children's playground, one comes to the Young Pioneers' Hydraulic Power Station built in 1956. To its east is the Spring Rain Forest Pool (Chunyulintang) and the Studio of Painted Pleasure Boat (Huafangzhai), while further to the north the path leads through a mulberry grove to the park's rear gate. Directly opposite the rear gate is the lock through which water flows into the lake. To the east of the gate is the Altar to the Goddess of Silkworms built by the Qianlong emperor, which is now the site of the Beihai Kindergarten. To the west the path leads on to the Tranquil Heart Study (Jingxinzhai), the Hall of Heavenly Kings (Tianwangdian), the Nine-Dragon Wall (Jiulongbi), the Hall for Gazing at the Water (Chengguantang), the Iron Screen (Tieyingbi) and the Five Dragon Pavilions (Wulongting).

East of the pavilions are docks for pleasure boats and the ferry that runs across the lake to the Hall of Azure Reflections (Bizhaolou) on Qionghua Islet. To the west of the pavilions stands the Little Western Heaven (Xiaoxitian), commonly called Haidao (Island in the Sea) or the "Land of Unlimited Happiness," which houses a collection of Buddhist images. To the north is the former site of the Temple of Revealing Happiness (Chanfusi), which is now a botanical garden, made up of ten display halls. Surrounding the halls are numerous decorative trees and shrubs as well as fruit trees, fragrant plants and other vegetation of commercial value. In 1980, a tropical greenhouse for displaying such exotic trees as mango, longan, litchee, carambola and coffee was erected.

To the west of the botanical garden is the Pavilion of Ten Thousand Buddhas (Wanfolou), with its entrance inscribed with "Wonderful Place of Dignity and Solemnity" (Miaojing Zhuangyan). This pavilion was built by the Qianlong emperor to mark his mother's 80th birthday. Inside the building are 10,000 tiny niches originally designed to hold an equal number of pure gold images of the Buddha. In 1900, all of these images were plundered by the Eight-Power Allied Forces when they invaded Beijing. At the same time, countless pearls and gems inlaid in the large Buddha which once stood in the Hall of Great Compassion and Truth (Dacizhenrudian) in the Temple of Revealing Happiness were also stolen.

Beihai's most famous structures deserve a more detailed introduction:

(1) Qionghua (Jade) Islet, also known as Qiong Islet or Penglai Mountain, covers an area of some 66,000 square meters. It was in accordance with the proposals of his Lamaist advisers that the Qing Shunzhi emperor (reigned 1644-61) built the 35-meter-tall onion-shaped dagoba on the site of the Jin dynasty Palace of the Moon (Guanghandian) and called it the White Dagoba. The top of the dagoba was damaged in the 1976 Tangshan earthquake, but was soon after repaired. The island is embellished with many large weirdly-shaped rocks, carved to resemble caves inhabited by Daoist immortals. At the summit of the hill stands an ancient hall, reputed to have been the dressing chamber of empress dowagers during the Liao dynasty (907-1125). On the slopes of the hill are the Hall of Correct Enlightenment (Zhengjuedian), the Hall of Universal Peace (Pu'andian) and the Hall of Beneficent Causation (Shanyindian).

The Hall of Beneficent Causation is built of glazed bricks with 100 glazed ceramic images of the Buddha set into its four walls. In the center of the hall is a statue of the Goddess of Mercy with 1,000 Arms, also called the Buddha who Calms the Lake (Zhenhaifo). The Pavilion for Evoking Victory (Yinshengting) which stands before the dagoba contains a stela inscribed with "A Complete Record of White Dagoba Hill." The Pavilion for Inspecting Old Script (Yuegulou) contains 495 samples of the works of famous Chinese calligraphers, which were carved in stone during the time of the Qianlong emperor. The collection is an excellent source for rubbings.

and west extremes of the circular "Echo Wall" and one speaks softly, the sound will be propelled around the wall enabling the person on the opposite side to hear it clearly.

Other items of interest in the Temple of Heaven are the bronze incense burner ornamented with the Eight Diagrams and the bronze tripod (*ding*) in front of the Hall of prayer for a Good Year, the Hall of Imperial Heaven (Huangqiandian), the Divine Kitchen and the Seventy-two Corridors, as well as the gnarled Nine-Dragon Cypress, the intertwined cypress and locust trees, and the Seven Meteorites.

Eight Ancient Altars in Beijing

Apart from the Temple of Heaven mentioned above, there were also a total of eight imperial sacrificial altars in ancient Beijing, all of which played an important part in the ritual life of the Ming and Qing emperors. They will be introduced briefly below.

Altar of Land and Grain (Shejitan)

The Altar of Land and Grain in Zhongshan Park was the site of imperial sacrifices to the gods of land (*she*) and grain (*ji*) in the Ming and Qing dynasties. The altar takes the form of a three-tiered square platform built of white marble, its shape symbolizing the ancient notion that the earth is square. There are four stone staircases, one on each side, leading up to the platform, which is 1.3 meters high and covers a total area of 17 square meters.

Five varieties of colored earth which were spread over the surface of the altar (yellow in the center,

green in the east, red in the south, white in the west,
black in the north) were received by the emperor as
gifts of tribute from subjects in every corner of the
empire. The gifts symbolized that "under heaven, all
belonged to the emperor," but according to an older
tradition, stood for the five elements (metal, wood,
water, fire and earth) which constitute the origins of
all things.

Ancient China was primarily an agricultural society.
The people felt the greatest reverence for the land and
the grain and elevated these things to the status of
gods. Prayers to the gods of land and grain were
originally offered up by the people in the hope of
obtaining a good harvest. But when the feudal emperors assumed the "mandate of Heaven" as their
personal responsibility, sacrifices to the gods of land
and grain came under the aegis of the imperial government. On the fifth day of the second month of spring
and autumn in the lunar calendar, the emperor conducted sacrifices here at dawn.

The altar is surrounded on its four sides by low red
walls set with glazed bricks in four colors representing
the four directions. The innermost wall, with a white
marble gate set in each side, is called the Altar Wall.
Between the Altar Wall and the northern outer wall
are the Hall of Worship (Baidian) and the Halberd
Gate (Jimen). On the west side are the sacred storage
chamber, sacred kitchen and a pavilion for slaughter-
ing sacrificial animals. The Hall of Worship is a solemn and elegant rectangular hall constructed entirely
of wood. The ceilingless roof section leaves the rafters
and corner brackets exposed in what is one of the
finest examples of classical architecture in Beijing.

Built in the Ming dynasty Yongle period (1403-24), the Hall of Worship originally served to shelter the emperors from wind and rain during the course of carrying out their sacrifices. When Sun Yat-sen died in Beijing in 1925, his coffin was temporarily kept here, and in 1928, the name of the Hall of Worship was changed to the Zhongshan Hall. (Zhongshan is Sun Yat-sen's alternate name.)

After 1949, extensive renovations were carried out on the temple building and grounds.

Altar of Earth (Ditan)

The Altar of Earth was the site of sacrifices to Earth. Located to the east of Andingmen (Gate of Peace and Stability), it was built in 1530 during the reign of the Ming Jiajing emperor. The square altar, representing the shape of the earth as conceived by the ancient Chinese, is made of two tiers of marble, each tier two meters high. In classical Chinese thought, the number nine stood for Heaven and the number six for Earth. The upper tier of the altar is 20 square meters or 60 *chi* and the lower tier is 22 square meters or 66 *chi*, both numbers multiples of six.

To the north of the altar is a small reservoir and to the south the House of the Imperial Gods (Huangqishi), where spirit tablets were stored.

The altar was opened to the public in 1925, and in 1957 the work of transforming the area into a public park was begun.

Altar of the Sun (Ritan)

The Altar of the Sun, originally known as the Altar of the Rising Sun (Zhaoritan), was built in 1530. As

its name suggests, it was the site of imperial sacrifices
to the God of the Sun. The altar is located in Beijing's diplomatic quarter to the northeast of Chaoyangmen (Facing the Sun Gate). A square white
marble platform once stood in the garden and although
it fell into disrepair long ago, traces of its ruins may
still be seen. In 1949, the People's Government began
a project of afforestation and turned the area into
Ritan Park.

In the fall of 1980, the construction of a large garden
was begun in the southeastern corner of the park. This
garden is called "The Curving Pond and the Roses
Which Surpass Springtime" (Quchi Shengchun). The
garden occupies a full hectare of land with the curving
pond set in its center. A stone toad sits in the center
of the pond with water gurgling from its mouth. It
is gazing up at a pair of stone swans with their wings
spread ready for flight — illustrating the adage "The
toad longs to eat the flesh of a swan."

Next to the pond are three tall snow pines and to the
east a number of peach and persimmon trees which
have been growing here for decades. A finely landscaped flower garden stands to the west of the pond
and to the north a square pavilion fronted by water on
two sides appears to be floating on the pond's surface.
In addition, at the foot of the little hill to the east is a
trio of graceful magnolias.

Altar of the Moon (Yuetan)

The Altar of the Moon was the site of imperial
sacrifices to the God of the Moon. It is located near
Fuchengmen (Mound-Formed Gate) on North Yuetan
Street. Here as in the other altars dedicated to the

celestial orbs there is a square white marble platform
1.5 meters high with an area of 13.3 square meters. In
the early 1930s, an old caretaker recalled how the last
imperial ceremony was held here 20 years before.

"It was on the evening of the autumnal equinox that
His Majesty came. When the Harvest Moon shone full
on the altar spread with white offerings, white silk,
white jade ware and milky pearls, the Lord of Ten
Thousand Years (the emperor) bowed before the creamy
tablet with the silvered characters meaning 'Place of
the Spirit of the Light of the Night.' Afterwards, four
animals were sacrificed, a pig, an ox, a sheep and a
deer, while the bell tolled from a nearby tower. Then
the emperor changed his sacrificial robes in the pavilion yonder while we humble folk," he added with a
chuckle, "shared the meat offerings with the moon."*

After 1949, numerous plants and fruit trees were
planted here, transforming the old temple into a public
park. In 1969, an immense television broadcasting
tower was erected in the park.

Altar of the God of Agriculture (Xiannongtan)

The Altar of the God of Agriculture was the site of
imperial sacrifices dedicated to the cult of Shennong,
the legendary "first farmer" of China. It is located in
the southern district of the city, directly to the west of
the Temple of Heaven, and occupies a total area of
three square kilometers. The altar itself, which faces
south, is 1.5 meters high and occupies an area of 15.6
square meters. The hall to the north houses the sacred

---

* From *Peking* by Juliet Bredon (Shanghai, 1931).

tablets and is provided with a platform for "observing the harvest."

According to the rites of the Qing dynasty, on the day of the spring equinox as fixed by the lunar calendar, the emperor would come here to sacrifice to the sacred tablet of Shennong. Following this ceremony, the emperor would plow several furrows of land with his own hands and retire to the observation platform to watch the princes, ministers and a representative group of common people finish the task. It was said that the emperor's plowing "set an example of industry to his subjects, thus dignifying the toil of the meanest agricultural laborer."

The area also contains an Altar to the Year God (Taisuidian) for carrying out sacrifices to the planet Jupiter and auxiliary halls on the east and west for carrying out sacrifices to the Deities of the 12 Lunar Months (Yuejiangshen).

After the establishment of the Republic of China in 1912, the main hall was turned into a Temple of Loyalty in memory of the 72 martyrs who died in an uprising at Huanghuagang in Guangzhou. Here there is also a dressing room where the emperor changed into the ceremonial robes worn during the sacrifices; a divine granary for storing the five grains used in the ceremony; and the Palace of Celebrating Completion (Qingchenggong), where the Ming emperors carried out their pre-sacrificial fast.

Altar of the Gods of the Sky (Tianshentan)

The Altar of the Gods of the Sky was the site of imperial sacrifices to the gods of wind, clouds, thunder and rain. It is located on the grounds of the Altar of the God of Agriculture (Xiannongtan). The altar is 1.5 meters high and occupies a total area of 17 square meters. A staircase of nine steps leads up to the altar on each of its four sides. To the north of the altar are four white stone shrines dedicated to the above-mentioned climatic forces. Each shrine is some three meters high and is carved with cloud and dragon patterns.

Altar of the Gods of the Earth (Diqitan)

The Altar of the Gods of the Earth was the site of imperial sacrifices to the gods of mountains and seas. Located in the western part of the Altar of the Gods of the Sky (Tianshentan), the altar is 1.43 meters high and occupies an area of 33 square meters. A staircase consisting of six steps leads up to the platform on all four sides.

To the south of the altar are five stone shrines, three of which are decorated with carvings of mountains symbolizing the Five Sacred Mountains (Wuyue)* and the Five Guardian Mountains (Wuzhen) among others, and two with wave patterns symbolizing the four great seas and four great rivers.**

---

* The Five Sacred Mountains (Wuyue): Taishan (Shandong), Hengshan (Hunan), Huashan (Shaanxi), Hengshan (Shanxi) and Songshan (Henan). The Five Guardian Mountains (Wuzhen): Yishan, Wushan, Huoshan, Kuaijishan and Yiwulüshan in the east, west, center, south and north respectively.

** The four seas are not named in classical books. The four rivers are the Huanghe (Yellow River), Changjiang (Yangtze River), Huai and Ji.

Ponds were dug at the bases of the shrines, but they were filled with water only when the sacrifices were being held.

To the east of the altar, two stone shrines engraved with landscape scenes were utilized for sacrifices to the important mountains and rivers in the capital environs. Another pair of shrines on the west side, also engraved with landscapes, were intended for sacrifices to other major mountains and rivers in China.

Altar to the Goddess of Silkworms (Xiancantan)

The Altar to the Goddess of Silkworms was the site where sacrifices to Leizu (wife of the Yellow Emperor), who is credited with the invention of silkworm breeding, were carried out by the empress. It is located to the northeast of Zhonghai (Central Lake) and is reached by passing north over a bridge from the Temple of the Dragon King (Longwangmiao). (See Zhonghai, page 133.)

The Altar to the Goddess of Silkworms was built during the Qianlong period (1736-96). Entering through the Gate of Admiration for Silkworms, one comes to the altar which is 1.3 meters high and occupies an area of 13.1 square meters. A staircase on each side of the altar leads up ten steps to the site where the sacrificial rituals were carried out.

Mulberry trees, which provide the regular diet for silkworms, are planted on three sides of the altar, and behind the temple there is a Hall of Admiration for Silkworms (Qincandian) and a Pool for Washing Silkworms (Yucanchi).

Zhongnanhai (Central and South Lakes)

Immediately to the west of the Forbidden City is a large area of lakes which the court officials of the Qing dynasty called the Western Lake (Xihaizi) or the Pool of Great Secretion (Taiyechi). Centuries ago, this stretch of water was divided into three sections — the North Lake (Beihai), the Central Lake (Zhonghai) and the South Lake (Nanhai). The area between New China Gate (Xinhuamen) on Chang'an Boulevard in the south and Yingtai (Sea Terrace Island) in the north is called the South Lake. The area north of the Hall of Diligent Government (Qinzhengdian) and south of the Temple of Endless Blessings (Wanshantang) is called the Central Lake, which is connected to the South Lake by a lock located near the old eastern gate of the area; and the area north of the Hall of Received Brilliance (Chengguangdian) and south of the Five Dragon Pavilions (Wulongting) is known as the North Lake or Beihai. A long white marble bridge — the Golden Tortoise Jade Rainbow Bridge — divides the Central Lake from the North Lake. The water supply for the lakes comes from the Jade Spring Mountain (Yuquanshan) to the west of Beijing and enters the city at the Gate of Moral Victory (Deshengmen) in the northwest corner of the old city limits.

The fine natural hills and ponds in this area inspired the emperors of the Liao dynasty (907-1125) to choose this area as their pleasure park and called the North Lake the Jade Islet. During the Jin dynasty (1115-1234), the North Lake became the site of the emperors' winter palace. In the Yuan dynasty (1206-1368), the lakes were enclosed to become part of the Imperial Palace in the new Mongol capital of Dadu, and the lakes were granted a new name — the Pool of Great Secretion (Taiyechi). At the same time, the lakes were widened and deepened, and the mud dredged from them was heaped up to the north of the Forbidden City to form Prospect Hill (Jingshan). The lakes attained their present dimensions of two kilometers from north to south and, at their widest point, 200 meters from east to west.

When the Ming Yongle emperor rebuilt the Imperial Palace in 1417, he extended the palace walls to enclose both the former Yuan palace and the gardens to the west. Hence in the Ming and Qing dynasties, the area became known as the Western Gardens (Xiyuan) and continued to serve palace residents as a place of leisure. During the Qing dynasty, refurbishment of the area continued on a grand scale, and the majority of the structures and relics which remain today date from that period.

After the demise of the Qing dynasty in 1911, Zhongnanhai (the Central and South Lakes) were turned into a park for a short period of time and served as the headquarters of the government of Yuan Shikai. This area is now the headquarters of the Central Committee of the Chinese Communist Party and the State Council of the People's Republic of China.

Nanhai (The South Lake)

The main gate of the South Lake is the New China Gate (Xinhuamen), which was originally known as the Precious Moon Tower. It is said that this tower was the famous Gazing Home Tower

(Wangxianglou) built by the Qianlong emperor for a favorite Moslem concubine, the Perfumed Consort (Xiangfei). To remind this homesick lady of her native Kashgaria (in present-day Xinjiang), Qianlong had a mosque and an Islamic style marketplace built within view of the tower. After the establishment of the Republic of China in 1912, the New China Gate (Xinhuamen) was refurbished and the signboard for Yuan Shikai's presidential residence was hung here.

The gate is today the official entrance to the headquarters of the People's Government, but visitors to the scenic areas must enter by a gate at 81 Nanchang Street. Once inside and a short distance to the north, one comes to a pavilion, the floor of which contains a stone-lined channel which makes nine turns. The bubbling sounds of the water in this channel give this spot the name Flowing Water Music (Liushuiyin). To the west of this pavilion is the Hall of Diligent Government (Qinzhengdian) where the Qing Guangxu emperor administered the affairs of state. When Yuan Shikai took up residence in Nanhai, he rebuilt the hall in Western style and used it to receive foreign guests.

Walking south from here, visitors cross a curving bridge to the Sea Terrace Island (Yingtai), which with its three sides surrounded by water is actually a peninsula in the South Lake. The tall granite structure on the other side of the bridge is the Southern Terrace (Nantai), the principal viewing place in this section of the park. The buildings here date from the reigns of the Shunzhi and Kangxi emperors (1644-1722). Among the dozen or so poetically named pavilions, gates, halls and towers, we shall only mention the fol-

lowing: the Hall of the Fragrant Screen (Xiangyi-
dian) where there is a room set aside for drinking tea;
the Fairy Isles Pavilion (Penglaige), next to which
stands a specimen of fossilized pine nearly three
meters tall — an inscription nearby attributes the stone
to the Six Dynasties period (220-589); on each side of
this stone are several flower beds, and in front of it
a stone bridge which leads to a pavilion on the water
known as the Welcoming Fragrance Pavilion (Ying-
xunting), where there are numerous stone inscriptions
praising the virtues and achievements of the emperors.
Looking south across the water from here, one can see
the north side of the screen wall which stands directly
inside New China Gate.

Among the other relics on the island are a group of
imitation stalagmites inscribed with the calligraphy of
the Qianlong emperor and another stone inscription in
the same emperor's hand commemorating a willow tree
in the shape of the Chinese character for "man" (人)
which once stood on this spot. A limb of this willow
was bent over by a strong wind, and some kind soul
moored one of its branches to the ground to support
the rest of the tree. This branch actually took root
and the resulting grotesquely shaped tree so delighted
the Qianlong emperor that he composed a prose poem
about it.

The Sea Terrace Island was one of the favorite summer resort spots of the Qing emperors. Kangxi and
Qianlong both administered the empire from here, and
after the failure of the Reform Movement of 1898, the
Guangxu emperor was imprisoned here by the Empress Dowager Cixi, and in 1907 died in the Hanyuan
(Cherishing the Origin) Palace. In the early years of

the Republican period, Yuan Shikai arranged for Li Yuanhong, the Vice-President of the Republic, to make his residence here. After the establishment of the People's Republic of China in 1949, various departments of the State Council made use of the many halls to hold private small-scale industrial exhibitions. A major restoration project was completed in 1975.

Walking northwest from the Sea Terrace Island, one comes to the Garden of Plenty (Fengzeyuan), in which there is a small plot of land called the Trial Sowing Grounds (Yangengdi) where the Qing emperors rehearsed on a somewhat smaller scale the plowing ceremony held at the Altar of the God of Agriculture (see page 123). One particular rehearsal which took place in 1888 is recorded in the diary of Weng Tonghe, the Guangxu emperor's tutor: "Shortly after 9 a.m. the emperor arrived at the yellow tent by palanquin, rested for a short while, and removed his long gown. Officials presented him with a plow and a whip, and with another official holding a basket, Weng Tonghe sowed the seeds. Two old peasants led the oxen, and with imperial guards supporting the plow, the emperor sowed four furrows in each direction. This accomplished, His Majesty rested in the yellow tent and drank tea before returning to the palace." Having been touched by the "dragon hands" of the emperor, this ceremonial plow became a sacred object. It is now on display in the Palace Museum.

Mao Zedong's former residence, a traditional Beijing home built around a courtyard, is also here in the Garden of Plenty. Chairman Mao occupied the rooms on the northern side of the courtyard; the rooms to the west now contain a display of his personal effects, while his office and bedroom to the east remain exactly as he left them, with the former Chairman's desk, bathrobe and slippers on display. In Qing times, these rooms were known as the "Library of Chrysanthemum Fragrance."

To the west of the Garden of Plenty is the Pavilion of Lotus Breeze and Orchid-Scented Dew (Hefenghuiluting), and immediately to the south, an elegant white marble gateway with the inscription "Peaceful Valley" (Jinggu) carved into its lintel. On either side of the gateway, the following couplet is inscribed: "Here we may revel in the splendor of strange clouds and rocks, while the numerous manifestations of nature reveal their particular wonders; in the green dark shadows of bamboos and pines, the luxuriant verdure remains unchanged throughout the year."

In addition to the places mentioned above, a number of other buildings not yet open to the public are worthy of mention. The Hall of the Calm Sea (Haiyantang) is the Western style structure formerly used by Cixi for entertaining her female guests. The hall is furnished with chairs and tables in Louis XV style imported from France. When Yuan Shikai came into power, he changed its name to the Hall of Benevolence (Jurentang) and continued to use it for entertaining visitors. In 1927, when the warlord Zhang Zuolin took over Beijing, he made the Hall of Benevolence his residence. And in 1923, when the warlord Cao Kun was President of the Republic, he too made his offices here. But when Cao was captured by the Christian General Feng Yuxiang, it became his prison.

In the South Lake district, there is an interesting set of ten square stones, each inscribed with a poem composed of lines written by different persons, and a preface to each poem. Though the nearby Corridor in the Shape of a Swastika (Wanzilang) has been torn down, to the south of its former site stands the Stone Chamber (Shishi), built entirely of white marble. Inside the chamber is a "golden casket" — actually a gilded safe — which played a critical role in the history of the early Republic. In 1914, Yuan Shikai reformed the "Laws for Electing the President" by having the names of three preselected candidates for his succession — including his own name — placed inside the safe. When the time came, his specially appointed parliament had little choice but to choose Yuan as the new president.

The most impressive natural scenery in the South Lake area is provided by the groves of old trees, with elms being the most conspicuous by their absence. The story behind this goes that on a certain day in 1883, the Empress Dowager Cixi was out for a stroll. When a caterpillar falling from an infested elm landed on her dress and stung her hand, Cixi became so enraged that she immediately ordered all of the elm trees in the South Lake district cut down.

Zhonghai (The Central Lake)

The area north from the Hall of Diligent Government (Qinzhengdian) to Fuhuamen Gate contains a number of pre- and post-Liberation buildings which, with the exception of the Hall of Embracing Benevolence (Huairentang), are not open to the public.

The Hall of Embracing Benevolence is the most important building in the Central Lake area. It was originally the site of the Hall of Imperial Pomp (Yiluan-

dian) which was destroyed by the Eight-Power Allied
Forces. When Cixi returned to Beijing from the court's
flight to Xi'an, she spent more than five million silver
dollars and erected a "Tower of Buddhist Reflections"
(Fozhaolou). During the first year of the Republic of
China (1912), the Tower's name was changed to the
Hall of Embracing Benevolence. The National Assembly
and other governing bodies of the early Republic met
in this hall, and after Yuan Shikai's death, the former
president's coffin rested here temporarily. After 1949,
the hall was used for meetings of the First People's
Political Consultative Conference and other important
political bodies. In front of the hall is a display of cultural relics: 12 bronze statues with animal heads and
human torsos; bronze lions decorated with cloisonne;
commemorative tablets; and images of the 12 animal*
signs used to symbolize the year in which a person is
born. Local school children are occasionally brought
here for a visit.

On the northwest bank of the Central Lake is another important structure, the Tower of Vermilion
Light (Ziguangge), also called the Flat Terrace (Ping-
tai), where the Ming Zhengde emperor (reigned 1506-
21) watched his troops practicing their calisthenics and
archery. These displays continued during the Qing dynasty when portraits of meritorious officials from past
dynasties hung inside the Tower's hall. In the first lunar
month of every year, the emperor would hold a banquet here in honor of his meritorious officials. A collec-

---

* Rat, ox, tiger, hare, dragon, snake, horse, sheep, monkey, fowl,
dog and pig.

tion of fine old maps and paintings is preserved in the
Tower in excellent condition.

The northeast bank of the Central Lake is the location of the famous Plantain Garden (Jiaoyuan) or Virtuous Garden, the former site of the Ming dynasty Palace of Sublime Wisdom (Chongzhidian).   The path
here leading north along the eastern side of the lake is
lined with scholar, willow and fruit trees as well as a
number of closely spaced pavilions and small decorative
buildings. During the Qianlong period (1736-96), the
Plantain Garden served as a schoolroom for the younger eunuchs who lived in the Palace. On the Buddhist
Ghost Festival, celebrated on the evening of the 15th
day of the seventh lunar month, numerous floating lanterns were sent out "to sea," turning the lakes into a
vast field of twinkling stars.

To the north of the Plantain Garden is the Temple
of Endless Blessings (Wanshandian). The main hall
contains images of the Three Buddhas — the Goddess
of Mercy (Guanyin), Manjusri (Wenshu) and Samantabhadra (Puxian) — and the Eighteen Immortals (Luohan). At the rear of the main hall is a statue of the
Goddess of Mercy of the Southern Seas (Nanhai Guanyin). The Hall of a Thousand Buddhas stands to the rear
of this temple complex and contains an octagonal sandalwood pagoda with seven stories dating from the
Ming dynasty. The other halls of the temple house
many fine sculptural representations of legendary emperors, Buddhas and other gods and immortals.   Of
particular interest is the Hall of the Dragon Kings
(Longwangtang) housing images of the dragon kings
which govern streams, rivers, lakes and seas.

Heading out of the eastern gate of the Plantain Gar-

den and walking north, one will pass a small hill and a
pond before coming to a thatched gate. Entering the
gate and continuing down a secluded path, one will
reach the Pavilion of Clouds on the Water (Shuiyunxie).
This pavilion is one of the principal sights in the Central Lake area. Its name is derived from the way it
appears to float amidst the images of clouds reflected
on the lake.

A large stone tablet in the pavilion inscribed with
the calligraphy of the Qianlong emperor, "Autumn
Winds on Taiye," immortalizes this spot as one of the
Eight Great Sights of Yanjing (see page 319).

Beihai (North Lake) Park

Beihai, situated in the center of downtown Beijing,
was the pleasure place of Liao, Jin, Yuan, Ming and
Qing emperors and is one of the most famous and exquisitely designed ancient parks in all of China.

In the middle of the 11th century, Beihai was
known as the "Jade Islet Palace" where the Liao dynasty rulers resided while visiting the suburbs of their
capital, Yanjing. In the Jin dynasty (1115-1234), it was
converted into an imperial villa, at which time Beihai
(North Lake) and Qionghua (Jade) Islet (the present
site of the White Dagoba) were incorporated into the
grounds. It is said that many of the Lake Taihu stones
found on Qionghua Islet were taken by the Jin rulers
from the Song emperor's garden in the Northern Song
dynasty capital, Bianliang (modern Kaifeng) and that
these in turn had been collected in Suzhou under the
Song Huizong emperor. After Kublai Khan destroyed

the Jin capital, he constructed his new capital Dadu with Beihai at its center. The name of the lake was changed to the Pool of Great Secretion (Taiyechi) and Qionghua Islet was named Longevity Hill. The Palace of the Moon (Guanghandian), built on the island by the Jin as a pleasure palace, was used by the Yuan leaders as a ceremonial hall and an office for issuing governmental decrees. The jade urn used to hold wine at imperial feasts held in the hall is on display today in its own tiny pavilion located in the Circular Wall (Tuancheng).

During the Ming and Qing dynasties, Beihai continued to be used as an imperial pleasure garden and several large-scale construction projects were undertaken to improve the park's facilities. In 1651, under the Qing Shunzhi emperor, the White Dagoba Temple was built on the site of the Palace of the Moon and the island renamed White Dagoba Hill. The dagoba was badly damaged in an earthquake in 1679 and rebuilt the following year. The Qianlong emperor (reigned 1736-96) also added several new structures. Apart from the halls, terraces and pavilions on the island, he also built the Temple of Revealing Happiness (Chanfusi), the Little Western Heaven (Xiaoxitian), the Hall for Gazing at the Water (Chengguantang) and the Tranquil Heart Study (Jingxinzhai), which is renowned for its curiously shaped stones. Beihai has changed very little since the time of the Qianlong emperor, save that in 1915 it was formally opened as a public park.

The park has two gates. The front gate stands at the eastern entrance to Wenjing Road and the back gate

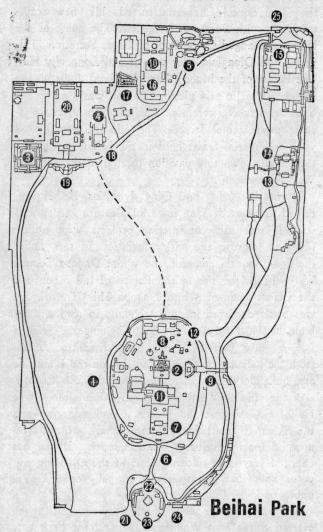

Beihai Park

leads onto West Di'anmen Street. The front gate,
known as the Gate of Received Light (Chengguang-
men), leads directly to the triple arched Bridge of Everlasting Peace (Yong'anqiao), built in 1332. Linking the
Circular Wall with Qionghua Islet, the bridge has memorial gateways at each end. The southern gateway is
named Accumulated Emerald (Jicui) and the northern
is named Piled-up Clouds (Duiyun). Beyond the northern geteway, 30 stone steps rise to the Temple of
Eternal Peace (Yong'ansi). Inside the temple gate is
the Hall of the Wheel of the Law (Falundian), with
pavilions on either side of it and a terrace to its north
laid with curiously shaped stones to form a tunnel and
six caves. The second cave from the east is inscribed
with the words, "Kunlun" (the Cosmic Mountain). The
caves connect with the tunnel which leads directly to
the White Dagoba Hill.

The White Dagoba is the aesthetic highpoint of Beihai Park. Below it on the southern slope of the hill
is the Hall of Beneficent Causation (Shanyindian),
where the view takes in the waters of Zhongnanhai

1. Jade Islet
2. White Dagoba
3. Little Western Heaven
4. Hall for Gazing at the Water
5. Tranquil Heart Study
6. Bridge of Everlasting Peace
7. Temple of Eternal Peace
8. Hall of Ripples
9. Mountain Climbing Bridge
10. Hall of Great Compassion and Truth
11. Hall of Correct Enlightenment
12. Jade Islet in Shady Springtime
13. Spring Rain Forest Pool
14. Painted Pleasure Boat
15. Altar to the Goddess of Silkworms
16. Hall of Heavenly Kings
17. Nine-Dragon Wall
18. Iron Screen
19. Five Dragon Pavilions
20. Botanical Gardens
21. Circular Wall
22. Hall of Received Light
23. Jade Urn Pavilion
24. Front Gate
25. Back Gate

(Central and South Lakes), the golden roofs of the Forbidden City and the tree-shaded buildings in nearby city streets.

Coming to the northern face of the hill, one notices that the neat layout of the southern side has given way to greater naturalness and intricacy, for this area of the park is a maze of pavilions and corridors leading around and between deep rocky crags. At the water's edge, a 300-meter semi-circular corridor follows the shoreline from the Tower Beside the Waters (Yiqinglou) in the east to the Pavilion of Sharing Coolness (Fenliangge) in the west. To the north in the central part of the corridor are the Hall of Ripples (Yilantang), which can also be reached by tunnel from the hilltop, and the Studio of the Peaceful Path (Daoningzhai). The corridor complex provides views of the eastern, northern and western sections of the park.

By crossing the Mountain Climbing Bridge (Zhishanqiao) to the east and passing through the children's playground, one comes to the Young Pioneers' Hydraulic Power Station built in 1956. To its east is the Spring Rain Forest Pool (Chunyulintang) and the Studio of Painted Pleasure Boat (Huafangzhai), while further to the north the path leads through a mulberry grove to the park's rear gate. Directly opposite the rear gate is the lock through which water flows into the lake. To the east of the gate is the Altar to the Goddess of Silkworms built by the Qianlong emperor, which is now the site of the Beihai Kindergarten. To the west the path leads on to the Tranquil Heart Study (Jingxinzhai), the Hall of Heavenly Kings (Tianwangdian), the Nine-Dragon Wall (Jiulongbi), the Hall for Gazing at the Water (Chengguantang), the Iron Screen (Tieyingbi) and the Five Dragon Pavilions (Wulongting).

East of the pavilions are docks for pleasure boats and the ferry that runs across the lake to the Hall of Azure Reflections (Bizhaolou) on Qionghua Islet. To the west of the pavilions stands the Little Western Heaven (Xiaoxitian), commonly called Haidao (Island in the Sea) or the "Land of Unlimited Happiness," which houses a collection of Buddhist images. To the north is the former site of the Temple of Revealing Happiness (Chanfusi), which is now a botanical garden, made up of ten display halls. Surrounding the halls are numerous decorative trees and shrubs as well as fruit trees, fragrant plants and other vegetation of commercial value. In 1980, a tropical greenhouse for displaying such exotic trees as mango, longan, litchee, carambola and coffee was erected.

To the west of the botanical garden is the Pavilion of Ten Thousand Buddhas (Wanfolou), with its entrance inscribed with "Wonderful Place of Dignity and Solemnity" (Miaojing Zhuangyan). This pavilion was built by the Qianlong emperor to mark his mother's 80th birthday. Inside the building are 10,000 tiny niches originally designed to hold an equal number of pure gold images of the Buddha. In 1900, all of these images were plundered by the Eight-Power Allied Forces when they invaded Beijing. At the same time, countless pearls and gems inlaid in the large Buddha which once stood in the Hall of Great Compassion and Truth (Dacizhenrudian) in the Temple of Revealing Happiness were also stolen.

Beihai's most famous structures deserve a more detailed introduction:

(1) Qionghua (Jade) Islet, also known as Qiong Islet or Penglai Mountain, covers an area of some 66,000 square meters. It was in accordance with the proposals of his Lamaist advisers that the Qing Shunzhi emperor (reigned 1644-61) built the 35-meter-tall onion-shaped dagoba on the site of the Jin dynasty Palace of the Moon (Guanghandian) and called it the White Dagoba. The top of the dagoba was damaged in the 1976 Tangshan earthquake, but was soon after repaired. The island is embellished with many large weirdly-shaped rocks, carved to resemble caves inhabited by Daoist immortals. At the summit of the hill stands an ancient hall, reputed to have been the dressing chamber of empress dowagers during the Liao dynasty (907-1125). On the slopes of the hill are the Hall of Correct Enlightenment (Zhengjuedian), the Hall of Universal Peace (Pu'andian) and the Hall of Beneficent Causation (Shanyindian).

The Hall of Beneficent Causation is built of glazed bricks with 100 glazed ceramic images of the Buddha set into its four walls. In the center of the hall is a statue of the Goddess of Mercy with 1,000 Arms, also called the Buddha who Calms the Lake (Zhenhaifo). The Pavilion for Evoking Victory (Yinshengting) which stands before the dagoba contains a stela inscribed with "A Complete Record of White Dagoba Hill." The Pavilion for Inspecting Old Script (Yuegulou) contains 495 samples of the works of famous Chinese calligraphers, which were carved in stone during the time of the Qianlong emperor. The collection is an excellent source for rubbings.

(2) The Temple of Eternal Peace (Yong'ansi), originally the home of the Lama Nuo Buhan, was built in 1651 and named the Temple of the White Dagoba. Inside the main gate lies the Hall of the Wheel of the Law (Falundian) and a number of other halls and pagodas. By climbing a flight of stone steps one comes to the Hall of Beneficent Causation which contains a bronze image of the Buddha. Above to the west stands the White Dagoba.

(3) The Hall of Heavenly Kings (Tianwangdian) lies on the west bank of Beihai Lake. A glazed tile memorial archway stands before the hall, and to the north is the Gate of Heavenly Kings which bears the inscription, "Western Heaven Buddhist Region." Inside this northern gate are two stone pillars, the eastern pillar inscribed with the *Diamond Sutra* (*Jingangjing*) and the western pillar with the *Yaoshi Classic*. The main hall is the Hall of Great Compassion and Truth (Dacizhenrudian). Up a flight of steps behind this hall is the Ten Buddha Pagoda (Shifota), behind which stands a two-story glazed tile pavilion surrounded on all four sides by corridors. To the west of the pagoda is the Beihai Stadium, built after the founding of the People's Republic. The Hall of Heavenly Kings has now become the Beijing Youth Science and Technology Hall.

(4) The Tranquil Heart Study (Jingxinzhai) lies to the east of the Hall of Heavenly Kings. This set of elegant buildings is the famous "park within a park," each building with its own original and poetic name; the Cherish the Search Study (Baosuoshuwu), the Tea Roasting Room (Beichawu), the Tower of Paintings Kiosk (Louhuaxuan), the Sweet-Sounding Zither Study

(Yunqinzhai), the Fresh Green Pavilion (Bixianting), the Room for Painting Peaks (Huafengshi), the Chilly Spring Corridor (Qinquanlang), the Rippling Emerald Tower (Diecuilou) and the Beside the Hill Pavilion (Zhenluanting). The buildings of the Tranquil Heart Study are the best preserved in the entire park. After 1949, this section of the park was entirely renovated and made available for use by the Central Documentary History Research Institute.

(5) The Five Dragon Pavilions (Wulongting) to the west of the Hall of Heavenly Kings were built in the Ming dynasty as a fishing spot for the emperors. The five pavilions on the water are linked by an angled corridor that resembles a swimming dragon, thereby giving the structure its name. The central pavilion, the largest of the five, is called the Pavilion of the Dragon's Benevolence (Longzeting). It has a double eaved roof which resembles a parasol and rectangular terraces extending from its front and back. To the east lie the Fragrance (Zixiang) and Auspicious Clarity (Chengxiang) Pavilions, and to the west the Surging Good Fortune (Yongrui) and Floating Emerald (Fucui) Pavilions.

(6) The Nine-Dragon Wall (Jiulongbi) stands to the south of the Beihai Stadium. Built in the Ming dynasty, it is 6.9 meters high, 25.5 meters long, 1.4 meters thick, and constructed entirely of glazed tiles. On each side nine coiling dragons are depicted frolicking among waves and clouds.

(7) The Iron Screen (Tieyingbi) stands in front of the Hall of Gazing at the Water (Chengguantang) and derives its name from its color and appearance, which resemble iron ore. The screen is four meters wide and two meters high. The strange creatures carv-

ed on both sides with primitive simplicity are reputed to date from the Yuan dynasty. Formerly the screen was stored inside the bell casting room at Deshengmen (Gate of Moral Victory), where it began to rust. In the winter of 1947 the "Beiping Cultural Relics Administration" removed it to Beihai for display.

(8) The Bronze Immortal Bearing the Dew-Collecting Dish (Tongxianchenglupan) stands on the northwest slope of Qionghua Islet. The statue, almost three meters tall, holds a large bronze dish for collecting dew sent down from heaven. It stands on a four-meter-high white marble column carved with dragons.

According to tradition, the Han dynasty emperor Wu Di was told that by drinking dew caught in a bronze dish he could live to be eight hundred years old. This was so intriguing to the middle-aged emperor that in 104 B.C. he had a bronze immortal bearing a dew dish cast and placed the sculpture in a palace outside the capital Chang'an (now Xi'an) especially for the purpose of collecting dew. The Qianlong emperor shared his early predecessor's dreams of longevity and had a new statue of the same image cast and placed on Qionghua Islet. Another explanation of the statue's origins relates that it was brought here by the Jin rulers from the Song capital of Bianliang (now Kaifeng) when they built the Xiang Palace.

The Three Rear Lakes (Housanhai)

The Three Rear Lakes (or Shicha* Lakes), which include Shicha Lake, Rear Lake (Houhai) and Jishuitan

---

* "Shicha" refers to ten temples which at one time stood on the banks of the lake.

(Reservoir Lake), are situated to the north of downtown Beijing between Di'anmen (Gate of Earthly Peace) and Deshengmen (Gate of Moral Victory). The lakes were given this name to distinguish them from the two lakes of Zhongnanhai and the lake in Beihai Park.

Shicha Lake, located to the southwest of the Drum Tower in serene and beautiful surroundings, has a long history. During the Yuan dynasty it was called the Great Lake (Dapozi), and assumed its present name in the Ming and Qing dynasties. Strolling along its shoreline, the visitor can appreciate the lake's glimmering blue water, its graceful weeping willows, its twisting railings and the flower-and-tree-covered central island. Boats are available for rowing and the banks are amply provided with shady places to rest. A swimming area in the lake is open every summer and autumn.

Northwards along the dyke is the gently arched stone Silver Ingot Bridge (Yindingqiao) which marks the boundary between Sicha Lake and Rear Lake. Rear Lake is much larger than Shicha Lake. Standing on the bridge looking westwards, it appears to be a silver river lined with brilliant green willows. The view at sunset, when the evening clouds atop the Western Hills become tinged with color, is known as "Gazing at the mountains from the silver ingot." Spread among the trees on the lake's southern bank are earth mounds, thatched pavilions, windbreaks of pine trees and flower beds, as well as swings, slides, seesaws and merry-go-rounds. Yet despite all these amusements, the general atmosphere remains peaceful and secluded.

Half a kilometer west of Rear Lake lies Jishuitan, which is also called Jingye Lake after the Jingye Temple on the northern bank of the lake. It is also known as Western Lake due to its position west of Shicha Lake.

In the northeastern corner of Jishuitan is a small island with a temple on it built by the Ming Yongle emperor (reigned 1403-24). At the time of its building, the temple was called the Convent of the Goddess of Mercy Who Calms the Waters. In 1761, the Qianlong emperor had the temple reconstructed and erected a stela in the shape of a sword in front of it inscribed with a poem written in the emperor's own calligraphy, which relates the story of the dredging of Jishuitan. Behind the temple is a massive stratified rock which, according to tradition, is a meteorite which landed here over 1,000 years ago. If you look very closely, a lion and a chicken can be discovered in this rock. For this reason, the local people also call this area Chicken and Lion Beach.

Today Jishuitan is a place of relaxation and fine scenery, but in ancient times it was actually a river port. According to the *Yuan History: Biography of Guo Shoujing*, "In 1293, the emperor (Kublai Khan) passed through Jishuitan on his way back from Shangdu and observed a convoy of boats linked stern to stern, so numerous as to render the water invisible." This suggests that grain transport boats were unloaded in these lakes as early as the 13th century.

By the time of the Ming dynasty (1368-1644) the canals had silted up to such a degree that grain could no longer be transported so far inland by boat. Jishuitan became a pleasure resort for high officials and members of the nobility, and pleasure boats replaced the grain convoys. In the early Ming, a scholar named

Wang Huang traveled to Beijing and wrote a poem with this line: "The wine boats on the lake are taller than buildings." At that time the shores of the lake were lined with the villas and gardens of the upper classes.

Under the Qing, Jishuitan remained largely unchanged save that the villas became the residences of Manchu imperial princes and high officials. And in Prince Chun's Mansion, for instance, water from the lake was led into gardens in streams to embellish the mansion grounds. Up through the Republican period, famous scholars continued to live on the lake's shores despite the fact that, although still quiet and peaceful, the banks of the lake had become rather dilapidated. In 1951 the People's Government dredged the lake and today the water is so clean that the bottom is clearly visible.

The Circular Wall (Tuancheng)

The Circular Wall (Tuancheng) is situated at the southern end of Beihai Park immediately to the east of the great marble bridge. There are two gates — the Clear View Gate (Zhaojingmen) to the east and the Gate of Extended Auspiciousness (Yanxiangmen) to the west. The latter was destroyed by the Eight-Power Allied Forces in 1900 and rebuilt by the People's Government in 1953.

The 4,500-square-meter Circular Wall is actually a round terrace five meters high. Planted with ancient trees and rich in cultural relics and classical architecture, it is situated in magnificent surroundings; to the east is Prospect Hill (Jingshan) with its five hilltop

pavilions; to the south the gold and green of the halls
and pavilions of Zhongnanhai (Central and South
Lakes); to the west the waters of Beihai (North
Lake); to the southeast the golden tiled roofs of the
Forbidden City; and to the north the awe-inspiring
form of the White Dagoba.

The main structure of the Circular Wall terrace is
the Hall of Received Light (Chengguangdian), a
spacious building with a double-eaved roof. Smaller
rooms with single-eaved roofs stand on the four sides
of the hall, giving it the overall shape of a cross. The
roofs are made of yellow glazed tiles with a border of
green and have upturned double eaves. Its rafters are
decorated with swirling golden designs. The building
is constructed to standards not commonly found among
ancient Chinese structures.

The hall contains a 1.6-meter tall Buddha carved
from a single piece of pure white jade inlaid with precious stones which legend says was presented to the
Guangxu emperor (reigned 1875-1908) by a Cambodian
king. The statue's left arm was damaged by the Eight-
Power Allied Forces when they invaded Beijing in 1900
and the scar is still visible today.

In the center of the Circular Wall stands the Jade
Urn Pavilion (Yuwengting) with its blue roof and
white pillars. The jade urn was placed in the Palace of
the Moon in Beihai Park in 1268 during the Yuan
dynasty. Under the Ming, the Palace of the Moon
was demolished and the urn was moved to the
Temple of the God of True Prowess (Zhenwumiao).
In 1745, the Qianlong emperor had the present stone
pavilion erected within the Circular Wall to house the
urn and had his poem *The Song of the Jade Urn*

engraved on the inside of the vessel. The pavilion itself was inscribed with poems written in a rhyme scheme
identical to the emperor's by members of the Imperial
Academy. The black jade wine urn is crossed with
streaks of white. Carved from a single block of jade,
its outside surface is carved with lifelike decorations of
fish, dragons and other sea creatures swimming among
the waves.

Like Beihai Park, the Circular Wall was part of the
imperial gardens under the Liao and Jin dynasties (907-
1234) when the land which it now occupies was a small
island in Taiye Lake. The Jin rulers built a small hall
on the island and planted pine trees, one of which is
still growing today. The Ming rulers constructed the
Circular Wall around the perimeter of the island, permanently fixing its dimensions. In 1669, during the
reign of the Kangxi emperor the Hall of Received Light
collapsed and was rebuilt the following year in its
present cross-shaped form. Major reconstruction was
also carried out by the Qianlong emperor in 1764 and
the buildings and layout of today's Circular Wall date
from that period.

Jingshan (Prospect Hill) Park

Prospect Hill (Jingshan) is situated in the central section of Jingshan Front Street with its main gate, the
North Upper Gate (Beishangmen), standing directly
opposite the Gate of Military Prowess (Shenwumen),
the northern gate of the Palace Museum. From the Yuan
dynasty (1206-1368) onwards, this area was a "forbid-

den garden" which was only opened to the general public in 1928. After 1949, it formally became a park.

Prospect Hill was built up from mud dredged from the surrounding lakes and moats at the time of the construction of the Yuan capital Dadu. At that time it was known as Green Hill. Under the Ming it was enlarged to its present size and because coal was stored at the foot of the hill, it became known as Coal Hill (Meishan). In the time of the Qianlong emperor (1736-96), a palace was built on the north face of the hill and a glazed tile pavilion built on its peak. Because the hillside was planted with numerous fruit trees, the park was also known for a time as the Garden of a Hundred Fruits (Baiguoyuan) and the name of the hill changed to Longevity Hill. Attention was lavished on the park and numerous trees were planted. Ancient cypresses thrived on the hill, and in tribute to its charming scenery, it was renamed "Prospect Hill."

Inside the North Upper Gate stands the Beautiful View Pavilion (Qiwanglou). In the past, memorial tablets used by the imperial family in their consecration of Confucius were stored here. Nowadays, it serves as an exhibition hall where cultural exhibitions are frequently held. Behind the building is the foot of Prospect Hill and a path lined with flowers leads to the hilltop.

The hill has five peaks, each decked with a pavilion constructed in 1751 by order of the Qianlong emperor. The pavilion on the central peak is called the Pavilion of Ten Thousand Springtimes. To the east are two pavilions named Admire the Surroundings and Gaze at Excellence, and to the west two others named Rich View and Accumulated Fragrance. Originally each pavilion held a bronze Buddha (collectively known as the "Five Flavored Immortals"), but four of these were removed by the troops of the Eight-Power Allied Forces in 1900, while the fifth, that in the Pavilion of Ten Thousand Springtimes, suffered the loss of its left arm, though a new arm was later cast to replace it.

The central summit can be reached via paths on both the eastern and western sides of the hill. In pre-skyscraper days, this was the highest point in Beijing's Inner City and offered the visitor an unequaled view of the capital and its surroundings. Northwards lies Gate of Earthly Peace (Di'anmen) Street and the lofty Drum Tower. Further to the southwest, the view takes in the Shicha Lakes and Beihai Park. The south-ward view reveals the entire symmetrical plan of Beijing, with the ancient capital's principal buildings lined up along a central north-south axis.

On the eastern pathway leading down Prospect Hill there once stood a diminutive scholartree slanting towards the east which was surrounded by a red brick wall. It was at this spot that the last emperor of the Ming dynasty hung himself on the morning of March 19, 1644. Two days earlier, Li Zicheng had led a peasant army into Beijing and accepted the surrender of the Ming troops outside the city. On the 18th, the troops guarding Fuchengmen (Mound-Formed Gate) and Xibianmen (Western Informal Gate) opened the gates and allowed the insurgent troops to enter the city. Before dawn on the 19th, the panic-stricken Chongzheng emperor ran out of the Palace without his crown and with his hair loose and unkempt. He wore a long white gown embroidered with a dragon and a single soft-soled shoe (history failed to record what happened to the other one) borrowed from Wang Cheng'en, a court eunuch. His hands stained with the blood of the concubine Yuan and two princesses, he reached the top of the hill and said, "I have always treated my subordinates well, yet today, finding myself in this wretched state, why is it that not a single one of them is here with me to sacrifice their lives. . . . Perhaps this is because they don't know that I am here, which would explain why they are not hurrying after me." He walked down the hill and hung himself with his belt on the old scholartree. In the past, there was a stone stela here with this inscription: "The place where the Ming Sizong emperor (his posthumous title) died for his country." In the 1950s, this stela was replaced by a wooden plague reading "The place where the Ming Chongzheng emperor hung himself."

On the north face of the hill are the Longevity of the Emperors Hall (Shouhuangdian) and the Hall for Observing Morals (Guandetang). The Longevity of the Emperors Hall originally contained a collection of portraits of the Qing emperors. During the Republican period, the Bureau of Cultural Relics confiscated the collection of so-called "Imperial Faces" despite the strong objections of the imperial family. According to the rules of the Qing court, the emperor visited the hall in person each season to offer sacrifices, and at the spot where the Chongzheng emperor hung himself, he was required to dismount from his carriage and walk. This diversion was intended to remind later emperors of the tragedy which befell one of their predecessors.

In the 1950s, the Longevity of the Emperors Hall was turned into the Beijing Children's Palace, a

recreational and educational facility for the capital's
youth.

Taoranting (Joyous Pavilion) Park

Taoranting Park, situated in the southwest part of
metropolitan Beijing, derives its name from the Joyous
Pavilion that once stood on the grounds of the Temple
of Mercy (Cibeiyuan).

The pavilion was built in 1695 during the reign of
the Kangxi emperor by Jiang Zao, a secretary in the
Board of Works. Hence it was also known as Jiang
Pavilion. In the Ming and Qing dynasties, a brick kiln
was built in the neighborhood of the Temple of Mercy
at what is now the Kiln Terrace. Jiang served as a director in the kiln and came to enjoy the grounds in the
vicinity of the temple so much that he decided to have
a pavilion built there. The original wooden inscription
belonging to the former pavilion still hangs inside the
gate of the Temple of Mercy. The characters inscribed
on it, "Taoran" (Joy), in Jiang's own calligraphy, are
drawn from the lines of a famous poem by the Tang
poet Bai Juyi: "Let us wait until the chrysanthemums
are golden and our home-brewed wine matured, then
with us all shall be intoxication and joy." The original
pavilion, which was built on a hill, stood higher than
the city battlements. For this reason, it was a favorite
destination for Beijing residents on the day of the autumn Double Ninth Festival, when tradition prescribed
that one should "ascend to a high place."

During the Jin dynasty (1115-1234) the Taoranting
Park area lay in the suburbs of the capital and contain-

ed streams and a small lake. On the southwestern side
of Central Island in the center of the lake was a small
hillock on which stood the ruins of the Liao dynasty
(907-1125) Temple of Mercy. Today Liao and Jin dynasty stone pillars inscribed with Buddhist scriptures
can still be found here.

In past centuries, scholars from all corners of China
wrote many poems and essays in praise of Taoranting,
though in imperial times, the scenery at Taoranting was
not particularly attractive. To the north of the pavilion
was a residential district of single-story dwellings and
to the east a group of desolate tombs. To the south
stood the bare city walls and to the west a stretch of
shallow water filled with reeds. Houses of ordinary citizens were not permitted to stand at an elevation higher
than the emperor's palace, and apart from the hillock
on the Central Island, all the highest points in the city
were occupied by the imperial family. Thus this was
the only place where the common people could come
and obtain a fine view of the city. The old temple
added extra interest and so the spot became very popular. As visitors increased, the original small pavilion was demolished to make way for a larger building,
which in turn was augmented by three buildings still
found today inside the Temple of Mercy.

In the past century several famous revolutionaries
were closely associated with the Taoranting Pavilion. At
the end of the Qing dynasty Kang Youwei, Liang Qichao and Tan Sitong came here to plan out the Reform Movement of 1898. Zhang Taiyan was imprisoned
in the nearby Dragon Spring Temple for his opposition
to the usurpation of state power by Yuan Shikai. In
the early years of the Republic of China, Sun Yat-sen

attended political meetings in the pavilion, and on several occasions Li Dazhao organized secret revolutionary activities in the most westerly of the three rooms in the northern courtyard of the Zhunti (Cundi) Hall. On the afternoon of August 6, 1920, five progressive societies from Beijing and Tianjin held a joint meeting in the pavilion which was attended by Zhou Enlai and Li Dazhao. Besides this, the tombs of the revolutionaries Gao Junyu and Shi Pingmei are situated on the northern side of Central Island at the foot of the slopes of Glorious Autumn Mound.

Noted bureaucrats and officials also flocked to Taoranting. The late-Qing official Zhang Zhidong, for example, frequently held political discussions here. The Baobingshi (Room Embracing Ice), once Zhang's villa, has been renovated and is now a hall for cultural activities.

Although Taoranting has a long history and contains numerous sites of historical interest, up till the eve of the founding of the People's Republic, it was little more than a foul smelling breeding ground for flies and mosquitoes. After dark, the area became a haven for criminals and the island's pines were frequently used by suicides to hang themselves. In 1952, the People's Government began dredging operations and transformed the stagnant pond into a lake. In the center of the lake is an island shaped like a bottle-gourd which divides the lake into three sections. The earth dredged out of the lake was heaped up to form seven small hills on the lake's perimeter, and these have been planted with flowers and various coniferous and broadleafed trees and shrubs. The two memorial archways that once towered over East and West

Chang'an Boulevards, and the Tower of Painted Clouds (Yunhuilou) and the Sweet-Sounding Pavilion (Qingyinge), both of which once stood on the eastern bank of Zhongnanhai (Central and South Lakes), have also been re-erected inside the park.

Inside the park, directly facing the northern gate, are two identical tall memorial archways painted in brilliant colors. A path leads through them to the spit of land which connects with the Central Island.

Arriving on the island, after passing through a fragrant wisteria arbor, one may ascend a series of steps made of stones from Lake Taihu in Jiangsu Province, which leads to the peak of the Glorious Autumn Mound. The mound's southern slope is the site of two tombs, the Fragrant Tomb and Parrot Tomb. The graveyard was originally part of the old Flower Spirit Temple and the two small tombs still have engraved stelae standing before them. In the past, several different stories have been attached to the Fragrant Tomb. One relates that after the Manchus took control of Beijing after the fall of the Ming dynasty, the people were forced to change their mode of dress. Adherents of the Ming dynasty, cherishing the memory of their old rulers, buried their Ming dynasty garments here in a gesture of loyalty.

Another story relates how a certain court official of the Qing submitted numerous memorials to the throne but received not a single response. In a fit of frustration, he gathered up all of his memorials and other writings and buried them all at this spot. Fearing that this action might arouse imperial wrath, he covered his tracks by naming the site the Fragrant Tomb. Still another legend explains that this is the tomb of the Fragrant

Concubine, a favorite of the Qianlong emperor, and yet another relates that this is the spot where an unsuccessful candidate in the national imperial examinations buried his brushes, ink and examination paper in a fit of frustration.

The Parrot Tomb stands a few meters to the west of the Fragrant Tomb. The writing on the front of the stela before the tomb is blurred, but on the back reads "Parrot Tomb." According to the *Notes from the Ten Thousand Willows Chamber*, the Qing calligrapher Deng Wanbai buried his pet parrot here after it was killed by a cat. From the text on the stela which reads, "Here lie brushes and writings, though under the name of a bird and of fragrant grasses," it can be inferred that the Fragrant Tomb and the Parrot Tomb were the efforts of a single hand.

To the east of the Glorious Autumn Mound is a small hill formerly called the Kiln Lump (Yaogeda). When the park was formally opened after the founding of the People's Republic, the hill was heightened and planted with trees, and a path was laid leading to its peak.

The Purple Bamboo Park (Zizhuyuan)

Purple Bamboo Park is one of Beijing's seven largest parks. It is situated at the southern end of Baishiqiao Road (White Marble Bridge Road), with its eastern gate directly across the street from Capital Gymnasium.

The park has three connecting lakes which occupy 11 out of the park's 14 hectares. Earth dredged from the lakes was piled up to form several small hills on the eastern shore to complement the natural hills that line the lakes' western shores. Five bridges connect the lakes, islands and hills into a single integrated recreational area. On the banks of the lakes and on the islands, flowering shrubs, trees and flowers have been planted with a generous hand. To the north of the lakes the famous Changhe River flows slowly by.

A temple, known in the Ming dynasty as the Temple of Longevity (Wanshousi) originally stood to the northwest of the lakes. Here the Qing rulers built a lodging palace where they and their retinues could rest as they floated to the Summer Palace or the Jade Spring Mountain on the Changhe River. Nowadays all that remains of the original temple are two stone stelae and traces of two landing platforms on the banks of the river.

The Purple Bamboo Park has a long history. According to early records, before the third century it formed the uppper reaches of the Gaoliang (Sorghum) River, and a famous Gaoliang Bridge stood nearby to the east. In the Ming dynasty, the bridge was a favorite visiting spot for city people on the Qingming (Clear and Bright) Festival, when the scene included "young girls riding in horse-drawn carts, and city folk competing with drums and banners." In the 13th century, the lakes of Purple Bamboo Park served as a reservoir providing an important part of Beijing's water supply. In the late Yuan dynasty, the mathematician and astronomer Guo Shoujing built a canal along the upper reaches of the Gaoliang River with locks to regulate the water diverted from the White River Dam, the Jade Spring Mountain, and other nearby waterways. In later years, however, the canal was neglected and gradually silted up.

During the Republican period it was filled in and rented out as paddy fields.

After 1949, the People's Government transformed the fields into a new park. Through several years of planting and construction, the park was provided with lush bamboos and shady trees, small bridges and open-air pavilions.

In 1981, on the eve of May Day, a new two-story 1,000-square-meter waterside complex on North Mountain (Beishan) Island opened to the public. This consists of the Purple Bamboo Pavilion, the Gallery for Watching the Moon, a winding walkway that leads out over the water, and a square pavilion. Though each structure is independent, from a distance the four components seem to blend into one. This in turn sets off the newly opened Lancui Pavilion on Central Mountain (Zhongshan) Island.

Yuyuan Lake Park and the Angler's Terrace (Diaoyutai)

Yuyuan (Jade Pool) Lake Park is situated in the southern section of Sanlihe Road, with its main gate directly opposite the Southern Road of the Altar of the Moon (Yuetan Nanjie). In the past it was known as the Angler's Terrace (Diaoyutai) because in the Jin dynasty (1115-1234), an official named Wang Yu lived here in seclusion in the guise of a fisherman.

Nowadays, a tall brick terrace runs from north to south along the southwestern portion of the wall surrounding the Diaoyutai State Guesthouse. The main western gate leading to the terrace still bears a stone plaque inscribed with "Diaoyutai" in the Qianlong emperor's hand. Three entrance-ways stand to the east of the terrace, the central one directly opposite the terrace's western gate. From the side gates, stone steps lead up to the terrace. All four sides of the terrace are lined with crenellations, which give it the appearance of a miniature castle.

This, however, is not the real Angler's Terrace, but merely a terrace built in honor of the emperor's inscription. The actual terrace stands to the north of the Room for Convalescence (Yangyuanzhai), and comprises a spacious hall and a pool where the emperors went fishing. In 1773, the Qianlong emperor had an imperial traveling lodge constructed here. At this time the lake was dredged and enlarged with spring water diverted from the Fragrant Hills (Xiangshan). The emperor composed a ballad here to commemorate the lodge, the ruins of which can still be seen inside the park.

As hinted above, the history of the terrace goes back much further than the time of Qianlong. According to local histories, the "Diaoyutai, to the west of Sanlihe, dates from the Jin dynasty.... Below the terrace is a small pool fed by a spring which never runs dry, even in the winter.... All the streams flowing from the Western Hills converge here." In addition, the great beauty of this natural scenic area was described in a poem written over eight hundred years ago:

> Grass grows lushly on Yuyuan Lake,
> The gurgling spring flows into distant streams.

Weeping willows line the dikes before the darkening hills,
Peach blossoms float on the water at sunset.

The Angler's Terrace served as a pleasure spot for emperors as far back as the Jin dynasty. One Jin emperor wrote: "His Majesty's carriage has made several trips here; the splendor of the Angler's Terrace compares with that of the Terrace of Gold."

The history of the park reflects the rise and fall of successive dynasties. Under the Yuan (1206-1368) it was renamed Yuyuantai and belonged to a family named Ding. In the Ming dynasty, from the time of the Wanli emperor (reigned 1573-1619) it was the personal villa of a nobleman named Li. Due to neglect, by the end of the Ming dynasty there was neither a terrace nor a pavilion to speak of, though the name of the park was passed down through the centuries by the local people. In the early 20th century, Puyi, the last Qing emperor, made a gift of the park to his teacher Chen Baochen, but Chen only came here to celebrate his birthdays.

At the time of the founding of the People's Republic, the entire area was reduced to desolation. Apart from the Room for Convalescence used by General Fu Zuoyi as a summer villa, there were few dwellings in the area and only a small number of fields and vegetable beds. In 1956, the People's Government expanded the area of the lake and diverted water from the Yongding River to fill the newly dredged 100,000-square-meter gourd-shaped lakebed which lies to the south of the old lake. The shores of the lake and the banks of the diversion were planted with poplar and willow trees. As a result, Yuyuan Lake serves both as a reservoir and as a place of great scenic beauty.

In October 1958, a state guesthouse known as the Diaoyutai State Guesthouse was built around the ruins of the ancient terrace. A stream which has its source in Yuyuan Lake winds its way through three artificial lakes on the grounds. The pools are well stocked with fish and hotel guests can enjoy fishing at their leisure. Graceful weeping willows line the shores of the lakes and white poplars are planted along the sides of the roads. Eighteen bridges combine with artificial hills, rockeries, rare flowers and exotic plants to provide a rich setting for the pine-shaded villas. In addition, there are various fruit trees — peaches, apricots, apples, pears and haws. Every spring lilac and flowering crabapple fill the air with their fragrance, while numerous species of peonies compete for the attention of the passing bees.

Beijing Zoo

The Beijing Zoo, situated to the west of the Beijing Exhibition Center, was for a short time after the founding of the People's Republic known as the Western Suburbs Park (Xijiao Gongyuan). The grounds combine cultivated flower gardens with stretches of natural scenery, including dense groves of trees, stretches of grassland, a small stream, lotus pools and small hills dotted with pavilions and halls.

In the 18th century, the zoo was known as the Sanbeizi Gardens, supposedly named after the third son of the Kangxi emperor, Prince Cheng Yin. Another explanation is that Sanbeizi referred to the Qing courtier Fu Kang'an, and that this was the site of his villa. In fact, as early as the Ming dynasty, an imperial mansion called the Garden of Happiness and Friendship constructed for Prince Kang stood here, and during the Qing, part of the Sanbeizi Gardens called the Garden of Continuity (Jiyuan) became the private property of an official in the Bureau of Palace Affairs.

In 1906, during the reign of the Guangxu emperor, the park area became an Agricultural Experimental Farm and a zoo. Known as the Garden of Ten Thousand Animals (Wanshengyuan), it opened to the public in 1908, though visitors remained very few.

Under the successive rule of the Northern Warlords, the Japanese and the Kuomintang, the park became increasingly desolate. The last remaining elephant died in 1937 and the Japanese imperialists, under the pretext of protecting themselves against air raids, poisoned the remaining lions, tigers and leopards. From then until the founding of the People's Republic, the park housed only 12 monkeys, two parrots and a blind emu. After Liberation the park was reopened to the public in 1950, and on April 10, 1955, it was formally named the Beijing Zoo.

The zoo has developed rapidly in the last three decades and by 1980 it covered an area of over 50 hectares. The areas displaying bears, elephants, pandas, lions, tigers, songbirds, hippopotamuses, rhinoceroses, antelopes and giraffes were all opened in the late fifties and a gorilla cage, leaf-monkey cage and aquarium were added soon afterwards. In 1980, a two-story reptile house was opened which contains specimens of over

100 species of reptiles from all over the world, including crocodiles and pythons.

At present, the zoo houses over 7,000 creatures belonging to 600 different species, including the giant panda, golden monkey, Manchurian tiger, white-lipped deer, red-crowned crane and Pere David's deer — all unique to China — as well as the African giraffe, rhinoceros, chimpanzee and antelope; Australian kangaroo and parrot; cougar from the American continent; wild ox from Europe; and elephant and gibbon from India.

Beijing Botanical Gardens

The Beijing Botanical Gardens are situated in the western outskirts of the city between Xiangshan Park and the Jade Spring Mountain. Although the gardens are not large, with only some 3,000 different plant species, many famous and rare plant specimens are on display.

The hothouse exhibitions are the highlight of the gardens, and consist of 13 different rooms. The first room is filled with evergreens, all members of the palm family.

The second room is given over to tropical aquatic plants, including water lilies and flowering taros. The third room in the hothouse contains commercial plants as well as the breeding and propagation section. Here there are specimens of the triple-leaved rubber plant, cocoa and coffee trees and the sugar producing sweet-leaved chrysanthemum which has recently been introduced into China from abroad.

The next room contains an exhibition of medicinal

plants, aromatic plants and succulents. The exhibition of ornamental plants is spectacular with its countless varieties of flowers and grasses. There are over 300 different types of orchid alone, among them a rootless variety which relies on fine hairs to absorb water vapor and nutrients from the air.

Besides the 13 hothouse rooms, the gardens also contain a Chinese national specimen collection housed in a 11,000-square-meter building made up of specimen rooms, plant classification laboratories, research rooms and a lecture hall. The buildings are arranged around a courtyard and are linked together with arches and trellises.

The Peony Garden was open to the public in 1981. It covers an area of 10 hectares and is divided into three sections. The Peony Grove is the most important of these, covering an area of 3.5 hectares. There is a Peony Terrace where specimens from famous growing areas in China can be found, including some from Heze in Shandong Province.

The plant collection includes many rare species. There is, for example, the metasequoia first discovered in the region of Hubei and Sichuan by a Chinese scientist in the 1940s. Since it was originally believed that it had become extinct during the Tertiary Period (65 million years ago), the discovery of living specimens in China came as a tremendous surprise to botanists.

Other plants in the gardens include specimens of the nepenthes or "pitcher" plant, which "eats" insects; the golden butterfly orchid with its lustrous yellow flowers; the American redwood; the Japanese blossoming cherry, and the famous "bo tree," the species of tree under which the Buddha sat when he gained enlightenment.

Summer Palace (Yiheyuan)

The Summer Palace, one of the finest and largest examples of garden architecture in China, is located in the northwest suburbs of Beijing. The more than one hundred examples of traditional architecture in the park include pavilions, terraces, temples, pagodas, waterside gazebos, covered corridors, stone bridges and the famous marble boat. In addition, there are also Kunming Lake, Longevity Hill, and countless quiet paths and natural streams. The palace occupies a total area of 290 hectares, three quarters of which is made up of shallow lakes.

The history of the Summer Palace dates back some 800 years when the first emperor of the Jin dynasty (1115-1234), Wan Yanliang, moved his capital to the vicinity of Beijing and built his "Gold Mountain Traveling Palace" at the present site of Longevity Hill. A subsequent emperor of the same dynasty diverted the water from the nearby Jade Spring to the Gold Mountain, naming the lake it flowed into the Gold Sea. Thus the general plan of the Summer Palace was laid out some 800 years ago. After the founding of the Yuan dynasty (1206-1368), Gold Mountain was renamed Jug Mountain (Wengshan), as explained in the following legend: There was once an itinerant old man who discovered a large rock on the slopes of Gold Mountain. Breaking it open, he found an earthenware jar hidden inside. The jar's surface was exquisitely carved with flowers, animals and dragons. Inside the jar were many objects of great value which the old man took away with him. Before his departure, however, he brought the jar to the sunny side of the mountain and inscribed it with the following couplet: "When this earthen jar is moved, the emperor's decline shall begin." During the Jiajing period (1522-66) of the Ming dynasty, the jar disappeared and, just as the old man predicted, the dynasty fell into decay.

In 1292, Guo Shoujing, a Yuan official in charge of irrigation work, suggested digging a riverbed and leading all of the springs in the vicinity of Jug Mountain into it to facilitate grain transport. Following Guo's proposals, spring water from the region of Changping, 50 kilometers north of Beijing, was led to the foot of Jug Mountain, and the lake was enlarged and renamed Jug Mountain Lake.

The names of the lake and the park and how they have changed over the course of their long history would make a study in itself. In the Yuan dynasty, Kunming Lake was known as the Big Lake, the West Sea or the West Lake. From historical records we know that in this period, visiting West Lake in April was already a popular custom among the people. And in the Ming dynasty a temple was built on the south side of Longevity Hill.

The Ming Zhengde emperor (reigned 1506-21) had his traveling palace built on the lake and called it the Fine Garden for Enjoying Mountains (Haoshan-yuan). At the same time, he changed Jug Mountain's name back to Gold Mountain and Jug Mountain Lake to Gold Sea. In the early 17th century, the infamous eunuch Wei Zhongxian took over the entire garden for his own private use.

When the Qing troops occupied Beijing in the middle of the 17th century, the Fine Garden for Enjoying Mountains was renamed Jug Mountain Traveling Palace. It was during the reign of the Qianlong emperor (1736-96) that the names of the mountain and the lake were changed for the very last time. In commemoration of the 60th birthday of Qianlong's mother, the emperor erected a Temple of Gratitude and Longevity (Dabao'enyanshousi) and renamed Jug Mountain Longevity Hill and, following the example of the Han dynasty Emperor Wu Di, who had conducted naval exercises on Kunming Lake in the Han capital of Chang'an many centuries before, the Gold Sea was renamed Kunming Lake. At this time, the name for the entire area was the Park of Pure Ripples (Qingyiyuan).

During its long history, the Summer Palace fell prey to two acts of destruction. The first took place in 1860 when the English and French Allied Armies invaded Beijing and ravaged both the Yuanmingyuan Garden and the Park of Pure Ripples. Every single building in the park was destroyed by fire except for uninflammable structures such as bronze pavilions and stone pagodas.

In 1888, Empress Dowager Cixi diverted 30 million taels of silver originally designated for the Chinese navy into the reconstruction and enlargement of the Summer Palace. Out of her admiration for the gardens of Suzhou and Hangzhou, she had the southern face of Longevity Hill laid out in imitation of West Lake in Hangzhou, while the northern face followed the architectural style seen along the canals of Suzhou. She also gave the park its present name: the Garden of Good Health and Harmony (Yiheyuan), known generally in English as the Summer Palace.

The second great act of destruction took place in 1900 when the Eight-Power Allied Forces invaded Beijing. The great temples rebuilt in the 1880s were completely demolished and almost every valuable object in sight plundered by the invading troops. In 1902, when Empress Dowager Cixi returned to Beijing from her flight to Xi'an, she ordered the reconstruction of the Palace. According to historical records, she "rebuilt the Summer Palace with unbounded extravagance and opulence, spending some 40,000 taels of silver per day. Singing and dancing went on without end."

After the 1911 Revolution, the Summer Palace became the private property of the deposed Emperor Puyi, who in 1914 opened the garden to the public. But the entrance fee was so high that the palace had very few visitors. In 1924, Puyi was forced to leave the Forbidden City by the "Christian" General Feng Yuxiang, and the Beijing Government turned the Summer Palace into a public park with the exorbitant entrance fee of one silver dollar. Over the course of the next 25 years, under the transient rule of the Japanese imperialists and the Kuomintang, the Summer Palace once again fell prey to full-scale devastation; pavilions and covered corridors were wrecked, lakes became silted up, vegetation withered and died, and antiques and other objects of value were lost.

Today, older Beijing residents can still recall some of the palace's former treasures: the statue of the

Goddess of Mercy and the watermelon made out of kingfisher jade (*feicui*), the huge jade disc (*bi*) which "could be traded for several cities," the pearl that glowed at night, and the pearl-embroidered shoes. When the Kuomintang troops fled the mainland, they absconded with these and other treasures, some of which ended up in Taiwan, while the remainder was bought up by museums and private collectors in the West. Before 1949, the Summer Palace was in a state of total dilapidation. After the founding of the People's Republic, local authorities began carrying out the painstaking task of restoration. Today, after more than 30 years of repainting and reconstruction, the Summer Palace plays host to approximately 2 million visitors per year.

Below, we will divide the Summer Palace into four areas — the Eastern Palaces, the south face of Longevity Hill, the north face of Longevity Hill and the South Lake district — and discuss each one separately.

The Eastern Palaces

The Eastern Palace Gate which serves as the main gate of the entire palace complex is guarded on each side by two brass lions which date back to the Qianlong period. Set in the center of the staircase leading up to the gate is a large slab of stone carved with two dragons amusing themselves with giant pearls. This elegant symbol of imperial power was moved here from the Yuanmingyuan Garden. On the lintel above the gate, the three Chinese characters of the name of the Summer Palace "Yiheyuan" have been inscribed in the calligraphy of the Qing Guangxu emperor. Im-

mediately inside the gate is a "spirit wall,"* beyond
which lies a bow-shaped "moon pond" crossed at its
north and south extremities by a pair of stone bridges.
In the days of the Empress Dowager only she, the emperor and the empress were permitted to come to this
part of the palace, all other mortals being denied entry
by a cordon of mounted guards. Walking west inside
the gate and passing through the Gate of Benevolent
Longevity, you come to the Palace of Benevolent
Longevity (Renshoudian). This edifice was originally
named the Palace of Encouraging Good Government,
but when it was restored in 1890, in order to pander
to the Empress Dowager's craving for longevity, its
name was changed to the Palace of Benevolent Longevity, an ironic notion derived from an old saying:
"Benevolent people live long lives." Here Cixi held
audiences with high officials and handled the daily affairs of government. This palace once contained the
famous screen behind which, out of propriety, Cixi
ruled China. Though the screen has long since rotted
away, the building still contains a number of interesting
treasures: bronze vessels from the Shang dynasty; a
screen bearing a scene on Dongting Lake made entirely of kingfisher feathers; lions carved from gnarled
roots of trees; and Chinese decorative mirrors dating
from the 18th century. Among these treasures is a
sandalwood mirror frame carved all over with dragons,
which took 3,600 days of labor to complete — the

---

* "Spirit wall" was erected inside the main gate of walled com-
pounds to keep out evil spirits (which traveled exclusively in
straight lines) as well as more innocent curiosity seekers.

equivalent of one person working non-stop for ten years.

North of the Palace of Benevolent Longevity is the Garden of Harmonious Virtue (Deheyuan). When Cixi rebuilt this section of the palace after it had been burned down by the English and French Allied Armies, she spent a total of more than 700,000 taels of silver. A good portion of this investment went into the outdoor stage, which stands 21 meters high and has a playing area 17 meters wide, more than five times larger than the average Chinese stage. Actually, the stage is composed of three levels, one on top of the other, and is impressive in several other respects: the ceiling of the lowest level stage is provided with seven traps through which actors playing the roles of immortals, spirits or other celestial beings could descend. The stage floor is also provided with seven traps which were used by ghosts and other underworld beings when they made their entrances. Beneath the stage is a deep well and five square water tanks. It is said that during certain productions, water was pumped up from the tanks at the appropriate moment to produce underwater scenes on stage. On Cixi's birthday every year, the same opera would be performed simultaneously on all three levels of the stage.

Walking south from the Palace of Benevolent Longevity and winding along a twisting mountain path, you come to the Hall of Jade Ripples (Yulantang). It is said that the name of this structure comes from a poem by Lu Ji (261-303) which contains the line, "Tiny ripples flow up from the Jade Spring." The hall was built in 1750 and destroyed by the English and

French Allied Armies in 1860. Upon its restoration, it
served as the private living quarters of the Guangxu
emperor, though this luxuriously appointed home soon
became his prison. Following the failure of the Reform Movement of 1898, to which Guangxu had lent
his support, the Empress Dowager had the emperor
imprisoned here, and a thick brick wall was built to
prevent him from escaping. Originally, a gate Dropping
Flowers Gate) connected Guangxu's Hall of Jade
Ripples directly with the Hall of Pleasing Rue (Yi-
yunguan), the residence of his concubines. As a further
punishment, Cixi ordered this gate to be sealed up with
bricks, thus confining Guangxu to his elegant prison.
To vent his pent-up resentment, Guangxu got into the
habit of tapping his walking stick on the brick floor of
his courtyard. Thus it is said that the uneven surface of
the patio floor is the personal handiwork of the second-
to-last emperor of China.

Directly between the Hall of Jade Ripples and the
Hall of Pleasing Rue stands the Tower of Fine Sunsets
(Xijialou). Offering an excellent view of the Western
Hills, it is an ideal spot for watching the sunset over
Kunming Lake. Its eastern wing contains rockery
hills and a Forest of (Stone) Lions modeled after the
Forest of Lions Garden (Shizilin) in Suzhou, though on
a somewhat smaller scale.

Walking north along the shore of the lake and heading west for a short distance, one comes to the Hall of
Joyful Longevity (Leshoutang), the residence chambers
of the Empress Dowager. The eastern and western
auxiliary halls were the center of daily activities. Each
year, Cixi would begin her summer residence here in

May, and not until the tenth day of the tenth lunar month (approximately the end of November), long past her birthday, would she move back to the Forbidden City. The current displays in the hall include a throne, imperial tables, screens, palace fans, and other imperial paraphernalia. Whenever "Old Buddha" (one of her favorite names) took a meal here, 128 different dishes would be served at a cost of 100 taels of silver, an amount which could buy enough millet to feed 5,000 peasants for one day. On display in the dining room are a basket made of pearls, agate and kingfisher jade (*feicui*), as well as a panoramic mural screen on which the flowers of the four seasons are depicted in inlaid designs of gold, silver and various precious stones. In the hall's courtyards are displays of magnolia, flowering crabapple and peony. When the magnolias bloom here in early April, the number of visitors increases dramatically. Directly south of the Hall of Joyful Longevity on the lake is a small dock provided with carved stone balustrades where Cixi would alight when arriving at the Summer Palace by boat.

Passing from the west auxiliary hall of the Hall of Joyful Longevity through the Gate for Greeting the Moon, one comes to the eastern end of the Long Corridor (Changlang). First built in 1750 and destroyed by the English and French Allied Armies in 1860, the current structure dates from the Guangxu reign (1875-1908). The total length of the corridor is 728 meters, making it the longest corridor in the history of Chinese garden architecture.

Skirting the northern shoreline of Kunming Lake, the corridor links up the principal structures in this section of the Summer Palace. Four poetically named pavilions have been built at regular intervals along its length: each pavilion is decorated with intricate paintings of flowers and historical figures, perhaps the finest examples of this genre in the entire Long Corridor. At the same time, every single crossbeam in the Long Corridor is decorated with a colorful painting — 17,000 in all. Among these are more than 300 paintings based on famous stories from Chinese history. Of additional interest are the two large stone kiosks which jut out over the water, making fine resting places on hot summer days.

The South Face of Longevity Hill

The main structure in the central architectural complex on the south face of Longevity Hill is the Palace of Parting Clouds (Paiyundian). This is fronted by a memorial archway built on the edge of the lake inscribed with the words "The myriad stars surround the Polar Star" on one side and "The radiance of the clouds shines through the jade firmament" on the other. Between the archway and the Palace of Parting Clouds there are a number of evergreens and 12 Lake Taihu stones chosen to represent the Chinese astrological animals. An elegant pair of bronze lions guards the Gate of Parting Clouds. Inside the gate is a courtyard with buildings on each side; to the east is the Hall of Brilliant Jade and to the west the Hall of Brocade Clouds. A lotus pond set in the middle of the courtyard is spanned by a stone bridge which leads to the gates of the inner palace. The Palace of Parting Clouds, standing on the northern side of the courtyard, was itself the site of the Empress Dowager Cixi's birthday celebrations. There was a temple here as early as the Ming dynasty, which was rebuilt during the Qianlong period and called the Temple of Gratitude and Longevity. After its destruction by the English and French Allied Armies, it was reconstructed in 1892 in its present form and renamed. The name itself is taken from a poem by Guo Pu (276-324): "The immortals emerge from between parting clouds; a terrace of silver and gold appears."

The Palace of Parting Clouds is built on a stone terrace with staircases on three sides and is surrounded by white stone balustrades. The terrace in front of the palace is called the "Cinnabar Staircase." Here a collection of bronze dragons, phoenixes, sacrificial vessels and large water vats is displayed. The display in the interior is similar to that in the Hall of Benevolent Longevity described above. However, it contains a unique portrait in oils of the Empress Dowager Cixi painted in 1903 by Katherine A. Carl, an American who also wrote a book about Cixi. Though the portrait was executed in Cixi's 69th year, to flatter the Old Buddha's passion for eternal youth, it was rendered after the likeness of a 30-year-old woman.

The covered staircases on either side of the Palace of Parting Clouds lead up to the Hall of Virtuous Light, and by climbing further one comes to the highest point in the entire Summer Palace, the Pagoda of Buddhist Fragrance. This pagoda, 38 meters high, is supported inside by four hardwood columns 30 meters tall. The pagoda is designed after the Yellow Crane Pagoda in Wuchang, Hubei Province. Due to prolonged poor maintenance, the pagoda was in poor condition at the time of the founding of the People's Republic, and in 1953 the immense task of restoration was begun. The job of repainting alone took 16,000 worker-days to complete and consumed some 600 kilograms of seagreen paint and 2.5 kilograms of pure gold leaf. On a trip to the Summer Palace, a view of the lake and the distant hills from this point should not be missed.

The Revolving Scripture Repository (Zhuanlun-zang) is the name given to a complex of buildings standing to the east of the Pagoda of Buddhist Fragrance which contains a large carved stone tablet and three small pavilions. The front of the tablet is inscribed with the words "Longevity Hill and Kunming Lake" in the hand of the Qianlong emperor, and on the back there is a short essay entitled "A Record of Kunming Lake," also in Qianlong's hand. The tablet stands nearly 10 meters tall. On either side of the stone tablet are pavilions which house miniature octagonal pagodas which revolve on vertical axles. These curious religious structures, designed for the storage of Buddhist scriptures, are modeled after similar objects in the Fayuan Temple in Hangzhou. The third pavilion is the so-called Bronze Pavilion or Precious Cloud Pavilion. Standing 7.55 meters tall and weighing more than 200,000 kilograms, every detail of its structure resembles that of a wooden pavilion. The decorative patterns of the surface of the pavilion were executed with the lost wax method, and on the interior surface of the pavilion there is a list of the craftsmen who took part in its construction.

The south face of Longevity Hill also contains a number of smaller buildings with picturesque names which will only be mentioned briefly. First, those to

the east: The House of Leisure (Zizaizhuang), dating
from 1903, which was built in the style of an old-fashion-
ed country teahouse; the Hall for Nourishing Clouds
(Yangyunxuan), divided into two side halls, which
served during the time of Cixi as a resting place for
higher-ranking concubines, members of the imperial
clan, and women who had been granted official titles;
the Hall of Limitless Pleasure (Wujinyixuan), which
faces a small lotus pond and is an ideal place of retreat from the heat of summer; and finally, the Hall
of Longevity (Jieshoutang), where some rare and
wonderful cypresses and magnolias are growing.

Now to the points of interest on the western slopes
of Longevity Hill. Shao's Nest (Shaowo) was named
after a Song dynasty philosopher, Shao Yong, who
called his retirement home the Nest of Peace and Joy.
Hoping to attain some peace and joy for himself, Qianlong chose this auspicious name. The name of another
"nest" here, the Nest of Pines and Clouds, is derived
from a line in a poem by the famous Tang poet Li Bai:
"Here I will make my nest in the pines and clouds."
The Pavilion of the Stone Gentleman (Shizhangting)
recalls the Song painter and calligrapher Mi Fei, who
would bow in reverence whenever he came upon a
strange stone. To the west of the Pavilion of the Stone
Gentleman is a group of buildings called the Four
Western Pavilions (Xisiting). Originally built by
Qianlong, they were refurbished in 1892 to serve as a
residence for the imperial concubines. After the failure
of the Reform Movement of 1898, the Empress Dowager temporarily imprisoned Emperor Guangxu's
favorite, the Precious Concubine (Zhenfei), in these
precincts.

The Listening to the Orioles Pavilion, the site of a popular restaurant, was first built in the 18th century and refurbished during the Guangxu reign (1875-1908). Fine old pine trees grow in its courtyards, while its exterior is planted with apricot trees and bamboo. To the rear of the pavilion stands the Strolling-Through-a-Painting Hall (Huazhongyou), a two-story building which is flanked by the Adoration for the Hills Pavilion on the east and the Borrowing from Autumn Pavilion on the west. Covered galleries connect these two side pavilions with the main hall. The name Strolling-Through-a-Painting Hall comes from the fact that standing on the exquisite veranda, it is easy to imagine oneself being part of a landscape painting.

To the west of the Stone Gentleman Pavilion, a rather unseaworthy boat sits permanently docked with its bow jutting out into the lake. This is the famous Marble Boat, an ironic reminder that the funds appropriated by the Empress Dowager to reconstruct the Summer Palace had originally been earmarked for the Chinese navy. The boat's hull is of stone and its two-story wooden cabin was designed by Cixi herself in the style of an old steamship. To the east of the Marble Boat is the Hall of Accumulated Ripples from where pleasure boats set out for rides around the lake.

The North Face of Longevity Hill

There is a great contrast between the southern and northern sides of Longevity Hill. While the southern side is lavish to the point of extravagance, the northern section is more peaceful and less crowded. With its winding hill paths, limpid flowing streams, luxuriant pines and cypresses, and numerous shrubs, the northern face of Longevity Hill reminds one of the countryside of southern China. There was originally a large number of fine buildings here, but with few exceptions they were all destroyed by the English and French Allied Armies.

Apart from the long Lilac Corridor, there are only two palaces worthy of mention: the Tower of Great Fortune (Jingfuge) and the Garden of Harmonious Delights (Xiequyuan).

The Tower of Great Fortune was known as the Palace of Epiphyllum (Tanhuage) during the Qianlong period and was rebuilt in its present form in 1892. This rather large square building is surrounded on all sides by corridors, and was frequented by the Empress Dowager for two main purposes: watching the moon, and admiring the scenery on rainy days. The elevation here permits a fine view of the Seventeen-Arch Bridge and the Knowing Spring Pavilion on Kunming Lake. Cixi often dined here on rainy days, for this was an ideal spot from which to gaze out upon the distant hills half-lost in clouds.

East of Longevity Hill in the very northeast corner of the palace grounds stands the "garden within a garden," the Garden of Harmonious Delights (Xiequyuan), perhaps the most peaceful and secluded place in the entire Summer Palace. Built during the Qianlong period, water from Kunming Lake was led here to form a pond, and a complex of ingeniously interconnected buildings was built around it. Since the buildings themselves were copied by Qianlong after a garden in the Huishan district of Wuxi, Jiangsu Province, the garden was first known as Huishan Garden. Its name was changed to the Garden of Harmonious Delights in 1893. The Hall of Embracing the Distance (Hanyuantang) is the central structure in the garden. Here the Empress Dowager would drink tea or perhaps take an afternoon nap. Everything in the hall remains as Cixi left it; there are sculptures of characters from the famous Qing novel *A Dream of Red Mansions* and an exquisite bamboo carved sailboat with 68 miniature figures of old men, each with their own distinct gestures and facial features.

Had the series of buildings on the banks of the Suzhou Creek in the rear section of the palace not been destroyed by the English and French Allied Armies, they would not only be a favorite spot for visitors, but also a valuable resource for studying the social economy of the Qing dynasty. In the old days, both sides of the creek in the vicinity of the Long Bridge were laid out with streets containing a variety of commercial establishments, such as teahouses, wineshops, bookstores and antique shops. Known as Suzhou Street, this area enabled the imperial family, entirely cut off from the normal society of the country they ruled, to taste Beijing urban life. The roles of the shopkeepers were played by court eunuchs, and when the imperial party approached, they would begin shouting to attract their customers' attention, just as in real life.

By crossing Long Bridge (Changqiao) and walking north, one will come to the North Palace Gate, which was originally the main gate of the Summer Palace.

At the eastern end of Suzhou Street stands a large gate-like structure which is inscribed on its eastern face with the words "Early morning light" and on its

western face with "Gathering brilliance." This is yet
another example of southern Chinese architecture.

The Palace Lakes

To the south of Longevity Hill is a vast expanse of
water embellished with a number of small islands and
a long embankment. The islands take their names
from the structures built upon them: the Knowing
Spring Pavilion; the Phoenix Pier; the Mirror Tower;
and the Hall of Ornate Mirrors. The most accessible
is the Southern Lake Island.

The Temple of the Dragon King is the main point
of interest on the Southern Lake Island. Seen from
afar, it resembles a mythical fairy mountain in the
middle of the sea. Southern Lake Island is connected
to the shore by the magnificent Seventeen-Arch Bridge,
which is decorated with numerous sculptures of lions.
A large bronze bull sits on the shore at the end of the
bridge, ostensibly for the purpose of suppressing floods.
An "Inscription to the Golden Bull" is cast in ancient
seal characters on the bull's back. The Tapestry of
Ripples Bridge (Xiuyiqiao) at the south end of the
lake marks the former site of a lock which connected
Kunming Lake with the old canal which leads to the
center of the capital. Nearby are the tomb of Yelü
Chucai, the famous advisor to Genghis Khan, and a
naturally formed swimming pool.

The Western Embankment leads from the Willow
Bridge in the south to the Lakes' Edge Bridge (Jiehu-
qiao) in the northwest corner of the palace, spanning
a total of 2.5 kilometers. Peach and willow trees grow
along its entire length and the bridges which interrupt
it at six points were designed in imitation of bridges

on the Su Dyke (Sudi) on Hangzhou's West Lake. The highest of the bridges is the superb Jade Belt Bridge (Yudaiqiao), known also as the Camel's Back Bridge, because of its tall and elegant arch.

Summer is naturally the finest time of year to visit the Summer Palace. By the end of April, winter jasmine and mountain peach make their early debut on the northern face of Longevity Hill. Not long after this, flaming-red flowering plums and sweet almonds come into bloom, followed by Chinese flowering crabapples and lilacs. Next, magnolias and peonies, the "king of flowers," begin their display, while Chinese wisteria and herbaceous peonies may be seen sprouting along the Long Corridor. The mockoranges in front of the Palace of Parting Clouds bloom in the middle of May, while the season for lotuses extends from July to October. At the height of summer, jasmine and osmanthus send forth their fragrance. The frost-defying autumn chrysanthemums bring this symphony of flowers to a splendid close, making their debut on October 1, China's National Day.

The Fragrant Hills (Xiangshan Park)

The Fragrant Hills (Xiangshan Park), also known as the Forest Park, is located on the eastern slopes of the Western Hills, approximately 10 kilometers to the west of Beijing.

Due to its high elevation and dense cover of trees, spring arrives late in this part of Beijing and summer days in the park are always pleasantly cool. Perhaps the best time of year to visit the park is late fall, when

The Fragrant Hills

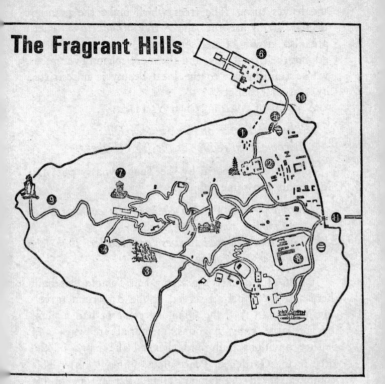

1. Retreat for Revealing the Mind
2. Temple of Clarity
3. Tree-Covered Imperial Audience Tablet
4. Chaoyang Caves
5. Eyeglasses Lake
6. Temple of the Azure Clouds
7. Western Hills Shimmering in the Snow
8. Xiangshan Hotel
9. Incense Burner Peak
10. Northern Gate
11. Eastern Gate

the leaves turn. The trees which make the grandest display of all are the smoke trees (*huanglu*). There are also groves of apricots, pears, peaches and lilacs adding their fragrance, and the more solemn evergreens, whose contribution to the local beauty is unrestricted by seasonal changes.

A poem of Marshal Chen Yi reads:

> *The red leaves of the Western Hills*
> *Become even redder as the frost thickens.*

And an earlier poem by the Tang dynasty poet Du Mu treats the same subject:

> *Stopping in my sedan chair in the evening, I sit*
> *   admiring the maple grove;*
> *The frost-covered leaves are redder than the*
> *   flowers of spring.*

In 1186 (Jin dynasty), a Xiangshan Temple was built here and for a period served as the emperor's traveling lodge. In 1745, the Qianlong emperor had a number of large halls, pagodas, memorial archways and leisure pavilions built and changed the name of the area to the Garden of Peacefulness (Jingyiyuan). This complex served the famous Qing ruler as one of his summer palaces and earned the garden a place among Qianlong's favorite "Three Hills," beside Jade Spring Mountain (Yuquanshan), and Longevity Hill (Wanshoushan) in the Summer Palace.

Qianlong's elaboration of the park consisted of a total of 28 separate vistas, each with a poetic name; Jade Chain Cliff, Toad Peak, Jade Milk Spring, Bell Separated from the Clouds, etc. Tragically, almost every trace of this carefully orchestrated symphony of landscape architecture, including the blueprints, was burned or destroyed by the French and English Allied Armies and the Eight-Power Allied Forces in the 19th and early 20th centuries. The more important extant sites are as follows:

Retreat for Revealing the Mind (Jianxinzhai): Built first in the Jiaqing period (1796-1820) and later rebuilt, this complex of buildings stands to the west of Eyeglasses Lake. The retreat contains a semi-circular pond and an adjacent pavilion, surrounded on three sides by covered galleries. Beyond the pavilion is rockery hill and a grove of trees concealing a gazebo.

Temple of Clarity (Zhaomiao): Constructed in 1780 in the Qianlong period, this Lamaist temple is said to have been built especially for the Panchen Lama. In its center, a Red Terrace (Hongtai) rises ten meters above the ground. On its eastern side is a memorial archway of white marble and glazed tile, while on the slope to the west is a seven-storied glazed tile pagoda, the eaves of which are hung with tiny bells. With even the slightest breeze the air fills with a pleasant tinkling sound.

The Tree-Covered Imperial Audience Tablet (Senyuhu): Located to the southwest of the Chaoyang Caves, this group of steep cliffs with its numerous trees resembles a giant *hu* — the rectangular tablet officials held before themselves in the presence of the emperor.

Worried Ghost Peak (Guijianchou): The main peak of Xiangshan Park, Worried Ghost Peak has an elevation of 560 meters. Its precipitously angled cliffs are often engulfed by clouds and mist, which give the two large stone excrescences of the peak a resemblance to incense burners. It is from this that the name

Xiangshan or Incense Mountains (and not Fragrant
Hills, as the area has been mistakenly called for
generations) is derived.

From the peak, the Yongding River and the Marco
Polo Bridge can be seen winding its way west like a
fluttering strip of white silk. Stone Vista Mountain
(Shijingshan), the Summer Palace and Jade Spring
Mountain can all be seen from here, and on a clear day
one can even make out the skyline of Beijing.

A Survey of Some Qing Private Gardens

The ancient private gardens of Beijing exhibit the
same high level of artistry and distinctly Chinese
genius as the famous gardens in other parts of China.

There are more than 50 extant private gardens
within the old city limits. Each of these gardens exemplifies the consummate skill of their designers who, with
a limited amount of space at their disposal, created a
seemingly unlimited number of constantly changing
vistas that not only imitate nature in miniature, but
also surpass it. Four such gardens will be introduced
here.

Lotus Garden

The Lotus Garden is one of the best-preserved
gardens in Beijing. Situated at 19 Hongyan Alley
in the East City District, it has a total area of about
3,600 square meters. The residence stands on the
west side, and the rectangular-shaped garden on the
east side is 60 meters long and 40 meters wide. The
main hall, with its hump-ridged gabled roof, stands in

the north part of the garden facing south. In front of it is a spacious brick terrace less than half a meter high, which adds an air of refinement to the surroundings. There are also two side halls connected to the main hall by covered corridors. The ground gradually rises to the south and the corridors follow the contour of this rise. At the highest point in the extreme south end of the courtyard stands a small pavilion with a hump-ridged roof. Set off against the main hall, with its back against the southern courtyard wall and its front overlooking a small pond, the pavilion's dominating position in the courtyard exaggerates the height of the incline and makes it seem as if it were standing on a "distant mountain."

The garden also contains two small pavilions with peaked roofs. The one in the center is surrounded on three sides by a meandering stream flanked by a white marble balustrade. The stream has its source in a rockery to the north of the pavilion and flows past it before collecting in a pond. It then continues southwest where it passes under a carved white marble bridge and disappears among some large stones.

Lining the sides of the pond are several large rock formations which together with the artificial hill give the impression of a vast mountain range with a gorge winding through it. At first glance, this arrangement of stones appears as an unbroken facade, but a closer look reveals a flight of stone steps winding through it. Just as in Chinese painting in which "A downward stroke three inches long represents a height of 10,000 feet; a line a few feet long forms a path of 100 miles," the vistas in this tiny garden appear as a vast panorama of majestic mountain peaks.

The six large locust trees in the garden seem to spread out their branches to welcome visitors to the garden. In front of the hall, lilacs, dwarf crabapple and walnut trees shade the courtyard with their rich foliage.

Sufficiency Garden

Sufficiency Garden is located at 9 Cap Alley (Mao'er Hutong) near the northeast corner of the Imperial Palace. It was built in the 1850s by Rong Yuan, an official who served in the Qing court, as part of his residence. Rong Yuan described an ideal garden as follows:

"Islets for ducks and cranes are most attractive when they are small. Miniature pavilions and flower beds can also add to the subtlety of a garden. Mine will never achieve the magnificence of Du You's villa or Hong Jing's mountain retreat, but if I can have a garden for strolling about in and fishing, and a few places to stop and rest, it will be sufficient. Hence I have chosen the name Sufficiency Garden."

Located in the eastern part of the residence, the garden occupies an area of about 3,000 square meters. It is rectangular in shape, 100 meters long and 26 meters wide. The buildings are the principal items of interest here, with the artificial landscapes playing a secondary role. The principal structures are laid out along a central axis, allowing the garden to be divided into front and rear sections. The front section is characterized by its brightness and spaciousness, while the rear section is more peaceful and secluded. The two sections are connected by side galleries. Entering the garden from the residence, one will notice that the

Soong Ching Ling's residence

The Temple *of the* Azure Clouds (Biyunsi)

The Eastern Qing Mausoleums

Ruins of the Yuanmingyuan Palace

Interior of the Hall of the Immortals in the Temple of the Azure Clouds

The Great Wall at Badaling

Exhibition Hall in the Beijing
Museum of Natural History

View of the Hall of Prayer for a Good Year
in the Temple of Heaven

Caisson ceiling in the Hall of Prayer for a Good Year in the Temple of Heaven

The Moon over the Lugou Bridge at Dawn

important buildings all face west, and that the buildings on the west are large in size but few in number,
while those on the east are small but numerous. Each
building has its own particular characteristics and the
arrangement of buildings is consciously casual and
random in order to avoid monotony.

The pillars in the various buildings in the garden are
carved with designs of pines, bamboos and plums.
Cypress trees predominate in the garden, but there are
also locusts and elms. Recent owners of the garden
also planted fruit-bearing persimmons.

Sufficiency Garden's rockery hills also deserve mention. The two examples in the rear garden are constructed with rocks from Fangshan near Beijing. One
lies along the central axis of the garden and breaks up
the rear garden into a number of separate sections
which cannot be viewed in their entirety from any one
point in the garden. The other hill stands near the
terrace and features a section which appears like the
entrance to a cave.

Sufficiency Garden has a strong northern Chinese
flavor and is a well-preserved example of the natural-
istic gardens of the late Qing period.

Half-mu* Garden

Half-*mu* Garden, located at 9 Glutinous Millet
Alley (Huangmi Hutong) in the East City District, is
one of the most famous Qing dynasty gardens in Beijing. It is repeatedly lauded in a number of old local

---

* *Mu* is a measure of area which has varied throughout the course
of Chinese history. In the late Qing it was equal to approximately
1,000 square meters. The name of the garden was chosen to de-
preciate its size rather than describe it scientifically.

histories for its complex structure, classical elegance and scholarly atmosphere.

The main hall, known as the Hall of Cloudshade, has a wooden model of a cloud formation dating from the Kangxi period (1662-1722) erected in its center. This peculiar decorative structure is designed to resemble purple clouds floating through the branches of trees. To the side of the main hall are the Chamber for the Appreciation of Stones, the Pavilion for the Display of Paintings, the Study of Approaching Brilliance, the Study for Withdrawn Contemplation, the Room for Enjoying Spring, and the Room of Congealed Fragrance. Each room had its own special purpose, as their names suggest: The Room for Preserving *Zun* and *Yi* was reserved for displaying ancient bronzes; The Langhuan Fairyland was a library; the Chamber for the Appreciation of Stones held exotic stones; and the Study for Withdrawn Contemplation contained various *qin*, or ancient Chinese zithers. To the south of the main hall is a pond with a small kiosk called the Flowery Residence of Flowing Ripples in its center. The kiosk may be approached by either of two bridges which connect it to the sides of the pool.

The garden was built by the Qing writer Li Yu (Li Liweng, 1611-ca. 1679) and the noted landscape architect Zhang Lian and his son. At the time, the artificial hills in the garden were known as the finest in Beijing.

From the early Qing dynasty on, the Half-*mu* Garden served as the residence of a number of officials, and at various times was used as a meeting hall and a theater. In the Daoguang period (1821-50) it was renovated, and certain features of southern Chinese gardens were incorporated.

Nuotongfu Garden

The Nuotongfu Garden at 1 Goldfish Lane (Jinyu Hutong) was the official residence of Nuo Tong, a senior Manchu official who served right up until the fall of the Qing dynasty. Originally the garden contained a goldfish pond, after which Goldfish Lane was named.

Nuotongfu Garden is one of the best-preserved residence gardens in Beijing. The western part of the grounds is taken up by the residence and the eastern part by the garden. A roofed gallery flanks the garden on the north, south and east sides, separating the garden itself from the living quarters but also serving to link the two together. Atop a high terrace at the western end of the garden is a small pavilion with a fine view of the entire premises. In the middle of the garden near the pond is a rockery hill, to the east of which is a six-sided pavilion. Another fine view of the garden may be obtained from a terrace built on top of the rockery hill. The garden is planted with elm, locust, silk and cypress trees, along with a great variety of flowers.

In addition to these four gardens, mention must also be made of Maguitang Garden at 44 Weijia Lane, which, with an area of 7,000 square meters, is one of the largest private gardens in Beijing. Maguitang Garden is best known for its rockeries.

Finally, Liu Garden at 129 Lishi Lane should be noted for its fine landscape gardening.

Chapter 4
Places Commemorating Famous
People

Sun Yat-sen Memorial Hall

The Sun Yat-sen Memorial Hall is located within the Temple of Azure Clouds (Biyunsi) at the foot of the eastern slopes of Fragrant Hills (Xiangshan) Park in the Western Hills, just over ten kilometers from downtown Beijing.

The Temple of Azure Clouds is a Buddhist temple some 600 years old. It is comprised of four large halls, the innermost of which is now the Sun Yat-sen Memorial Hall. Before 1949, the hall contained nothing more than a portrait of Sun Yat-sen (1862-1925) and it was not until 1954 that the government renovated the building and enlarged the display to its present form.

A bust of Sun Yat-sen stands opposite the main entrance to the hall. Immediately to its right is an empty coffin, covered in bronze and lined with glass which was a gift from the government of the Soviet Union. Because it arrived two weeks after Sun Yat-sen's remains had been entombed, this coffin was not used. On the left side of the hall is a display of letters and manuscripts left behind by Sun at his death. On the wall is a white marble inscription of a letter Sun Yat-sen addressed to the Soviet Union.

There are exhibition rooms on each side of the Memorial Hall. The first displays photographs of Sun Yat-sen in his youth and the second shows his activities during the period of democratic revolution.

Behind the Memorial Hall is the Pagoda Courtyard (Tayuan) which is shaded by pine trees. The Diamond Throne Pagoda (Jingangbaozuota) was constructed in 1748 during the reign of the Qianlong emperor and modeled after the Five Pagoda Temple (Wutasi) in the northwestern suburbs of the city. In March, 1925, Sun Yat-sen's coffin was temporarily placed inside the pagoda before being moved to the Sun Yat-sen Mausoleum (Zhongshanling) in Nanjing on June 1, 1929. His clothing and personal effects, however, were left behind inside the pagoda. In front of the pagoda stands a stone stela with an inscription by Hu Hanmin, a senior leader of the Kuomintang. The pagoda itself is 34.7 meters high and is built of large blocks of marble. The four sides of its base are carved with images of the Buddha. Above the terrace and surrounding the central pagoda there are seven miniature nine-story pagodas.

Honglou (The Red Building)

Honglou, the former site of Beijing University, is situated at the eastern end of Shatan Street. The four-story red brick building dates from 1918 and is particularly famous today because Li Dazhao, one of the founders of the Chinese Communist Party, and Mao Zedong both worked there. In the southeastern corner of the first floor of the building, two west-facing rooms have been designated the Mao Zedong and Li Dazhao Memorial Rooms.

Born in 1888, Li Dazhao went to study in Japan and there in 1913 took part in movements to oppose Yuan Shikai. On his return to Beijing, he became the general editor of the magazine *Morning Bell Journal* (*Chenzhong Bao*) and in 1917 joined the staff of Beijing University as a professor of economics and director of the library. He organized a diverse group of idealistic youth and on June 30, 1918, founded the Young China Study Society. The members included Mao Zedong, Gao Junyu, Yun Daiying, Cai Hesen and Xu Deheng. Their aim was "... with a scientific attitude, to work for society and create a new young China." Nowadays, the room that was Li Dazhao's study contains a display of items of historical interest such as photographs, letters, manuscripts and books. Also on display are some of the magazines that carried his essays — *New Youth*, *New Tide*, *Weekly Review*, as well as copies of his posthumously published works *Essentials of Historiography* and *Populism*. His old desk and chair, its back worn out from long use, are still in their original positions. A more sinister exhibit is a photograph of the gallows used by the warlord Zhang Zuolin to execute Li Dazhao in 1927.

From August 1918 to 1919, Mao Zedong worked in Beijing University as a library assistant. Today the room where he worked contains a display with his three-drawer desk and wooden chair. Here is also a copy of the *Beijing University Monthly* which published a notice about Mao's receiving an auditor's permit for a series of lectures given by the Beijing University Journalism Society, and the letter that he wrote to the

Beijing University Students' Self-Governing Society in 1949.

Honglou was the birthplace of the May 4th Movement. On the morning of May 4, 1919, it was from this building that Beijing University students set out on their way to Tian'anmen (Gate of Heavenly Peace) and on May 7 it was in the square north of here that the students gathered once again to welcome back classmates released after their arrest during the demonstrations.

The Tomb of Li Dazhao

The Cemetery of Eternal Peace (Wan'an Gongmu) is situated in the foothills of Jade Spring Mountain, 15 kilometers from Beijing. Here, under the shade of groves of pine trees, lies Li Dazhao, a leader of the Chinese revolution, one of the key promoters of the May 4th Movement, and a founder of the Chinese Communist Party. To the north the tomb is overshadowed by undulating ridges and peaks which form a natural screen. To the south, the flat fertile plains of the Beijing suburbs stretch away into the distance.

The tomb is in the southern part of the cemetery and is constructed of concrete. Before it stands a white marble tablet, one meter square, on which six characters are engraved, "The Tomb of Li Dazhao," in the calligraphy of Liu Bannong, a noted scholar of the May 4th Movement period.

From 1916, when Li published the first issue of the *Morning Bell Journal* (*Chenzhong Bao*) in Beijing, until his death by hanging in April 1927 at the age of 51, Li Dazhao devoted his life to the service of his country.

Li left behind a corpus of over 350 writings which were praised by Lu Xun as "the legacy of a pioneer, a monument of revolutionary history."

Lu Xun's Former Residence

The Former Residence of Lu Xun (1881-1936), a typical Chinese style home built around a courtyard, is situated near Fuchengmen in the West City District. The easternmost room on the northern side of the courtyard belonged to Lu Xun's mother and the western room to Lu Xun's wife. The rooms on the southern side of the courtyard served as a sitting room and library. Attached to the northern side of the courtyard is a small room known as the "Tiger Tail" (Laohuweiba), which was used as his study and bedroom.

Lu Xun bought the house in February 1923 with money borrowed from friends, and in the two years and three months that he lived there he completed *Tomb*, *Wild Grass*, *Aureole Anthology*, *Aureole Anthology Part II* and the famous collection of short stories entitled *Uncertainty*, as well as a large number of translations. Next to the "Tiger Tail" is a tiny garden with a thorny plum tree which, together with the lilac tree in the front courtyard, were planted by Lu Xun himself.

After 1949, Lu Xun's wife Xu Guangping donated the residence to the state, and in 1956 the government created the Lu Xun Museum. The Museum's courtyard is filled with flowers and trees. Inside the main entrance

of the exhibition hall facing the doorway is a commemorative verse, in front of which stands a bronze
bust of Lu Xun.

The first section of the exhibition displays photographs, unpublished manuscripts and letters the writer
left behind on his death. Included here are photographs
of his hometown of Shaoxing in Zhejiang Province and
pictures of the childhood scenes described in his short
stories. Here also is the anatomy notebook that he
used while a medical student in Japan, a copy of the
magazine *New Youth* which carried his first short story
"Diary of a Madman" and a proof copy of Qu Qiubai's
Collected Narrations Written at Sea (Haishang Shulin)
which Lu Xun proofread for the author. The exhibit
which attracts the most attention is the facsimile of the
diary that Lu Xun wrote the day before he died.

The second section of the exhibition displays a collection of photographs of Chinese and foreign memorial
gatherings held on the occasion of Lu Xun's death, a
display of Lu Xun's works translated into 24 different
languages, and a set of the *Complete Works of Lu
Xun* published in 1938.

Lu Xun's library of 16,000 books stands to the west
of the exhibition hall. Many of the volumes on display
were re-bound by Lu Xun himself.

The Lu Xun Museum was officially opened on the
20th anniversary of the writer's death on October
19, 1956. In 1980, a project to expand the Museum was
begun. The completed Museum now houses an exhibition of the author's life divided into eight periods, from
his youth in Shaoxing to his death in Shanghai.

Soong Ching Ling's Former Residence

The Former Residence of Soong Ching Ling, late Honorary Chairman of the People's Republic of China, is situated at 46 North River Street (Beiheyan) in the Rear Lake (Houhai) area of the West City District. The residence was once a garden in one of the Qing dynasty princes' mansions. The area along the banks of Rear Lake is quiet and beautiful, with shady willows lining the streets. Water from Rear Lake has been diverted through an underground channel into a stream that wends its way through the garden.

This lovely Beijing garden is elegantly laid out with rockeries and ponds set off by pines, cypresses and flowers. Traditional style halls and pavilions in the garden are linked by winding corridors. The tasteful layout gives the whole garden an atmosphere of elegant antiquity.

Originally, the grounds of the mansion contained numerous buildings; the front hall, called Happiness on the Hao River Bridge, after a story from Zhuang Zi; the rear hall, called the Changjin Study; the side hall, the Pavilion for Listening to the Orioles; and the eastern hall, called the Hall for Gazing at Flowers. Linked to the South Building by a winding corridor was the Waves of Kindness Pavilion. Exquisite large rockeries were dotted with structures such as the Fan Pavilion and the Room for Listening to the Rain. Ponds, fine rocks, shady trees, flowers and lawns all added to the enchantment of the garden. But over the years the whole garden fell into disrepair.

After the founding of the People's Republic, the Party and government made plans to build a residence for

Soong Ching Ling in Beijing, and decided to renovate one of the princes' gardens for the purpose. New buildings were constructed to the west of the mansion's main hall to create the quiet secluded courtyard as it stands today. Soong Ching Ling moved into the mansion in 1963 and worked, studied and lived here until she passed away on May 29, 1981.

A short way inside the main gate is a grape arbor, and beneath it a flower bed upon which stands a wooden tablet carved with a brief introduction to the history of the mansion.

Walking northeast from the grape arbor, one comes to the exhibition halls. The auxiliary exhibition hall served as a guest room where Soong Ching Ling received guests from China and abroad. A dignified portrait of Soong Ching Ling hangs on the wall directly opposite the main door.

The first exhibition hall is divided into eight sections, each representing a period in Soong Ching Ling's life. The exhibit contains large numbers of photographs, documents and objects of interest depicting her childhood and student days, her marriage to Sun Yat-sen, her participation in political activities, her organization of the Association to Safeguard the Rights of the Chinese People and her support of the advocates of resistance to the Japanese invasion. Also on exhibit is a copy of one of Soong Ching Ling's most famous sayings, taken from her essay "Sun Yat-sen and His Cooperation with the Chinese Communist Party":

"Sun Yat-sen's forty years of political struggle for the Chinese nation and people reached their peak in the last years of his life. The high point of his development came with his decision to cooperate with the Chinese Communist Party and work for the Chinese revolution."

The second exhibition hall is divided into seven sections with the following titles: Invitation to Come to the North; One of the Founders of New China; Close Comrade-in-Arms of the Party, Beloved Leader of the People; Pioneer in Safeguarding Peace-Envoy of the Chinese People; Study, Life and Work; Great Communist Fighter; and the Grief of a Nation, the Sorrow of the World.

The third exhibition hall is the Children's Hall, reflecting Soong Ching Ling's great affection and concern for the youth of China. She once said; "Children are our future, our hope; they are our country's most valuable asset." Included in the exhibition is a painting of a basket of longevity peaches, presented to Soong Ching Ling by the four-year-old artist Enge, symbolizing the affection which the children of new China feel for her.

The fourth exhibition hall is a small two-story building. The ground floor contains a small drawing room and a dining room, while Soong Ching Ling's study, office and living quarters are on the second floor. The bedroom, study and dining room are all arranged as they were when Soong Ching Ling lived at the residence. The layout is simple and tasteful. Formerly, Soong Ching Ling would spend her time here playing the qin (Chinese zither), doing embroidery and writing poetry and prose.

Xu Beihong Memorial Hall

Xu Beihong (1895-1953) was an outstanding modern Chinese painter and teacher. An advocate of realism, he produced a great variety of works, though he was particularly skillful at painting horses.

The Xu Beihong Memorial Hall was originally located in Xu's old home. In accordance with the artist's will, Xu's wife, Liao Jingwen, donated the house and all of his works, books and calligraphy to the People's Government, which established the Xu Beihong Memorial Hall on the site. Later, when the house was demolished to make way for Beijing's underground railway, the Memorial Hall was moved to 53 North Xinjiekou Street.

At the new hall, Xu's studio was reconstructed just as it had been before his death. On the walls are Xu's copy of "Bumper Harvest" along with works by Ren Bonian and Qi Baishi and a photograph of Xu taken with Rabindranath Tagore. Two small cabinets containing Xu Beihong's personal seals, a collection of antiques and a number of gifts presented to him by foreign friends are also on display.

A pictorial summary of Xu Beihong's life contains photographs of Xu's visits to the Soviet Union, Italy, Czechoslovakia and India. In addition, there are original specimens of his correspondence with the People's Volunteer Army and primary school children, and telegrams and letters of condolence sent on the occasion of his death.

Among the Chinese paintings, oil paintings and sketches in the Memorial Hall collection are many of Xu's representative works, including four outstanding pieces: the oil paintings "Tian Heng and His 500 Troops," and "Wait for My Lord," and the Chinese paintings "The Foolish Old Man Who Removed the Mountains" and "Jiu Fanggao Appraises a Horse." There is

Beiping (as the city was then called) Judiciary to commemorate the Southern Song national hero Wen Tianxiang.   Today the memorial stands on the northern side
of the entrance to South Fuxue Alley near Beixinqiao.
According to historical records, there was once a memorial archway outside the memorial's eastern wall inscribed with "Teaching Loyalty District" (Jiaozhongfang),
the old name of that section of Beijing.

The temple once housed three ancient scholartrees,
as well as a "Prime Minister" elm and one date tree
with its branches and trunk leaning very noticeably
southward. According to local legend, this tree represents Wen Tianxiang's longing for his old home in the
south.   The three scholartrees disappeared long ago,
but the date tree is still thriving.

A eulogistic couplet reading "The Song Dynasty's
Top Ranking Scholar and Prime Minister, the West
River's Filial Son and Loyal Subject," is carved into the
columns of the memorial's main hall. In the center of
the hall stands a sculpture of Wen Tianxiang holding an
official tablet before him. To the left of the statue is a
tablet engraved on its upper half with Wen's likeness
and below with the 32-character "Clothes and Belt Inscription" which ends with the lines ". . . and today and
ever after his conscience is clear." Four large inscribed
wooden plaques hang inside the hall. They read, "Loyalty and devotion to old friends"; "Righteousness in
heaven and on earth"; "The utmost in benevolence and
justice"; and "The Song dynasty survives here." A
screen bears the complete text of Wen Tianxiang's *Song
of Righteousness* (*Zhengqige*).

Wen Tianxiang (1236-1282) was born near present-day
Ji'an in Jiangxi Province.   In 1256 he was the top scholar

in the imperial examinations and successively held posts in the Board of Punishments and in local government offices in Hunan and Jiangxi. When the Yuan (Mongol) armies began moving southward and steadily closed in on Hangzhou, Wen Tianxiang received orders to negotiate a truce, but was arrested by the Yuan forces. He escaped and returned to Wenzhou where he led the Song troops into battle. In 1278, Wen was taken prisoner after suffering a defeat at Haifeng and made two unsuccessful suicide attempts. Later, he was taken by the Yuan army to Chao'an County and in the following year ordered by the Yuan general Zhang Hongfan to write a letter to the anti-Yuan faction headed by Zhang Shijie, advising them to surrender. Wen sternly refused and wrote a poem which ends with two famous lines:

What man is ever immune from death?
Leave me with a loyal heart shining in the pages of history.

In April, 1279, Wen was sent north under armed escort and reached the capital Dadu on October 1. Here he was held captive for four years and despite all manner of threats and inducements on the part of the Yuan rulers to win him over, he refused to yield. In 1282, at the age of 47, he was put to death. Before his execution he is reputed to have said; "I have done all I can for my country." When the chief executioner asked him if he wished to petition the emperor for clemency, he refused and said, "Because I am dying for my country, there is nothing to say." His remains were removed to his hometown by his old friend Zhang Qianzai. According to legend, after Wen's death, his wife was made a captive in Dadu, and when the news of her husband's death reached her, she said, "My husband has remained faithful to his country; I shall not betray him," and with that seized a knife and cut her throat.

Wen Tianxiang's execution site was traditionally thought to have been the firewood market in the "Teaching Loyalty District" near the present-day entrance of Fuxue Alley, and thus the memorial was established here. But according to one modern scholar, the execution grounds in the 13th century were located in the southern part of the city and, because the majority of executions during the Ming and Qing dynasties were carried out there as well, Wen's memorial should properly be located there.

Many of the patriotic poems and essays in Wen Tianxiang's complete works were widely known in China by the time he was incarcerated in the capital. His famous *Song of Righteousness* was written while he was in the Yuan dynasty military prison.

The Memorial to Prime Minister Wen is located on the grounds of the Fuxue Alley Primary School in the East City District. The memorial contains only a fragment of a stela, while the remainder of its contents have become part of the permanent collection of the Beijing Bureau of Cultural Relics.

Yu Qian Memorial Temple

Yu Qian (1398-1457) was a famous politician and military strategist of the Ming dynasty. In 1449, he repulsed the invasion of the Oyrats (a general name used during the Ming dynasty for the Mongolian tribes occupying the western part of China), safeguarded the city of

Beijing and rescued the Ming dynasty from subjugation. Later, however, he was put to death as a result of plots against him by the Ming court. To commemorate his service to the country, a shrine was constructed at the site of his old home at 14 West Biaobei Alley in Dongdan.

Yu Qian was born in 1398 during the reign of the Ming emperor Hongwu to a family from Qiantang (modern Hangzhou) in Zhejiang Province, and from his earliest youth was an avid student. The young Yu greatly admired the conduct of the patriotic statesman Wen Tianxiang and wrote a eulogy in praise of him which he hung beside his desk. Two lines from this eulogy read: "He would rather die in uprighteousness than live in corruption." Years later these words would tell Yu Qian's own story.

After working his way up through the local and provincial imperial examinations, Yu Qian passed the national palace examination and was assigned to a succession of administrative posts in Shanxi, Jiangxi and other places. His outstanding achievements in office won him the deep affection of the people whom he governed.

In the autumn of 1449, the Oyrats took advantage of the seizure of power by the eunuch Wang Zhen and the resulting political chaos and military corruption to mount a large-scale invasion. Urged on by Wang Zhen, the Zhengtong emperor (reigned 1436-49 and 1457-64) gave orders to mount a defensive campaign despite a glaring lack of preparations, and naturally numerous battles were lost. After retreating to Tumubao, the emperor was finally besieged by the Oyrats and taken prisoner by the enemy. The defeat at Tumubao threw the

Ming dynasty into unprecedented peril and set off a
general panic at the capital.

At this critical juncture, Yu Qian took upon himself
the task of restoring peace and safety to China. He
began by instigating a purge of the government and ex-
posing how Wang Zhen had brought disaster to the
country. Next, he took several steps to protect the
capital, bringing together military units from all over
the country, recruiting a people's militia and arranging
for the transport of grain to feed the army. Military
materiel was repaired, new men were promoted to positions of leadership and defensive units were positioned
in outlying regions. In addition, the common people
were mobilized to resist the invaders.

On October 11, 1449, the Oyrats, holding the Zhengtong emperor as hostage, advanced on Beijing. Yu Qian
engaged them in a fierce battle and after several days
of fighting, repulsed the invading army and saved Beijing from falling into enemy hands.

After the victory, Yu Qian was given the honorary
title of Shaobao and continued to supervise military affairs as Minister of the Army. He reorganized border
defenses and eliminated the threat of enemy troops ma-
rauding the outlying areas. The Oyrats suffered heavy
losses on several occasions and in 1450 were forced to
return the emperor to the Ming court.

After his release, the emperor, along with Shi Heng,
Xu Youzhen, Cao Jixiang and others, formed a conspir-
acy, and on the 17th day of the first lunar month in
1457 overthrew the Jingtai emperor (reigned 1450-56)
and regained the throne. In order to eliminate all opposition, when the Zhengtong emperor entered the hall
to carry out the enthronement ceremonies, his supporters

issued a memorial for Yu Qian's arrest. Claiming that Yu had planned to enthrone the son of one of the emperor's brother, they accused him of being a traitor and sentenced him to death along with General Fan Guang. When Yu's property was confiscated it was discovered that his wealth consisted mainly of a large collection of books, as well as a number of gifts from the Jingtai emperor which demonstrated his loyalty to the court.

Yu Qian died on February 16, 1457. It is said that when the news of his death became known, "every single woman and child in the capital was moved to tears." Before long, a children's rhyme became popular in the city:

> In the capital rice is expensive;
> Where can we obtain rice in plenty?
> The egret walks through the waters,
> Seeking everywhere for fish.

The last two words of the second and fourth lines are homophones for Fan Guang and Yu Qian respectively.

In 1466, nine years after his death, Yu Qian was posthumously restored to his former posts by special imperial decree and the site of his old home renamed the Shrine to Loyalty and Integrity. In 1590, during the reign of the Wanli emperor, a statue of Yu Qian was placed inside the shrine, but this was destroyed along with the rest of the shrine in the early years of the Qing dynasty. The present Yu Qian Memorial Temple was constructed in the Guangxu period (1875-1908), but all the objects placed in the temple at the time have long since disappeared. A commemorative altar to Yu Qian, a horizontal tablet that reads "His blood burns for a

thousand years," and several other memorial inscriptions
are now on display on the second floor of the Kuiguang
Pavilion.

The Tomb of Li Zhi

The Tomb of Li Zhi, a progressive thinker and writer
of the Ming dynasty, is situated to the north of Tongxian County on the highway leading from Beijing to
Shanhaiguan. The tomb was originally in another part
of Tongxian County, but in 1953, the Ministry of Health
established a tuberculosis sanatorium in the neighborhood of the tomb and moved Li Zhi's remains to their
current site. The tomb was renovated in 1954.

The one remaining stela at the tomb is inscribed on
the front with "The Tomb of Li Zhuowu" (Li Zhi's
courtesy name) written in the hand of Li's friend Jiao
Hong, and on the back with a "Record in Commemoration of Li Zhuowu" and two poems entitled "In Memory
of Li Zhuowu" written in 1612 by Zhan Zhenguang.

Li Zhi was born to a Hui nationality family in Quan-
zhou, Fujian Province, in 1527. He became the prefect
of Yao'an in Yunnan Province, but retired from office
in protest at the age of 54 after an official career lasting
over 20 years. After his retirement he wrote and
taught in Macheng and Huang'an in Hubei Province, and
was unusual in the fact that he accepted female students.

Li Zhi openly adopted the stance of a heretic and
wrote, "I dislike Confucianism, I don't believe in Daoism
(Taoism) and I don't believe in Buddhism; so whenever
I see Daoist priests I detest them, whenever I see Buddhist monks I detest them, and whenever I see Confu-

cian scholars I detest them even more." At that time, political power in China lay in the hands of the Confucian scholars and the Confucian ethical code was regarded as sacred. Nevertheless, Li Zhi had the courage to advocate abandoning Confucian ethics. At the same time, Li denounced the Song and Ming schools of Confucian idealist philosophy as hypocritical, proposing a version of utilitarianism instead. In the field of literature, Li held that a writer must express his own personal opinions with the "pure, true heart of a child."

In 1591, "upright" high officials, annoyed at Li's exposure of the hypocricy of Confucian morals, sent their lackeys to Li's residence at the Yellow Crane Pavilion (Huanghelou) in Wuchang to expel him from the province. Li was accused of "having defamed Confucius and of lacking moral principles" and of being an "absolute heretic."

In his later years, Li moved from place to place trying to avoid persecution, and finally took refuge in Tongzhou (present-day Tongxian County) in Beijing's eastern suburbs with an old friend, Ma Jinglun. At the time, the authorities considered Li's progressive thought to be a serious menace and labeled him as "an advocate of irresponsible and immoral doctrines" and as "one who seeks to mislead the people."

In the spring of 1602, during the reign of the Wanli emperor, Li, then 76, was arrested, imprisoned and hounded to death. His body was later buried by his friend Ma Jinglun. After Li's death, an order was issued that all his published and unpublished works be burned, and no further copies made. Despite this order, however, the great majority of Li Zhi's works have survived.

Yuan Dushi Temple

The Yuan Dushi Temple was built to commemorate Yuan Chonghuan, a national hero who was active during the last years of the Ming dynasty. Yuan, originally from Dongguan County in Guangdong Province, passed the imperial examination in 1619, and in 1622 became an official in the Board of War. His growing awareness that the Manchus presented an ever-increasing threat to the Ming dynasty led him to make a personal investigation of the situation by traveling to the Shanhaiguan Pass. At that time, Manchu forces under the dynastic title of Later Jin occupied over 70 towns and cities to the east of the Liao River. Many Ming officials proposed that the area beyond the Shanhaiguan Pass should be relinquished, but Yuan Chonghuan petitioned to be allowed to defend it.

On arriving in Ningyuan (present-day Xingcheng in Liaoning Province), he strengthened the city's fortifications and repulsed numerous attacks from the Later Jin armies. In January 1626, the Manchu armies once again attacked the city and Yuan personally mounted the walls to direct the defense. Heavy losses were inflicted on the attacking forces, and the Later Jin Emperor Nurhachi was injured, later dying of his wounds. As a result of this victory, Yuan was promoted to the position of Governor of Liaodong and the following year, after successfully defending the city of Jinzhou against further attacks, he was again promoted by the Ming Chongzhen emperor to the post of Minister of War and commander of the troops of Jiliao.

In 1629, the Later Jin armies, skirting the protected

areas along the Liaoning coast, made a detour inland, crossed the Great Wall at Gubeikou Pass and headed towards Beijing. The Ming court was taken by surprise, but fortunately Yuan had gathered intelligence about the enemy's movements and led 9,000 cavalry on a rescue mission to the capital. After riding non-stop for two days and two nights, Yuan reached Beijing before the invaders and after a fierce battle under the city walls drove the Later Jin into retreat, thus rescuing the capital from the Manchu menace.

Despite his meritorious service to the emperor, Yuan Chonghuan nevertheless came to an inglorious end. Agents deployed by the Later Jin framed a case against him and the Chongzhen emperor was duped into believing that Yuan had colluded with the enemy. On August 16, 1630, he was found guilty of treason, sentenced to death and brutally executed beneath the Western Four Archways (Xisi Pailou).

After Yuan's death, his body was carried from the Inner City by his bodyguard, a man named She, and buried on the east side of Sleeping Buddha Temple Road (Wofosijie) on a site that now belongs to the Beijing No. 59 Middle School. She's reverence for Yuan was such that he not only tended Yuan's grave for the rest of his life; he also ordered his sons and grandsons to carry on this task in his place, a tradition that was maintained for three hundred years.

To commemorate Yuan's name, the Yuan Dushi Temple was built on the banks of the Dragon Pool (Longtandonghu), the site of Yuan's general headquarters when his troops bivouacked in Zhang's Garden, an area between Dragon Pool and 4 Xinsili (New

Fourth Street). The original memorial to Yuan was destroyed by Kuomintang troops in 1948. Nevertheless, two Chinese characters carved in stone in Yuan's own script, "Ting Yu" (Listen to the Rain), remained preserved in the walls of Zhang's Garden and after 1949 they were set in the inside wall of the hall built at the site of Yuan's tomb.

In 1952, the People's Government completely renovated the Temple and adorned its surroundings with flowers and trees. Yuan's grave was also renovated and an exhibition of historical relics related to Yuan Chonghuan opened to the public.

Gu Yanwu Memorial

Gu Yanwu (1613-1682) was born in Kunshan, Jiangsu Province. In 1645, when the Qing army invaded Nanjing, Zhang Huangyan, acting on behalf of the Prince of Lu, attempted to re-establish the Ming dynasty, and Gu raised an army to support him. Gu's admiration for Wang Yanwu, a disciple of the Southern Song national hero Wen Tianxiang, led him to change his own name to Yanwu. Despite his political activities, Gu Yanwu is primarily known as a scholar. After the fall of the Ming, he repeatedly refused official positions in the Qing government and devoted himself to literary pursuits. The Gu Yanwu Memorial on Baoguosi (Recompense the Country Temple) Road in the Guang'anmen district was originally his home. In 1843, during the reign of Daoguang emperor, the poets He Shaoji and Zhang Mu made his house into a memorial. The site was abandoned long ago and little remains of the original buildings, yet on a wall lining the paved path leading to the main hall there are two stone stelae; one recording how He Shaoji and Zhang Mu erected the memorial; the other inscribed with a commemorative text by Xu Shichang (1855-1939), a president in the Northern Warlord government.

Gu Yanwu spent little time in Beijing as he became implicated in the "Case of the Huangpei Poetry Counter-Current" and was imprisoned in Jinan (Shandong Province) for seven months. While Gu was in Beijing, however, he devoted himself to scholarship, and his famous works *Notes on the Daily Accumulation of Knowledge* and *The Strategic Economic Advantages of Districts and States of the Empire* were both compiled while he was living at the capital. His work *Five Volumes on the Study of Phonology* was said to have taken him 30 years to complete and to have undergone five revisions.

Yuewei Cottage (Yuewei Caotang)

Yuewei Cottage, located at 45 Tiger Lane Bridge Road (Hufangqiao Dajie), is the former residence of the Qing dynasty scholar Ji Yun (1724-1805).

It was here that Ji wrote the famous collection of literary essays called *Yuewei Cottage Sketchbook*, which ranks among the most important works of its kind in Chinese history. The writer's most assiduous work, however, was not done on this book but on the *Synopsis of the Library of the Four Branches of Literature*, which took 13 years to complete. For only after reading the more than 36,000 volumes of the *Complete Library of the Four Branches of Literature* could the synopsis, which takes up more than 200 fascicles, be compiled.

Ji Yun (courtesy name Ji Xiaolan) was born in Xian County, Hebei Province, and was a successful candidate in the imperial examinations during the reign of the Qianlong emperor. He had a carefree, humorous disposition and was generally regarded as something of a comic. A man of profound learning and an eloquent and out-spoken writer, Ji Yun made many valuable contributions to Chinese scholarship. Nevertheless, his fate under the feudal monarchy was an unfortunate one. One of his relatives, Lu Yayu, was Commissioner of Salt Affairs headquartered in Yangzhou, Jiangsu Province. Lu held feasts and entertained guests at the government's expense so frequently that he nearly exhausted the salt tax revenues which rightfully belonged to the state. When the emperor discovered this, he decided to confiscate Lu's property.

Ji Yun got wind of the plan and sent Lu a letter of warning. Without writing a single word, he sprinkled a few tea leaves inside and added salt to the glue with which he sealed the envelope. Lu understood this to mean that there was trouble about the salt business, while the tea leaves (*cha*) warned of a raid (also pronounced *cha*) on his house. Lu immediately transferred all of his valuable property to a secret place for safekeeping. Unfortunately, an old enemy of Ji Yun's named He Shen, a vice-minister of the Board of Revenue and Population and member of the Imperial Privy Council, learned of the secret and informed the emperor. As a result, the scholar was banished to distant Xinjiang Province. Despite the fact that Ji was subsequently pardoned and promoted to become a senior member of the

Imperial Academy, there acting as Chief of Editing and Compiling, his official career never recovered from this serious setback.

In 1931, the noted Peking Opera stars Yu Shuyan and Mei Lanfang organized the Chinese Opera Society, the Chinese Opera Pictorial and the Society for the Teaching and Practice of Chinese Opera, all of which gathered at the Yuwei Cottage for meetings. A stage was constructed in the courtyard and it was here that the Society for the Teaching and Practice of Chinese Opera staged its premiere performance. After 1949, the cottage became the headquarters of the Society for Democratic Construction.

The courtyards of the Yuewei Cottage house two rare old trees which deserve mention. The first is a 100-year-old Chinese wisteria growing in the front courtyard. The other is a double-forked crabapple found in the rear courtyard.

Kang Youwei's "Sweat-Soaked Boat"

Kang Youwei (1858-1927), who was born in Nanhai County, Guangdong Province, and popularly known as the Master of Nanhai or Kang Nanhai, was a progressive reformer who throughout his life "sought truth from the West." The Sweat-Soaked Boat was the small boat-shaped room Kang lived in while in Beijing and originally was part of the Nanhai Guildhall. It now stands at 43 Mishi (Rice Market) Alley, opposite Caishikou (Vegetable Market).

In his "Sweat-Soaked Boat," Kang Youwei wrote poetry and prose, compiled a number of famous books and, along with his colleagues, formulated plans for the Reform Movement of 1898.

When Kang lived there, the northern courtyard of the Nanhai Guildhall contained seven trees and was thus known as the Seven-Tree Court. A roofed gallery running through the center of the courtyard was flanked by picturesque rockeries and its walls decorated with an inscription of Su Dongpo's verse, "On Seeing a Flowering Crabapple." When Kang Youwei arrived in Beijing for the first time in June 1882 to take part in the national imperial examinations, he resided at the Nanhai Guildhall. Although he was unsuccessful in the examinations, his experiences in the capital were an education in itself. After returning home via Shanghai, he read a number of translated works on such subjects as modern industry, international politics, medicine, and military strategy, from which he became aware that the Western nations drew on a set of ideologies which were entirely different from Confucian thought. The theories presented in these books were the catalyst for Kang Youwei's reformist plans to bring constitutional monarchy to China.

In the summer of 1888 at age 30, Kang returned to Beijing for a second unsuccessful attempt at the imperial examinations, once more staying at the Nanhai Guildhall. By this time, the corruption and decadence of the Qing government and the general situation brought about by China's defeat in two Opium Wars further reinforced his belief that China's only hope lay in reform. Kang wrote several lengthy memorials to the throne enumerating his beliefs, expressing his grief at the sorry state of the nation and suggesting reform. Unfortunately, his memorials fell into the hands of arch conservatives at court and never reached the emperor. Despite this, Kang's name became well-known in Beijing.

Between 1890 and 1897, Kang Youwei completed two major works which laid the foundation for constitutional reform and modernization and gave further impetus to the reform movement. In 1894-95, he and his student Liang Qichao met twice in Beijing. Their meetings coincided with the outbreak of the Sino-Japanese War and the subsequent defeat of China's army and navy which for over a decade had been in the hands of advocates of Westernization. The panic-stricken Qing government dispatched Li Hongzhang to Japan to surrender and negotiate a peace settlement, and in March 1895, the Treaty of Shimonoseki was signed. According to the terms of the treaty, the independence of Korea was recognized, the Liaodong Peninsula, Taiwan and the Pescadores (Penghu) Islands were ceded to the Japanese, and China was to pay an indemnity of 200 million taels of silver. News of this treaty set off vigorous opposition from the Beijing public and Li Hongzhang was strongly criticized for betraying his country. Kang Youwei immediately called upon the 1,300 successful provincial examination candidates (*juren*) currently in Beijing to join him in presenting a memorial to the throne requesting that the emperor nullify the treaty and institute progressive reforms.

In 1897, Kang founded a number of politically oriented societies and in 1898, he and Liang Qichao organized candidates in Beijing taking the imperial examinations into the Society to Preserve the Nation, which issued the following warning cry: "China's territory is diminishing; China's power is being eroded; the people of China face increasingly greater difficulties."

After a period of deliberation, on April 23, 1898, the Guangxu emperor issued a decree to "determine China's correct policy" wherein he agreed to realize the requested reforms. But the weakness of the emperor's clique resulted in the Reform Movement lasting for only 100 days before it was quashed by an arch-conservative clique led by the Empress Dowager Cixi. Kang Youwei was forced to flee Beijing in disguise on the eve of the coup d'etat.

Kang's final visit to Beijing took place in August 1926. He died at Qingdao on March 31, 1927.

Tan Sitong's Misty Room

Tan Sitong, the late-Qing politician, reformist and philosopher, was born in 1865 at Lanman Alley near Beijing's Xuanwumen to a family from Liuyang in Hunan Province.

Diagonally opposite present-day Caishikou Department Store in Beijing is an alley named Beibanjie, and at 41 stands the building that in Tan Sitong's time was the site of the Liuyang Guildhall. Tan Sitong lived in a room in the courtyard which he named the "Misty Room" and it was here that he compiled the poetry anthology *Verses from the Misty Room* in 1895. As a radical reformer, Tan maintained close ties with Kang Youwei and Liang Qichao, and at the time of the Reform Movement lived just one alley away from Kang, whose residence was in Mishi (Rice Market) Alley. Most of Tan's essays, poems and letters were written during this period.

With the outbreak of the Sino-Japanese War in 1894, 29-year-old Tan Sitong secretly circulated a number of progressive works, including the *Mingyi Interviews*, a late Ming work which was critical of autocratic monarchy and advocated democracy, industry and commerce, and *Ten Days at Yangzhou*, which told how the Qing army had occupied the city and massacred its citizens in ten days of slaughter.

In a burst of patriotic ardor, Tan returned to his hometown in Liuyang and established the Current Affairs School, the School for Preparing Defenses and the Southern Institute. He also ran periodicals such as the *Hunan New Studies* and the *Hunan Daily*.

Tan Sitong came to be recognized and admired by the reformist sympathizer Xu Zhijing, a vice-minister in the Board of Ceremonies who recommended him to the Guangxu emperor. On September 5, 1898, the emperor summoned Tan to an audience and asked him to become a member of the cabinet of the newly established reformist government. On the night of September 18, he went alone to the Fahua Temple to visit Yuan Shikai and attempted to persuade him to give his support to the Reform Movement. Yuan, however, double-crossed him and betrayed the reformers to the Empress Dowager who sent Qing soldiers to arrest Tan Sitong at the Liuyang Guildhall on September 26.

Some days before his arrest, friends advised Tan to leave Beijing and seek refuge in Japan. Tan's father repeatedly urged him to return south for a "family visit" to avoid the imminent disaster, but Tan refused. He explained: "Reform has never come about in any country without the flow of blood. No one in China in modern times has sacrificed himself for the cause of reform, and because of this China is still a poor and backward country. Therefore, I request that the sacrifices begin with myself."

On the afternoon of September 28, 1898, Tan Sitong, Kang Guangren (Kang Youwei's younger brother), Yang Shenxiu, Yang Rui, Lin Xu, and Liu Guangdi were executed by command of the Empress Dowager Cixi at Caishikou. Tan Sitong, only 33 at the time, faced the executioner and the crowd of thousands which had gathered to watch, and recited the words he had composed the night before:

> I am yet determined to kill my enemies
> but I cannot escape my fate.
> For the sake of the ideals have been striving for
> I shall die joyfully!

The Tomb of Matteo Ricci

The tomb of the Jesuit missionary Matteo Ricci stands behind the French Church at 12 Horsetail Ditch Road (Maweigoulu) in the Fuchengmen district. Ricci died in Beijing in June 1610 at the age of 58. According to the code of the Ming dynasty, foreigners who died in China had to be buried in Macau. The Jesuits made a special plea to the court, requesting a burial plot in Beijing in view of Ricci's contributions to China. The Ming Wanli emperor granted his permission and designated a Buddhist Temple which had been appropriated from a court eunuch for the purpose. In October of 1610, the Jesuit Father's remains were transferred to the tomb.

Constructed of square bricks and surrounded by a brick wall, the tomb is entered through a decorative iron latticework gate. A pair of carved Ming stone vases still stands before the tomb, and a stone tiger from the same period stands outside the gate.

Matteo Ricci was born in 1552 of a noble Italian family. He first went to China in 1582 after studying the Chinese language in Macau. He worked for a period in Zhaoqing, then the capital of Guangdong Province, and a number of other places before receiving permission to enter Beijing in 1601. Upon his arrival at the capital, Ricci presented the Wanli emperor with maps of foreign countries, a chiming clock and other gifts, which induced him to permit Ricci to carry on missionary work in Beijing, and to approve the building of the Southern Cathedral (Nantang), the first Catholic church in the city, near Xuanwumen.

Ricci proposed a synthesis of Confucian ideology and the ancestor worship of the patriarchal clan system with Catholicism. He also introduced Western scientific achievements into China. His books include *Basic Geometry*, translated with the help of Xu Guangqi; *Astronomy: Fact and Fiction*; and *On the Introduction of the Society of Jesus to China*. Ricci gained the respect of the high officials of the time, who addressed him as the "Wise Man of the Great West."

Chapter 5
Muscums and Libraries

Imperial Historical Archives

The Imperial Historical Archives (Huangshicheng) is situated on the eastern side of the southern end of Nanchizi Street. Construction of the building was begun in 1534 during the reign of the Jiajing emperor of the Ming dynasty, and although it was rebuilt by the Qing Jiaqing emperor in 1807, the basic structure of the main part of the building remained unchanged.

The Imperial Historical Archives is China's oldest state archives. In the early century, it housed a copy of the *Yongle Encyclopedia* (*Yongle Dadian*) and later it was used to store important historical documents of the emperors such as the "True Narration" (*shilu*), "Imperial Teaching" (*shengxun*) and "Precious Records" (*yudie*). These were preserved inside 20 wooden cabinets decorated with brass fittings patterned with clouds and dragons.

The complex is built on a north-south axis with its entrance on the west side of the front courtyard. At the northern end of the rectangular courtyard lies the library itself, a long building with an overhanging roof. Stone was used exclusively in the construction of the library so as to reduce the risk of fire. Though the library resembles buildings made of wood, it is in fact constructed

225

of a single, long tube-shaped stone arch with five arched entrances on its southern facade. For this reason, it is also known as the "Hall Without Roofbeams" (Wuliangdian). The outer layer of the double-layered doors is also made of stone. Inside the hall is a low marble platform on which the 20 cabinets stand.

The walls of the library are made from polished gray stone, and all the columns, crossbeams, brackets and rafters beneath the exterior eaves are designed in the manner of wooden building. The only noticeable difference is that the eaves are much shorter than those on most wooden buildings, and the roof corners do not curve upward.

The library is tastefully decorated. Between the gray walls and the roof of glazed, yellow tiles, the crossbeams and rafters are painted blue and green and decorated with gold. Below, a pure white marble terrace helps to give the building a cheerful and elegant appearance.

Despite the fact that many examples of this style of architecture were built during the Ming dynasty, the Imperial Historical Archives is the only example of its kind in Beijing.

Exhibition Hall of Ancient Astronomical Instruments

On South Jianguomen Street in the East City District stands the Exhibition Hall of Ancient Astronomical Instruments, the descendent of an observatory first built in 1279 during the Yuan dynasty. This was the workplace of Guo Shoujing, the noted astronomer, hydraulic engineer and mathematician.

The observatory's name was changed several times. In the Yuan period, it was called the Terrace for Managing Heaven (Sitiantai), and in the Ming, the Terrace for Observing the Stars (Guanxingtai). In modern times, it was opened to the public as a museum in 1956.

The bronze astronomical devices on display here are not only scientifically accurate; they also exemplify the finest tradition of Chinese craftsmanship. Note particularly the exquisite decorations provided by the "heavenly" dragons.

Seven of the 15 instruments were moved to Nanjing in 1931 and are now on display at the Zijinshan (Purple Gold Mountain) Observatory. The eight instruments remaining in Beijing are as follows: three armillary spheres, a quadrant, a celestial globe, a horizon circle, a quadrant altazimuth and a sextant.

Beijing Museum of Natural History

The Beijing Museum of Natural History is housed in an unpretentious building in the Yongdingmen district in the southern part of the city, just opposite the Tianqiao Department Store. The first museum of its kind in China, it houses more than 5,000 specimens which are displayed in the Halls of Paleontology, Zoology and Botany.

Featured in the Hall of Paleontology are fossil remains from the Paleozoic, Mesozoic and Cenozoic eras, forming a wordless chronicle of prehistoric life that flourished between 500 million and one million years ago. Among the exhibits is a piece of ocher marble with a cloud-like pattern on its surface formed by fossilized seaweed. This is all that remains from a period of floods dating back some 500 million years when algal life dominated the earth. When the floods receded, the algae had to adapt to a more terrestrial existence, and pteridophytes (early ferns) and gymnosperms, the predecessors of terrestrial plant life, came into being.

Aquatic plant life was soon followed by primitive animal life, and trilobites became the dominant animal species in the seas of the Cambrian era. It was not, however, until millions of years later that fish — the earliest vertebrates — appeared on earth. Their fossilized remains, such as that of the bothriolepis are on display in the Hall of Paleontology. Here is also a chart suggesting the life cycle of the crossopterygill, the purported ancestor of the reptiles and other terrestrial animal life. In the center of the hall is a large petrified skeleton of a High-Nosed Qingdaosaurus, so called because it was found at Qingdao, Shandong Province, and has a nose with a large bump on it. Twice as large as this is the skeleton of a Mamenchisaurus unearthed at Mamenxi Village in Sichuan Province. As a contrast to these giants the remains of a Lufengosaurus from Yunnan Province, no more than two meters high and six meters long, and those of a parrot-beaked dinosaur no larger than a cat are also on display.

The Hall of Zoology houses more than 2,000 specimens arranged to show the course of evolution from simple aquatic to complex terrestrial forms. These include a vast range of Chinese fauna, from the lynx and

otter of the northeast to the peacock and parrot of the
southwest; from sea dwellers such as the whale and
giant clam to such terrestrial creatures as the giant
panda.   There are also enlarged models of protozoons
and finely colored models of jellyfish and coral.

The fish specimens number in the hundreds, representing both sea and freshwater aquatic life.   Among the
reptile specimens, two items catch the visitor's eye: an
enormous leatherback sea turtle (Dermochely's coriacea)
and a Chinese alligator.   Equipped with a vocal cord-
like organ, the latter growls in stormy weather and during fights.

The museum also houses a rich collection of specimens of avian life.   The hornbill, for instance, is a rare
species in China.   Its long scythe-like bill surmounted
by a horny casque gives it its Chinese name, "rhinoceros bird."

The mammal section houses a specimen of a three-
year-old sei whale which weighed over seven tons when
it was caught.

In the Hall of Botany, the aquarium contains a collection of various forms of algal life, including kelp,
laver and agar in a range of strikingly beautiful colors.

China has a rich variety of plant life, including almost
every one of the 300,000 known species of seed plants.
The dawn wood (metasequoia), for instance, long considered extinct, is found in China's Sichuan and Hubei
Provinces.   Among other rare species on display is the
Lingzhi Cao (Glossy ganoderma), considered by pur-
veyors of traditional Chinese medicine to be a potent
elixir of life.

Beijing Planetarium

When it was built in 1957 the Beijing Planetarium was the first of its kind in China.

It is located diagonally opposite the Beijing Zoo in the northwestern section of the city and is composed of a planetarium, an exhibition hall, a lecture hall and an astronomical observatory.

The planetarium, with its cupola measuring 25 meters in diameter, is the main focus of interest of the entire complex. At regular intervals, 45-minute presentations take the visitor on a trip through the heavens made possible by projectors installed in the center of the hall which faithfully reproduce an image of the starry sky on the inside of the cupola.

Geological Museum

The Geological Museum stands at the eastern end of Mutton Alley (Yangrou Hutong) in the Xisi district. The Museum was built in 1958 and its total area of 10,000 square meters is divided into five exhibition halls: Mineral Resources; Earth History; Stratigraphy and Paleontology; Rocks and Minerals; and Mineral Deposits of China. The museum is responsible for collecting and storing geological specimens from both China and abroad and for disseminating geological knowledge. It also carries out scientific and technological exchanges, geological research, and the exchange and supply of specimens to scientific entities at home and abroad.

The Mineral Resources Hall displays a rich collection

of specimens from various parts of China. Of the standard 150 useful minerals, China has verified deposits of 132, including important deposits of coal, tungsten, tin, lead, zinc, mercury and antimony. There is an extensive display of iron ore specimens which includes magnetite, hematite and siderite, as well as dozens of nonferrous metals. In addition to specimens of coal, shale and petroleum, there are more than 80 examples of non-metals, such as diamonds, crystal, Iceland spar and mica.

The exhibits in the Earth History Hall depict, by means of various working models and dioramas, the origin and development of the earth, its internal structure and the characteristics of the earth's surface. In addition, many geological phenomena unique to China are displayed here, for example, the karst of Guilin and the Stone Forest in Yunnan; the Wudalianchi Volcanoes in northeast China; and the Rongbu Glacier, the highest glacier in the world.

The Stratigraphy and Paleontology Hall displays in chronological order a collection of fossils representing each of the geological eras beginning from the late Precambrian period in China.

The Rocks and Minerals Hall exhibits typical specimens arranged according to their chemical composition and genesis. Among these specimens are a replica of the Changlin diamond (the biggest discovered so far in China), perfect cinnabar crystals, antimony and wolframite crystal druses, large crystals of topaz, as well as the recently discovered hsianghualite and baolite.

The Mineral Deposits of China Hall displays specimens and geological maps and models which illustrate the geological conditions for the formation of China's major ore deposits and the distribution of each mineral type.

Military Museum of the Chinese People's Revolution

The Military Museum of the Chinese People's Revolution stands on the north side of the central section of Fuxing Road directly south of "August 1" Lake (Bayihu). The museum is composed of two four-storied wings and a main building of seven stories topped with the gilded emblem of the Chinese People's Liberation Army.

The museum occupies a total area of 60,000 square meters. After passing through the lobby, one comes to the central exhibition hall, which contains over 500 photographs and over 1,000 mementos of the Chinese revolution led by Mao Zedong over the course of half a century. On the eastern side of the main building, the three floors are taken up with specialized exhibits, the titles of which are in the calligraphy of Chen Yi, who penned them at the request of Zhou Enlai. The first floor is devoted to the Second Revolutionary Civil War (1927-37), the second floor to the War of Resistance Against Japan (1937-45) and the third floor to the Third Revolutionary Civil War (1945-49). The exhibits in these three sections depict the 28 years from the founding of the Chinese Communist Party in 1921 to the establishment of the People's Republic of China in 1949. They treat in detail the organization of the Party and the army, the establishment of rural revolutionary bases, and the seizing of state power by the armed forces. Included in these more than 5,000 exhibits are the oil lamp used by Mao Zedong during the Jinggang Mountain Struggle, and photographs showing Mao writing his essay "On Protracted War" and delivering his famous speech at the celebration of the founding of the People's Republic. Also on display here are photographs of Zhou Enlai, Zhu De and other veterans of the revolution along with a collection of their personal effects. Sections devoted to the People's Liberation Army and the masses show the importance of their participation in the revolutionary wars. There is also a special exhibit devoted to noted revolutionary martyrs such as Norman Bethune and D. S. Kotnis. In the western wing, the first floor exhibition hall contains a general exhibition while the second and third floors house a display entitled "The Protection of Socialist Revolution and Construction." The outdoor plazas on either side of the central hall exhibit representative weapons used by the People's Liberation Army and enemy weapons captured during various periods of the revolutionary war.

Cultural Palace of the Nationalities

(Minzu Wenhuagong)

On the northern side of Fuxingmen Street directly to the east of the Nationalities (Minzu) Hotel stands the Cultural Palace of the Nationalities. The palace is designed after the Chinese character for mountain (山), with a central section towering above two wings. The pagoda-like tower of 13 stories is exactly the same height as the famous White Dagoba in Beihai Park. The symmetrical, three-story east and west wings extend to the south along the sides of the large square in front of the main gate.

Pine trees encircle the square and a decorative fountain stands in its center. Three colors predominate in the building itself: the earthen-gold of the granite foundation, the white of the unglazed wall-tiles, and the peacock blue of the roof tiles on the pagoda-like tower.

The palace has a total floor space of 30,700 square meters and consists of six sections — a museum, a library, an auditorium, a dance hall, a restaurant and a guesthouse. The glazed roof tiles and double eaves of the tower, the two decorative pagodas on the wings, and the pair of large palace lanterns hanging before the main gate give the structure a pronounced Chinese flavor.

One enters the palace by climbing a granite staircase to the white marble portico, with its two large bronze doors decorated with the words *tuanjie* (solidarity) and *jinbu* (progress). Inside is the four-story central hall with its floor and walls of green and white marble. From the octagonal ceiling hangs a large bronze chandelier, and on the four walls are relief carvings in white marble, each depicting the various minority peoples of China. The relief carving on the southwest wall is a representation of spring time, showing the Tibetan, Miao, Yi and Bouyei (Puyi) nationalities. The southeastern relief depicts coconut trees on the sea shore as well as the people of Zhuang, Li and Yao nationalities celebrating a rice harvest. The relief on the northwestern side of the hall shows a flock of sheep, and members of the Hui and Uygur nationalities harvesting wheat, cotton and grapes. The northeastern relief shows a group of people gathered around a number of industrial products tied with colorful ribbons. The museum is in the north section of the building and consists of five main exhibition halls and 35 small display rooms spread out on the first and second floors and throughout the tower. The library is located in the basement below the exhibition hall to the north of the central hall. It can accommodate 600,000 volumes and serves as a source center for research related to China's 55 minority peoples. The library has two large reading rooms for newspapers and magazines and ten smaller rooms for use by researchers.

The east wing of the Cultural Palace contains the well-equipped 1,500 seat auditorium, each seat provided with earphones capable of transmitting eight separate channels. There are also facilities for radio and television broadcasting and a sound recording studio.

The west wing of the palace contains the amusement rooms, indoor dance hall, restaurant and a roof-top dance floor. The range of facilities includes: billiards, ping-pong, chess and bowling, a small-scale gymnasium, a small theater, a Chinese music room, a sitting room and a shop.

On the second floor, the dance hall and coffee shop are separated by a large elaborate screen decorated with a scene entitled "One Hundred Birds Admiring the Phoenix." The third floor contains a Muslim restaurant serving the typical dishes of the Hui and Uygur nationalities. Above the restaurant is the roof-top dance floor, which is enclosed by a white marble balustrade.

The large staircase in the main hall leads up to residence facilities used by minority peoples. There are

40 rooms altogether complete with private meeting
rooms, dining rooms and kitchens.

On the 13th floor of the tower is an observation
room completely enclosed in glass. From here or from
the surrounding balcony one may obtain an unobstruct-
ed bird's-eye view of the city.

China Art Gallery

The China Art Gallery, one of the ten major construction projects carried out in Beijing in 1959, is situated at
the eastern end of May Fourth Road. The high multi-
eaved roof section of the central portion of the building
is balanced on both sides by long corridors. The roofs
of these structures and the eaves of the wings of the
building are embellished with yellow glazed tiles in
traditional Chinese style. The cream color of the brick
walls blends harmoniously with the colorful glazed tile
decorations on the pillars, giving the entire facade a
tasteful appearance. The 14 exhibition halls have a
total floor space of more than 6,000 square meters.
There are, in addition, studios where artists do their
own creative work or inspect the works of other artists
past and present. The gallery frequently holds exhibitions of Chinese and foreign art. There is also a
sales department which deals in folk art, reproductions,
art posters and postcards.

Beijing Library

The Beijing Library, formerly known as the Jingshi
(Capital) Library, is the oldest and largest library in

China. An important part of the library's holdings is the Wenyuange (Pavilion of Literary Profundity) collection of the Ming emperors which includes rare Southern Song editions from the 13th century. In 1949, the library contained about 1,400,000 books and the rapidly increasing collection now numbers nearly ten million. These include rare books such as hand-written Buddhist scriptures from Dunhuang dating from the Tang dynasty, Song and Yuan woodblock editions, early Ming volumes of the *Yongle Encyclopedia* and a set of the Qing dynasty *The Complete Library of the Four Branches of Literature* (*Siku Quanshu*). The library has books in 80 different languages, including more than one million books in Russian, Japanese, English, French and German. There is also a collection of books in 20 different Chinese national minority languages. The serials section contains 2,000 journals published in China since 1949 and 10,000 foreign newspapers and journals.

The library's collection spans a wide spectrum of Chinese history. Bindings range from the ancient "butterfly" style which originated in the Tang dynasty and the so-called "wrapped spine" (*baobei*) binding developed in the Yuan, to modern cloth and paper bindings. The collection also contains specimens of Karl Marx's letters and the original manuscripts, hand-written volumes and proof copies of the works of many distinguished scholars. Of particular interest are 110 such manuscripts and hand-written volumes by Lu Xun, totaling over 5,000 pages. In addition, there are examples of the design models of the Qing architect Yang Zilei.

The founding of the Beijing Library was first officially proposed by Zhang Zhidong, a scholar of the Grand
Secretariat in charge of a Qing dynasty forerunner of
the Ministry of Education. In 1908 Zhang commissioned the Governor-General of the Jiangsu, Jiangxi, and
Zhejiang areas, Duan Fang, to buy up two wealthy
scholars' private libraries. After being brought to Beijing, the collections were stored in the Guanghua Temple and were later placed together with the surviving
Song and Yuan woodblock editions from the library of
the Grand Secretariat, the remaining volumes of the
Yongle Encyclopedia from the Imperial Academy, and
over 8,000 hand-written scrolls from Dunhuang. The
following year, the Jingshi Library was formally established at the Guanghua Temple.

From early times, China's rulers attached great importance to the storage of books and records in libraries. The Han dynasty imperial family kept a size-
able library known as the Tianlu Pavilion, and by the
Song dynasty, classical academies throughout the country housed collections of books for scholarly use. It
was not until the end of the Qing dynasty, however,
that public libraries appeared in China. Under the influence of the Reform Movement of 1898, Zhang Zhidong presented a memorial to the throne citing the importance of establishing a library in Beijing and recommended the famous bibliographers and epigraphers
Miao Quansun and Xu Fangren to act as supervisor and
deputy supervisor. After the Revolution of 1911, the
Jingshi Library was formally opened to the public on
October 7, 1912, with its reading rooms located in the
side halls of the Guanghua Temple. The Temple, however, was in an inaccessible part of the city and its rooms

were small and damp. Readers were so few in number that it closed to the public in October 1913. In June 1915, the library was moved to the Imperial Academy (Guozijian), and in 1917, the facility was reopened to the public with a ceremony attended by Cai Yuanpei and Lu Xun. At the time, Lu Xun was section chief of the Social Education Section of the Ministry of Education, and the management of the library fell under his jurisdiction.

At the end of 1928 the library was moved to the Juren Hall on the banks of the Central Lake (Zhonghai) and its name was changed to the National Library of Beiping. The following year the library was amalgamated with the Beiping Beihai Library and under the direction of Cai Yuanpei, plans were made to construct a new building to alleviate the shortage of storage space. The main building, the library's present site, was completed in 1931. After the founding of the People's Republic, it became the Beijing Library, and in 1954 a six-story building with a capacity of 1,200,000 volumes was constructed behind it. As a result, the majority of materials in storage became available for readers' use. In the summer of 1982, work was completed on the East Building, a thoroughly modern addition to the library. The new building's facilities include reference and periodical reading rooms, microfilm equipment, a computer cataloging center and extensive open stacks.

The Beijing Library is situated on the west bank of Beihai Lake, separated by the lake from the park's famous White Dagoba. Because the library contains the *Complete Works of the Four Branches of Literature* brought from the Wenjin Pavilion in the summer palaces at Chengde, the street in front of the library's main gate

was named Wenjin Road. The library is surrounded
by a red wall topped with green glazed tiles.

The site of the library had enjoyed a high reputation
from the time of the Ming dynasty when the Palace of
Brilliant Splendor (Yuxigong) stood here. The Ming
Jiajing emperor (reigned 1522-66) lived here briefly after
the Wanshou (Longevity) Palace burned down, and
under the Ming Wanli emperor (reigned 1573-1619), over
300 of the emperor's maidservants studied drama and
singing here. This remained the site of the imperial
family's private theater until the end of the Ming dynasty. Under the Qing the palace fell into disrepair and
it was not until the late 1920s when the new library
was being built that the site was renovated and ornamental columns, stelae and stone lions brought from
Yuanmingyuan Garden were placed inside the library's
courtyard.

Nowadays, the library serves as the classification
center for over 2,000 libraries throughout China and is-
sues catalog cards for all new Chinese publications. It
also maintains relationships with libraries in other countries and handles inter-library exchanges with over 2,000
libraries around the world. At present the library has
more than 20 reading rooms with seating for over one
thousand people. Anyone with a work card, a student
card or letter of introduction may read there.

In addition to the basic task of providing materials
for both scientific researchers and the general public, the
Beijing Library frequently holds exhibitions, lecture pro-
grams and reader's conferences, compiles special subject
catalogs and answers readers' inquiries. Recently, preparations were begun for a new library to be built in
Beijing's western suburbs. The structure will be a mod-

ern library complex more than double the size of the present facility.

Capital Museum

The Capital Museum, located on the grounds of the Confucian Temple on Guozijian Street southeast of Andingmen (Gate of Peace and Stability), was opened to the public on October 1, 1981. The permanent "Brief History of Beijing" exhibition traces Beijing's 3,000-year history with a display of more than 1,000 objects.

The exhibition presents the city's history in six sections: (1) The development of an organized community from ancient settlements; (2) Historical remains of the former cities of Yan and Ji; (3) Gradual development as an important northern center; (4) The capital of half of China during the Liao and Jin dynasties; (5) The world renowned Yuan dynasty capital of Dadu; (6) The political center of the Ming and Qing dynasties.

The majority of the objects on display were unearthed in the Beijing area by archeological workers or donated to the museum by local citizens. The archeological treasures include a Shang dynasty (c. 16th-11th century B.C.) bronze wine vessel decorated with three rams; a Western Zhou (c. 11th-8th century B.C.) bronze tripod; and a bronze ox cast during the Tang dynasty (618-907). Other ancient pieces include an earthenware teapot from the Spring and Autumn Period (770-476 B.C.); a gilded Buddha inlaid with turquoise from the Yuan dynasty; a Ming blue and white lotus plate; and a Qing dynasty folding fan with an ivory handle inlaid with precious stones and a tiny watch.

A separate exhibit at the Capital Museum commemorates Comrade Li Dazhao. As a herald of communism in China, Li was active in many revolutionary activities carried out in Beijing. The exhibit traces Li Dazhao's life in great detail through photographs, letters, publications and a number of personal effects collected after his death.

Capital Library

The Capital Library is located southeast of the Andingmen Gate, just west of the Confucian Temple. The library, established more than 70 years ago, was originally founded in 1913 by Lu Xun as the Metropolitan Popular Library. Before that it was the famous Imperial College (Guozijian).

The history of the Capital Library is long and complex: In 1924, the Metropolitan Popular Library and part of the Jingshi Library were transferred to the former site of the Imperial Academy beside Toufa Alley near Xuanwumen. In 1927, the two were consolidated and renamed the First Metropolitan Popular Library under the Ministry of Education. Later it was managed by the Municipality of Beijing and again renamed the First Normal Library. Then, just prior to the liberation of Beijing, its name was changed again to Beijing City Library. At this time, the library in the Zhongshan Park known as the Zhongshan Library or the Revolutionary Library became a branch.

The library was taken over by the People's Government after the liberation of Beijing in 1949 and renamed Beijing Municipal Library. In 1953, it was moved from

Toufa Alley to Xihuamen and a Xidan branch was opened at Toufa Alley. In 1956, the state appropriated a
large sum of money to refurbish the Imperial College
(Guozijian) and transfer it into what is today called the
Capital Library.

In the past, libraries were not considered important
for the common people. This, coupled with repeated
changes of address, accounts for the fact that after several decades the collection consisted of only 110,000
volumes. According to 1980 statistics, however, the
books and resources have increased 17 times since 1949.

Next to the Beijing Library, the Capital Library is
the largest public library in the municipality of Beijing.
Besides offering books on political thought, many scientific, cultural and historical books are available. It also
plays an important role in assisting and developing the
library network in Beijing's 20 suburban districts and
counties. In addition to its managerial office and general affairs department, the library is divided into a
number of other departments: editorial, reading, scientific and technological, social science reference (including foreign and domestic periodicals), book preservation, and research and assistance departments. It is also
temporarily in charge of the Beijing Youth and Children's Library.

A number of reading rooms (with more than 440
seats) are open to the general public. More than 24,000
library cards have been issued to scientific and technological personnel, workers, cadres, students and collec-
tives. More and more people are enjoying Capital Library services. In 1980, it received 300,000 readers and
some 800,000 books were borrowed. It also reproduced a large number of books and data for scientific re-

search departments and personnel. The library, under the direction of the Cultural Bureau of Beijing Municipality, is open more than 60 hours a week.

The Confucian Temple (Kongmiao)

The Confucian Temple (Kongmiao) stands next to the Imperial College (Guozijian) in the northeastern section of the city. It was built in Beijing during the Yuan dynasty (1206-1368).

A glazed tile memorial archway stands before the temple's main gate, the Gate of the Foremost Teacher (Xianshimen), which leads into a courtyard shaded by pines and cypresses. The four courtyards which make up the temple grounds occupy a total of 20,000 square meters. In the first courtyard are a number of pavilions housing a collection of 188 stone tablets bearing the names of scholars from all over China who passed the triennial imperial examinations.

At the northern end of this courtyard is the Gate of Great Achievements (Dachengmen), near which stone drums were found. These treasured drums, inscribed with a series of odes reputed to date from the reign of King Xuan (828-782 B.C.) of the Zhou dynasty, are now on display at the Palace Museum. The drums near Dachengmen today are reproductions executed during the reign of the Qianlong emperor (1736-96).

Leading to the central Hall of Great Achievements (Dachengdian) is a pathway flanked by 11 stela pavilions containing stone tablets recording military expeditions ordered by the Qing emperors. The hall was rebuilt in 1906 during a period of Confucian revival.

The double-eaved roof is covered with imperial yellow glazed tiles and the entire hall is surrounded by a stone balustrade. Between the two rows of stone steps leading up to the main hall is a marble slab with relief carvings of two pairs of flying dragons playing with pearls encircling a coiled dragon spouting mist and clouds. A memorial tablet to Confucius stands inside the rather austere hall. To the east and west are auxiliary halls that once housed stone tablets inscribed with the names of Confucius' disciples and other famous Confucianists down through the ages.

Directly behind the central hall is the Shrine of the Noble Sage (Chongshengci), used in the past for holding memorial services to Confucius' ancestors.

The Imperial College (Guozijian)

The Imperial College is located immediately to the west of the Confucian Temple (Kongmiao) and, in fact, connects with the temple through a side gate. Generally recognized as the highest official institution of learning in imperial China, it was first established in 1287 during the Yuan dynasty and subsequently enlarged several times, attaining its present dimensions during the reign of the Qianlong emperor (1736-96) of the Qing dynasty. After the founding of the People's Republic, the Imperial College was completely renovated and the Capital Library was incorporated within its grounds.

After entering the main gate, the visitor will be confronted by a pair of wells and the Gate of Highest

Scholarship (Taixuemen), also known as the Gate of Assembled Virtuous Men (Jixianmen). Inside this gate is a glazed tile memorial archway with bell and drum towers to the east and west. Directly in front of the gate is the famous Biyong (Jade Disc) Hall. The square pavilion, which stands in the center of a circular pond, has a double-eaved roof surmounted by a gilded sphere. The pond is crossed by four marble bridges and provided on four sides with stone spouts in the shape of dragon heads. It was here that the emperor came occasionally to expound the classics to an audience composed of civil and military officials from the imperial court and students of the Imperial College.

The east and west auxiliary halls of the Biyong Hall originally housed the Qianlong Stone Scriptures. In the middle of the 18th century, the Qianlong emperor ordered to have the Thirteen Classics* engraved in stone. To carry out this order, Jiang Heng, a scholar from Jiangsu Province, spent 20 years carving the 630,000 Chinese characters onto 189 stone tablets. Today these tablets are located to the east of the Gate of Highest Scholarship.

Behind the Biyong Hall stands the former Pavilion of Exalted Literature (Chongwenge) which was used as a library during the Yuan dynasty. Later its name became the Hall of Ethics (Yiluntang). Here the emperor and other noted scholars gave lectures during the period

---

* The Thirteen Classics: The Book of Changes; the Book of History; the Book of Songs; the Rites of Zhou; the Record of Rituals; the Book of Rites; the Zuo, Gongyang, and Guliang Commentaries (on the Spring and Autumn Annals); the Analects of Confucius (Lunyu); the Classic of Filial Piety; the Dictionary of Terms (Erya); and the Works of Mencius (Mengzi).

before the Biyong Hall was built. It is now one of the reading rooms of the Capital Library.

The Museum of Chinese History and the Museum of Chinese Revolution

The Museum of Chinese History and the Museum of Chinese Revolution share a single building complex which runs more than 300 meters north and south along the eastern side of Tian'anmen Square. The four-storied main building with its two symmetrical wings was built in 1959 as part of the project to build ten monumental buildings in Beijing.

Rising 40 meters at its highest point, the creamy yellow structure is decorated with a band of alternating green and yellow glazed tiles surrounding its eaves. On each side of the entrance stands a pylon in the form of a burning torch, symbolizing Mao Zedong's famous prophecy "A single spark can start a prairie fire."

Climbing up the granite steps the visitor will find himself inside a vestibule which to the east leads into the Central Hall, to the north the Museum of Chinese History, and to the south the Museum of the Chinese Revolution.

The Central Hall is dedicated to the memory of Marx, Engels, Lenin and Stalin, and sculptured representations of their heads appear on the wall, lit by a skylight framed with ornamental white flowers.

The two museums are arranged symmetrically, each with an introductory hall and 17 exhibition halls. The exhibits housed in the museums are arranged over the course of hallways two kilometers long. The solemnity of the Central Hall contrasts with the airy simplicity of the exhibition halls.

The Museum of Chinese History opened to the public in 1926, when it was known simply as the Museum of History. Despite the 14 years of preparatory work which preceded its opening, the museum disappointed the public with its paltry collection, which included Han dynasty (206 B.C.-220 A.D.) pottery and bricks excavated from three tombs at Xinyang, Henan Province; Song dynasty (960-1279) furniture and pottery found in the Song city of Julu in Hebei Province; as well as several jade seals from the Taiping Heavenly Kingdom (1851-64).

After 1949, however, the collection expanded rapidly to include over 30,000 pieces. Some of these came from official sources, such as the North China Administration of Cultural Relics, while more than 16,900 pieces came from private collections. Among these are a number of precious items such as a blue glazed lamp of the Six Dynasties Period (222-589), Tang stone figurines, and a Ming embroidered silk portrait of the Heavenly Kings (Devarajas).

Exhibitions held in the Museum of Chinese History can be divided into those of a permanent nature, such as the present exhibition of the Comprehensive History of China, which begins with the period of primitive tribes and ends with the May 4th Movement in 1919; and those of a temporary nature, which include local history exhibitions and traveling exhibits from foreign museums.

Chapter 6
Temples, Mosques and Churches

The Eight Great Temples of the Western Hills (Badachu)

The Eight Great Temples (Badachu) is the traditional name given to eight Buddhist temples "nestled among the clouds on Cuiwei Hill and Lushi Hill" in Beijing's Western Hills district.

The Temple of Eternal Peace (Chang'ansi)

The Temple of Eternal Peace is situated on the plain at the foot of Cuiwei Hill. Constructed in 1504 during the Ming dynasty, the temple is comprised of two court-yards, the first containing the Hall of Sakyamuni Buddha and the second the Niangniang (a female deity) Hall. The Hall of Sakyamuni Buddha contains a bronze statue of Guan Yu, a hero of the Three Kingdoms period (220-280) who was later worshipped as the God of War. Guan Yu was worshipped as a temple guardian by Chinese Buddhists. In the south corner of the covered corridor in the rear part of the hall is a bronze bell cast in 1600 by imperial command. It is perfectly preserved after nearly 400 years. In front of the Sakyamuni Hall there is an urn-shaped bell struck as part of Buddhist rituals which also dates from the Ming dynasty. In the rear courtyard there are two white pines (also known as dragon-claw pines) reputed to date from the Yuan dynasty (1206-1368).

The Temple of Divine Light (Lingguangsi)

Less than half a kilometer up Cuiwei Hill one comes to the Temple of Divine Light. Originally called the Dragon Spring Temple, its name was changed to the Mountain of Awakening Temple in 1162. In 1428, during the Ming dynasty, it was restored and resumed its old name, and in 1478, it was finally given its present name.

The only extant component of the original temple is the fish pond located behind the halls at the foot of a small cliff. The pond is filled with unusually large and colorful goldfish, some more than half a meter long. It is said that fish were placed in the pond before 1851.

To the west of the pond is a small kiosk known as the Pavilion of the Water's Heart (Shuixinting). A spring to the side of the kiosk bubbles with fresh cool water.

The Temple of Divine Light originally contained a number of fine old buildings, carvings and statues, but these were all destroyed by the Eight-Power Allied Forces when they occupied Beijing in 1900. One notable structure was a large octagonal Liao dynasty pagoda constructed of carved bricks built in 1071. Originally situated to the east of the goldfish pond, it was called the Pagoda for Entertaining Immortals. All that remains now is its foundation. The pagoda is important in the history of Buddhism in China since, according to the records, when Buddha was cremated all that remained in his ashes were four teeth, one of which was brought to China in the 11th century and placed here. The Liao dynastic history records that the Daozong emperor (reigned 1055-1100) placed the tooth in a pagoda here. After the destruction of the pagoda in 1900, monks searching through the rubble found a stone chest containing a wooden box in which they discovered the Buddha's tooth. In the year 855 — 108 years before the building of the pagoda in 963 — the monk Shan Hui carved the words "The Tooth of Sakyamuni," the date and some Buddhist incantations in Sanskrit on the inner and outer surfaces of the stone chest. The tooth remained in the temple until 1955 when it was removed to the Guangji Temple by the Chinese Buddhist Association and placed in the Hall of Buddhist Relics.

In 1956, the People's Government erected a new 13-story pagoda on the site of the Liao foundation and named it the "Pagoda of the Buddha's Tooth." A row of old monastery buildings to the north of the pond was restored and a visitors' service center installed. To the northeast is the Mahavira Hall (Daxiongdian) dating from 1920, which was not part of the original temple. The two Ming-style stone tablets in front of the hall are also later copies.

Three Hills Convent (Sanshan'an)

A short distance from the Temple of Divine Light stands the Three Hills Convent, which derives its name from the fact that it is situated between Cuiwei Hill, Pingpo Hill and Lushi Hill. Though the convent is not large and consists of only one courtyard, it is of rather exquisite construction. At the doorway of the main hall there is a rectangular "Cloud and Water Stone," carved with images of scenery, human figures and animals. To the east of the main hall is a small kiosk with an inscribed plaque which reads "Cuiwei

Hill is part of a painting." Looking out from here, one can see many peaks covered with pines and cypresses. The temple is set in the midst of a dense forest that provides a cool and pleasant place for a stroll. During the dog days, a visitor will find this an excellent place to escape the heat.

The Three Hills Convent is a common starting point for a climb into the hills.

The Temple of Great Compassion (Dabeisi)

Climbing up from the Three Hills Convent, one passes many strange rock formations before arriving at the fourth of the Eight Great Temples, the Temple of Great Compassion. The three main halls in the temple complex date from different eras of the Ming dynasty, the most recently built being the rearmost Hall of Great Compassion (Dabeidian). On the front hall hangs a plaque inscribed with the words "Sea of Compassion," and the courtyard before it is thickly planted with a rare species of bamboo which remains green throughout the winter. The courtyards also contain potted landscapes, fragrant plants and decorative rockeries. Also of interest to sightseers are the two huge ginko trees in the rear courtyard, reputed to be more than 800 years old.

The carved statues of the Eighteen Luohan (Immortals) in the front hall of the temple are some of the finest in all of the Eight Great Temples. Legend has it that they were made by the famous Yuan dynasty sculptor Liu Yuan.

The Dragon King Temple (Longwangtang)

The Dragon King Temple, located to the northwest of the Temple of Great Compassion, is also known as

Dragon Spring Convent. It was built during the early Qing dynasty (1644-1911).

Entering the temple, one first notices the sound of a bubbling spring breaking the stillness. The spring bubbles up from beneath a cliff behind the second courtyard and flows through the first courtyard and out of a carved stone spigot in the shape of a dragon's head into a pond. The water of this eternally flowing spring is clear and sweet and never freezes in winter. A Pavilion for Listening to the Spring stands nearby.

Behind the pond is the Hall of the Dragon King which, according to local legend, is the residence of the Dragon King. The hall is surrounded by luxuriant green bamboo.

The Pavilion of Reclining Leisure and the Pavilion for Listening to the Spring, both of which are built up against the side of the mountain, are fine spots for viewing the distant hills.

At several places in the temple, inscriptions in the calligraphy of the Qianlong emperor, who reigned from 1736 to 1796, can be seen.

The Temple of Fragrant World (Xiangjiesi)

Also known as the Pingpo Temple, the Temple of the Fragrant World is the largest temple complex in the entire area. In the past, it served as the summer villa of Chinese emperors and today the Traveling Palace (Xinggong) and Scripture Repository erected by the Qianlong emperor can still be seen. The temple also contains numerous historical relics as well as paintings and calligraphy by known artists.

Several hundred stone steps lead the visitor to the Mahayana Gate and the entrance to the temple. Inside,

the courtyard is full of fine flowers and trees. Near
the eastern corner there is a large magnolia tree as tall
as the building. It is said that this tree was planted in
the Ming dynasty, and is the only specimen of its kind
in all the Eight Great Temples.

The central structure in the temple is the Scripture
Repository, with drum and bell towers to the left and
right of it, and the Qianlong Traveling Palace to the
east. Inside the Scripture Repository are statues of
Kasyapa, Sakyamuni and Maitreya, the Past, Present
and Future Buddhas, which are flanked on both sides
by polychrome statues of the Eighteen Luohan (Immortals). In the entrance hall of the Traveling Palace
there is a Study for Distant Viewing, offering a fine
view of the hills, plains and trees of the area west of
the capital.

The Pingpo Temple, named after the hill on which
it was built, has a history traceable back to the Tang
dynasty (618-907). In the 15th century, when a Ming
princess named Cuiwei was buried here, the hill
was named after her. The temple was rebuilt and renamed three times, its present name being bequeathed
to it in 1748 by the Qianlong emperor. The extant buildings all date from the Ming and Qing dynasties.

The Precious Pearl Cavern (Baozhudong)

On the steep path that leads up the hill from the
Temple of the Fragrant World, there stands a memorial
archway with the inscription, "Place of Happiness"
(Huanxidi) on one side and "Forest of Solidity" (Jian-
gulin) on the other. There is also a large grotesque
rock inscribed with poems in the calligraphy of various
emperors. The hall erected behind this archway is the

famous Precious Pearl Temple. This is the highest
point in all the Eight Great Temples, and thus the open
gazebo in front of the temple is named "The Pavilion
for Distant Viewing." On clear days one can see the
entire Municipality of Beijing, with Kunming Lake to
the east, the Yongding River to the southwest, the plains
to the south and the city skyline in the center. Immediately below are the other seven temples and the Asian
Students' Sanatorium.

The temple's name comes from the cavern behind the
main hall and a stone near its mouth which resembles a
large pearl. Though the floor area of the cave is no
more than 25 square meters, a Qing monk named Hai
Xiu lived there for 40 years. A statue of this long-
term resident standing inside the cavern is popularly
known as the "King-of-the-Ghost Bodhisattva."

The Mysterious Demon Cliff (Mimoyan)

Heading north down the hill from the Precious Pearl
Cavern and climbing up Lushi Hill, one passes through
a dense grove of trees before coming to an old temple
known as the Temple of Buddhahood (Zhengguosi) or
the Temple of Pacifying the Nation (Zhenguosi — the
two Chinese names are nearly homonymic). Inside the
temple courtyard there are exquisitely wrought rockery
hills. Directly in front of the main hall is a stone tablet
testifying to the Buddha's mercy, and behind it a two-
meter-high bronze bell, both dating from the Ming
dynasty.

Following the winding path from the western gate
of the temple past another pavilion, one comes to the
last of the Eight Great Temples, the Mysterious Demon
Cliff. The main feature of the cliff is a large over-

hanging rock which, when seen from afar, suggests the image of a roaring lion. On the stone are carved the words, "Natural Secluded Valley" and a number of inscriptions by visitors from all over the world. A stone house built into the cliff is reputed to have been the home of the monk Lu Shi, who in the seventh century traveled from southern China to the outskirts of the capital in a rowboat. The legend has it that a pair of dragons he had accepted as his disciples came to the aid of the local people by ending a terrible drought, whereupon the hill was dubbed Lushi Hill and the Mysterious Demon Cliff renamed Lushi Cave. Down through the ages, the two dragon-disciples have been the subject of numerous folktales and the object of respect and worship for their good deeds.

The Temple of Buddhahood, one of the older and larger temples in the area, was first built in the Sui and Tang period more than 1,200 years ago. The name was changed several times during the ages, yet each of these changes reflected the temple's close association with Lu Shi and his auspicious dragons. The present name of the temple was fixed in 1460 during the Ming dynasty, and many of the buildings that remain show evidence of Ming architectural style.

White Cloud Temple (Baiyunguan)

The White Cloud Temple is in southwestern Beijing, directly behind the Broadcasting Building. It was called the Temple of Heavenly Eternity (Tianchangguan) during the Tang dynasty (618-907) and the Temple of the Great Ultimate (Taijigong) during the Jin period

(1115-1234). It is the largest-scale Daoist (Taoist) architectural complex in Beijing and was the headquarters for the Dragon Gate sect. Although historical records indicate that there were Daoist temples in Beijing during the Tang dynasty, it was not until the early Yuan period that they came to be built on a large scale. The Yuan emperor Shizu (Kublai Khan), whose reign lasted from 1260 to 1293, appointed a Daoist priest from Shandong Province to the position of "National Teacher" (Guoshi), which nominally put him in charge of all Chinese Daoist affairs. This priest's name was Qiu Chuji, but he was commonly known as the Sage of Eternal Spring (Changchun Zhenren). While Qiu Chuji was in Beijing, he resided in the Temple of the Great Ultimate which he expanded and renamed the Temple of Eternal Spring (Changchungong). From then on, it became the center of Daoism in northern China. It was not until the Zhengtong era of the Ming dynasty (1436-49) that its current name was adopted.

The extant temple was rebuilt in the Qing dynasty and exemplifies the Daoist architecture of the period. The complex is composed of multiple courtyards set out on a central axis. From front to back the structures are as follows: a memorial archway, the main gate, a pool, a bridge, the Hall of Officials of the Heavenly Censorate (corresponding to the Buddhist Hall of Heavenly Kings), the Hall of the Jade Emperor and the Hall of Religious Law (corresponding to the rear hall of a Buddhist temple).

In the center of the rear courtyard is the Hall of the Patriarch Qiu, devoted to the worship of Qiu Chuji, and behind this, the Hall of the Four Heavenly Emperors,

the second story of which is the Hall of Three Purities
(corresponding to the Sutra Repository of Buddhist temples and housing the Daoist Tripitaka*). Here one can
see the similarity between Daoist and Buddhist temple
architecture, though the decorative details and paintings
make use of specifically Daoist motifs such as *lingzhi*
fungus, Daoist immortals and cranes, and the Eight
Diagrams.

The temple contains a stela with calligraphy by the
Qianlong emperor recording in detail the history of
the temple and the life of Qiu Chuji.

Temple of the Pool and the Wild
Mulberry (Tanzhesi)

The Tanzhesi (Temple of the Pool and the Wild
Mulberry) was first built in the Jin dynasty (265-420),
when it was known as the Temple of Excellent Blessings
(Jiafusi). In the Tang dynasty it was renamed the Dragon Spring Temple (Longquansi) and in the Jin period
(1115-1234) rebuilt as the Temple of Longevity (Wanshousi). Additions were made to it in the Yuan, Ming
and Qing dynasties, and during the Kangxi reign (1662-
1722) it was rebuilt and renamed the Hill and Cloud
Temple (Xiuyunchansi).

The present name of the temple refers to the Dragon
Pool (Longtan) above the temple and the wild mulberry
(*zhe*) trees growing in the surrounding hills. From

* The Daoist Tripitaka is the complete compendium of Daoist
religious texts.

the old saying, "First there was Tanzhe and then there was Youzhou (a name for the Beijing region dating back to the sixth century)," one can imagine the antiquity of the temple.   Legend has it that the pool was originally called the Green Dragon Pool (Qinglongtan). When the famous Tang monk Fa Zang came here to preach, a green dragon residing in the pool was so frightened of the monk's supernatural powers that it fled. That day at dusk a violent storm broke out and the pool was transformed into a flat plain.

Tanzhesi is located in Beijing's Western Hills on Mount Tanzhe, 13 kilometers west of Mentougou. The temple is laid out along three axes.

The central axis consists of the main gate and the front, main and rear halls.   Many cultural relics are to be found in this architectural group, the most interesting being a statue of Princess Miaoyan, daughter of Kublai Khan.   According to legend, the princess shaved her head and lived in the temple as a nun.   She worshipped the Bodhisattva Guanyin so devoutly that the particular flagstone upon which she stood and kowtowed soon developed three indentations in it — two from her feet and one from her head.   Among the other relics is an image of the monk Yao Guangxiao, an imperial tutor during the Ming dynasty.   On the eastern side of the Mahavira Hall (Daxiongbaodian) stands an ancient ginko tree known as the Emperor's Tree.   It is nearly 30 meters high and is said to have been planted in the Liao dynasty (907-1125).   There is another symmetrically placed ginko growing on the western side of the hall called the Emperor's Companion Tree.   The pines along the central axis are particularly grand and besides them there are magnolia and sal trees and a variety of other rare flowers and shrubs. Climbing up to the Vairocana Hall (Piluge), one can obtain a good view of the entire temple. Hanging under the eaves of the Hall of the Dragon King (Longwangdian) is the famous stone fish. This one-meter-long "sea creature" weighs 150 kilograms and is carved out of a meteorite. When struck it resounds with a clear bell-like tone.

On the eastern axis are the rooms where the Qing emperors rested during their visits to the mountains. The architectural style employed here differs substantially from that in the temple.

A bamboo grove has been planted in the northern section of this part of the temple, and through a dragonhead spout set in an adjacent wall, water from two mountain springs bubbles forth and flows through a curving watercourse carved in white marble which forms the base of a small kiosk.

The western axis is comprised of a number of scattered buildings, although the overall layout gives the impression of solemn regularity. The highest point in this section is the Hall of the Goddess of Mercy (Guanyindian). Great numbers of tiny bells hang from its corners and make a delightful tinkling sound when the wind blows.

Outside the main gate are two other points of interest: the Hall of Peaceful Joy (Anletang); and the stupa park, containing the tombs of monks from the Liao and Jin dynasties. Originally, there were numerous wild mulberry trees in the park, but now only one remains in the eastern section.

Temple of Heavenly Peace (Tianningsi)

The Temple of Heavenly Peace (Tianningsi) is located on Guang'anmenwai Street in the southwestern part of Beijing. In the time of the Xiaowen emperor of the Northern Wei dynasty (late fifth century), a Buddhist temple stood on this spot. A stone pagoda was added in 602 and the name of the temple changed. In the Tang dynasty, it was rebuilt and repaired on several occasions. In the early Ming period it fell into temporary disuse, but its present name, Tianningsi, was adopted in 1404. The pagoda at the temple is now the oldest extant building in Beijing. According to historical records, there was a pagoda here in the Sui dynasty (581-618). However, the extant pagoda dates from the Liao period (907-1125), though some of its superficial decorations were added in the Ming and Qing dynasties.

The octagonal pagoda rests on a large square platform and is clearly divided into three sections: the base, the body and the 13-story tower. The pagoda is exactly 57.8 meters high and is constructed entirely of stone bricks. The base is ornamented with a single band of relief-carved arched niches. Above them is a platform with its perimeter decorated with a series of brackets and balusters. This in turn supports three rows of lotus petals and the body of the pagoda itself. The lower part of the pagoda is decorated with large arched openings and numerous relief carvings. Above this, the 13 levels rise in a slightly bowed profile. Bells hanging from each story tinkle pleasantly in the wind. The uppermost level is surmounted by a pearl-shaped symbol which represents the Buddhist faith.

In Liao times (907-1125), the Tianningsi stood in the most flourishing market district of the imperial city; thus one can imagine the important role it played in embellishing the skyline of ancient Beijing. Today it is an integral part of the city plan, and the recently built Tianningsi Road, which runs opposite the old monument, provides a fine view of the site.

Temple of the Origin of the Dharma (Fayuansi)

The Fayuansi, one of the oldest Buddhist temples in Beijing, is situated in the Xuanwumen area in the southwest quarter of the city. According to the Shuntian Prefecture Annals, the temple was built in 645 by Li Shimin, the second emperor of the Tang dynasty, to commemorate those officers and soldiers who lost their lives in battles. At the time it was called the Minzhongsi (the Temple in Memory of the Loyal). It was rebuilt in the Zhengtong period (1436-49) of the Ming dynasty and renamed the Temple of Exalted Happiness (Chongfusi). Its present name dates from 1734.

When the Qinzong emperor of the Northern Song dynasty (reigned 1125-27) was captured by troops of the Jin dynasty, he was held prisoner in the temple. When the Southern Song official Xie Fangde was taken to Beijing by the troops of the succeeding Yuan dynasty, he refused to surrender and starved himself to death here.

Occupying an area of 6,700 square meters, the temple contains a number of fine early cultural relics. The bronze sculptures of the Four Heavenly Kings (Devarajas) and lions date from the Ming dynasty, as do the rare gilded figures of the three Buddhas — Vairochana (Piluzhena), Manjusri (Wenshu), and Samantabadra (Puxian). The huge stone urn in the form of a Buddhist alms bowl which stands on a double base before the Hall of Pure Karma (Jingyetang) rivals the jade urn in the Circular Wall (Tuancheng) in Beihai Park in terms of size and decoration. The sides of the Platform in Memory of the Loyal (Minzhongtai) is inscribed with a cursive rendering of *The Ode to the Pagoda* by Zhang Shijin in the calligraphy of Su Lingzhi, who lived in the Tang dynasty. There are also many fine examples of stelae, stone carvings, stone pillars inscribed with Buddhist sutras, plaques inscribed in the calligraphy of emperors and printed Buddhist scriptures, all dating from the Ming and Qing dynasties.

In the past, the temple was so famed for its lilac gardens that it was also known as the Sea of Fragrant Snow. Each year when the trees came into bloom, the monks would hold vegetarian banquets which were attended by all the celebrities of the day. Pines from the Tang dynasty are found in the front courtyard, and cypresses from the Song stand before the drum and bell towers. A ginko reputed to be several hundred years old is growing next to the Sutra Tower (Cangjingge).

Temple of the Ordination Altar (Jietaisi)

The Jietaisi stands at the foot of Ma'anshan (Saddle Hill), about eight kilometers to the southeast of the Tanzhesi (The Temple of the Pool and the Wild Mulberry). The temple takes its name from its ordination altar, which has a history of 1,300 years.

The famous Ming marble ordination altar stands nearly five meters high and is decorated with unusually fine carvings. Most of the buildings in the temple, however, date from the Qing dynasty.

Inside the main hall is a second three-story wooden altar with steps linking its upper and lower sections. In the northwest part of the compound stands the Hall of a Thousand Buddhas, provided inside with spiral staircases. Seemingly countless niches, each containing a finely carved Buddha image less than one foot high, cover the walls.

Surrounding the main hall on all sides are a number of intimate courtyards containing exquisite rock formations, old pines and cypresses. The famous trees in the compound include the Sleeping Dragon Pine, the Nine-Dragon Pine and the "Mobile Pine." If you pull on any one of the branches of this peculiar tree, all of its branches and leaves will be set into motion as if a strong wind were blowing. The "Mobile Pine" was known at least two hundred years ago; the Qianlong emperor left a small stela inscribed with a poem about it.

The temple also contains a Liao dynasty (907-1125) stupa and a Jin dynasty (1115-1234) stela. Many of the stone pillars covered with the texts of Buddhist sutras have been preserved in near-perfect condition.

Temple of the Reclining Buddha (Wofosi)

The Temple of the Reclining Buddha (Wofosi) is located in the Western Hills at the southern foot of Jubaoshan (also called Shou'anshan) Mountain, about

20 kilometers from the city. The rear of the temple is set against the mountain cliffs; at its front are open fields.

The temple was first built during the Zhenguan period of the Tang dynasty (627-649), when it was also known as the Temple of Peaceful Longevity (Shou'ansi). In later periods it fell into ruin and was rebuilt and renamed a number of times. One of the last major renovations was completed in 1724.

As early as the Tang dynasty, the temple contained a sandalwood sculpture of the reclining Buddha. In 1330-31 during the Yuan dynasty, a large-scale bronze image of the Buddha attaining Nirvana was cast, and from that time on, the temple was popularly called the Reclining Buddha Temple. According to the official history of the Yuan dynasty, the casting of this Buddha required 250,000 kilograms of bronze and 7,000 laborers. At the main entrance of the temple stands a glazed tile ornamental archway, and inside there is a semi-circular pool flanked by a bell tower and a drum tower.

The temple compound is built on an enormous scale. Four large halls aligned along the central axis are linked by covered galleries and auxiliary halls to create a completely enclosed series of courtyards. The first structure, the *shanmen*, serves as the main gate. The second large building is the Devaraja Hall (Hall of the Heavenly Kings) and the third is the Hall of the Buddhas of the Three Worlds. In traditional temples, this would be the largest hall in the compound, but because the fourth hall contains the image of the Reclining Buddha, the situation here is reversed. The famous bronze Buddha is more than five meters long. It lies in a sleeping position, with one arm extended and the other

propping up its head, and is surrounded by 12 smaller Buddhas. According to legend, this scene represents the Buddha on his deathbed giving instructions
to his 12 disciples, who are seated under a pair of
sal (*poluo*) trees. The temple courtyard contains several
of these sal trees, which bloom in late spring or early
summer. At very rear of the temple is a sutra repository built against a cliff. On the western side are
rockeries, pavilions and mountain vegetation, all which
contribute to the beauty of the garden-like setting.

Miaoying Monastery White Dagoba

The Miaoying Monastery is situated on the north
side of Fuchengmennei Street in the West City District
of Beijing.

It was first built in 1096 (Liao dynasty) and was con-
siderably expanded and elaborately redecorated in 1271
during the reign of Emperor Shizu (Kublai Khan) of
the Yuan dynasty.

A passage from *Chats of a Visitor to the Capital*
(*Chang'an Kehua*), written during the Ming dynasty,
describes the monastery in these words: "From the corners of the buildings hang pestle-like jade ornaments.
Stone balustrades line the platform. Beneath the eaves
dangle countless strings of wrought iron flowers. Bells
tinkle overhead in the wind. The golden apex of the
dagoba glitters in the sun. Seen from afar, the lustrous
ornaments appear like a galaxy of stars." The present-
day brilliance of the dagoba's surface is due to the fact
that it is painted with an expensive whitewash containing a high percentage of pulverised seashells. A local

joke relates that if it were not for this whitewash, the monument would soon become a "black dagoba."

In 1279, the monastery was renovated and renamed the Temple of the Emperor's Longevity and Peace (Dasheng Shou'ansi), but was destroyed by fire 12 years later.

In 1457, a new monastery was built in its place which was given the name it retains to this day, the Monastery of Divine Retribution (Miaoyingsi). At the same time, 108 iron lanterns were installed around the base of the dagoba.

A verse from an early description of the monastery runs as follows: "The Monastery embellishes the capital with its lofty dagoba rising above the skyline. In the wee hours of the night, the fragrance of incense drifts about beneath the lone bright moon."

The Miaoying Monastery dagoba is today the largest structure of its kind in Beijing. It rises to a height of 50.9 meters, making it 15 meters taller than the dagoba in Beihai Park, and has a diameter of over 30 meters at its base. Thirteen broad circular bands of molding, called the "Thirteen Heavens," divide its surface. At the apex of the cone is an umbrella-like bronze disc structure with 36 bronze bells hanging from its rim. At the very top is a small bronze pagoda, in itself a work of art.

Today the White Dagoba stands as a symbol of cultural exchange between China and Nepal. In the Yuan dynasty, a Nepalese architect named Arnico played an important role in its design and construction. It is said that while in China, Arnico helped to build three pagodas: one in Tibet, another on the Wutai Mountain in Shanxi Province and the third the White Dagoba in

Beijing. For his work, the Yuan court posthumously
conferred on him the title of "Duke of Lianguo."

Down through the centuries, many wonderful legends
have been woven around the White Dagoba, the most
popular of which relates to Lu Ban, the "master car-
penter" who lived in the Spring and Autumn Period
(770-476 B.C.). It is said that Lu Ban repaired the
dagoba when it cracked by binding it with seven broad
iron hoops. Though impossible to authenticate, this
story attests to a high level of skill in forging and rivet-
ing in early times.

In 1976, the tremors of the Tangshan earthquake caus-
ed serious damage to the monastery buildings. The top
of dagoba tilted to one side, bricks and mortar in the
conical neck supporting the cupola crumbled off, and
the main trunk cracked in several places.

In September, 1978, the Beijing Department of Cultural Relics undertook the work of repair and reinforce-
ment. The courtyards, the four corner-pavilions, the
Hall of the Buddhas of the Three Ages, the Hall of the
Heavenly Kings (Tianwangdian) in front of the dagoba, the Hall of the Seven Buddhas and the dagoba
itself were repaired and renovated.

At this time, a number of valuable objects were discovered. A square box, a round box and two oblong
boxes of different lengths were found in a hidden recess
inside the dagoba. And at its apex a box containing
numerous Buddhist scriptures was discovered.

The square box is covered with copper and contains
a folded map wrapped with finely-woven multi-colored
silk threads. The design of the dagoba appears on both
sides of the map.

The larger oblong box contains: calligraphy of the Qianlong emperor, four silver urns filled with jewelry, rosaries and coins of different dynasties, bronze images of the Buddhas of the Three Worlds, a *hada* (a piece of silk used as a gift among the Tibetan and Mongol nationalities) and several pieces of brocade.

The small box contains only a colorful image of the Goddess of Mercy (Guanyin), and at the bottom of the image's lotus-flower throne, an almsbowl containing 33 pieces of *shelizi* (luminous stones reputed to have been drawn from the ashes of Buddha's cremated body). The round box contains a pentagonal Buddhist headdress and an applique brocade robe, which were encrusted with a total of approximatley 1,000 rubies, sapphires and coral beads.

Temple of Enlightenment (Dajuesi)

The Temple of Enlightenment (Dajuesi) stands at the foot of Yangtai Hill in Beijing's western suburbs. The rolling hills here are said to resemble a sleeping lion. The vista of two flanking temples — the Lotus (Lianhuasi) and the Universal Grace (Puzhaosi) — sitting atop hilltops to the west and east of the Dajuesi, is popularly described as "A Lion Rolling Two Embroidered Balls" or "A Buddha and Two Bodhisattvas."

Visitors must go north beyond the Summer Palace (Yiheyuan), pass through Heishanhu, Xibeiwang, Heilongtan (Black Dragon Pool) and the Wenquan (Hot Springs), and then go through the two villages of Beianhe and Zhoujiaxiang before coming to the steep path which leads to the main gate of the temple.

The principal structures in the temple are the Laughing Buddha (Maitreya) Hall, the main hall, the rear hall, the northern and southern courtyards, and at the very rear of the complex, a peaceful courtyard. The roof brackets and columns of the main halls date from the early Ming period. A mountain spring flows by the Restful Clouds Pavilion (Qiyunxuan) in the rear courtyard. Here too is a stupa, which stands at the highest point in the temple complex.

Inside the temple is a Liao dynasty (907-1125) stela on which it is recorded that more than a thousand years ago, the temple was named the Clear Stream Court (Qingshuiyuan) after the nearby springs. Although the carving is blurred and the stela itself broken into two pieces, most of the inscription remains legible. After 1949, the broken stela was repaired and installed in a specially built brick niche.

There are many flowers and trees in the various courtyards, the finest being the magnolias in the northern and southern courtyards. It is said that two specimens in the southern courtyard were brought from Sichuan by a monk during the Qianlong era (1736-1796), and one of them survives today. Another magnolia in the northern courtyard was transplanted here about one hundred years ago, and grows alongside a gingko tree.

There are a number of interesting sights in the immediate vicinity; Vulture Peak, the Tombs of the Seven Kings, Yang Family Garden (Yangjia Huayuan) as well as the Lotus Temple and the Temple of Universal Grace, all of which are accessible by following paths through the hills.

Temple of the Azure Clouds (Biyunsi)

The Temple of the Azure Clouds is situated in the eastern part of the Western Hills. The temple buildings are spread out on the gradually sloping hillside and, from the foot of the temple's main gate to the highest point, rise almost 100 meters.

The temple was first built in the early 14th century and named the Nunnery of the Azure Clouds (Biyunan). It was expanded in the early 16th century and again during the reign of the Qianlong emperor in 1748. At this time, the Hall of the Immortals (Luohantang), modeled after the Jingcisi Temple at Hangzhou, was built in the temple's southern courtyard, and the Diamond Throne Pagoda (Jingang Baozuo) erected to its rear.

At the time of the founding of the People's Republic in 1949, the temple buildings were in a state of disrepair. In 1954, the government undertook the task of rebuilding and renovating the temple, which included the reconstruction of the Sun Yat-sen Memorial Hall.

A stone-paved road leads from the front gate of Xiangshan (Fragrant Hill) Park directly to the entrance gate of Biyunsi. A brook runs outside the temple and passes before this gate. On entering the temple, the visitor will pass two huge statues of lions measuring 4.8 meters in height. Inside the first compound are the Bell Tower and Drum Tower, while in the center stands the Devaraja Hall (Hall of the Heavenly Kings), which houses a bronze image of Maitreya Buddha cast in the Ming dynasty. A goldfish pond in this courtyard is surrounded by ancient sal trees, white-bark sandalwood trees and gingko trees. The second courtyard contains

the main hall of the temple complex. Inside the Hall
stand images of Sakyamuni and his disciples. A series
of clay figurines standing against the walls make up
a diorama of the monk Xuanzang's passage to India
in quest of Buddhist scriptures.

The principal building in the third courtyard is the
Hall of Bodhisattvas. The two roofed corridors that
once stood here have fallen into decay.

The buildings in the fourth courtyard consist of the
Rear Hall and its auxiliary halls, all of which are laid
out in an orderly and harmonious manner. This complex now serves as the Sun Yat-sen Memorial Hall. Behind this is a stone memorial archway which leads to
the Diamond Throne Pagoda. (See the description of
the Sun Yat-sen Memorial Hall, page 194.)

The principal building in the western courtyard is the
Hall of the Immortals (Luohantang), designed in the
form of a Greek cross. There are altogether 500 gilded
wooden images and seven Buddha images crowded into
the hall. Each of these fine specimens of Qing dynasty wood carving has its own individual personalities and
expressions.

In addition to these life-sized images, there is also
a miniature statue of Jigong in the hall. But rather
than sitting on a pedestal among his fellows, he is found
perching on an overhead beam. The legend tells that
having arrived late, he was unable to find a seat among
the other immortals.

In the northern part of the compound are the Spring
Garden, the Azure Hall of Study and the Eyeglasses
Pond. In the Spring Garden on the western side of
the temple, underground streams from a mountain spring
can be seen gushing out of the crevices in the rocks.

Rocks, pavilions, pines and cypresses embellish the spot, making it ideal for relaxation and meditation.

Temple of Great Charity (Guangjisi)

The Temple of Great Charity, situated at the eastern end of Fuchengmennei Street, is one of the best-known Buddhist temples in Beijing. Today the temple is a center of Buddhist learning and serves as the headquarters of the Chinese Buddhist Association.

The Guangjisi was first built over 800 years ago by the architect Liu Wangyun of the Jin dynasty (1115-1234). In the Tianshun reign (1457-64) of the Ming dynasty, it was rebuilt by the Monk Pu Hui and named the Temple of Great Mercy and Great Charity (Hongci Guangjisi). In the ensuing years, it went through a series of repairs and renovations. In 1699, the Kangxi emperor ordered the entire temple to be renovated and expanded, at which time the following structures were added: an inscribed stela; a horizontally inscribed plaque; a stone tablet engraved with the calligrapher Mi Fu's rendering of the Eulogy to the Goddess of Mercy copied by the Kangxi emperor himself; and a number of gilded Buddha images.

An ancient tree once stood in the temple compound, but it was consumed in a fire. A stone tablet inscribed with "The Ode to the Iron Tree" composed by the Qianlong emperor stands on the spot where the tree once grew. An inscribed tablet bearing the words, "Temple of Great Mercy and Great Charity — Bestowed by the Emperor" was placed over the front gate.

On January 8, 1934, fire suddenly swept through the

temple, destroying dozens of halls, countless scrolls of calligraphy and painting, and numerous valuable objects of porcelain, bronze and jade. More than 100 volumes of the *Fahuajing* (a Buddhist scripture) were lost, along with the "iron tree" mentioned above. Generous donations enabled the temple to be speedily rebuilt. Two other major reconstruction projects were carried out in 1952 and 1972, restoring this ancient temple to its former magnificence.

Inside the temple's front gate is the Hall of the Heavenly Kings and, to each side, the Bell Tower and the Drum Tower. In the center of the compound is the Mahavira Hall (Daxiongbaodian), where offerings were made to the Buddhas of the Three Ages. The images here are the work of the noted craftsman Jiao Wanli of the Kangxi period (1662-1722). Further inside the courtyard is the Hall of Perfection (Yuantongbaodian), in which 11 bronze images of the Goddess of Mercy are displayed.

At the rear of this hall is the Hall of Bhaisajya-guru, the God of Medicine (Yaoshidian), and on its second story, the Sheli Pavilion, which serves as a depository for a Ming dynasty Tripitaka (the complete collection of Buddhist scriptures) and a collection of fine Buddhist paintings.

Ox Street Mosque

The Ox Street Mosque, located in the Guang'anmen-nei area in the southwestern section of the city, is the oldest and largest of the 80-odd mosques in Beijing.

The Islamic faith was introduced into China during the Tang dynasty (618-907) and has followers among more than ten Chinese minority nationalities, including the Huis, Uygurs, Ozbeks and Kazaks.

When it was first built some thousand years ago, the architecture of the Ox Street Mosque was in pure Arabic style. During its many phases of reconstruction and renovation, however, elements of Chinese traditional architecture were adopted. Today, in terms of organization and general layout, Islamic features still prevail.

The mosque was originally built by Nasruddin, the son of an Arabic priest who came to China to preach the Islamic faith in 996 (Northern Song dynasty).

Major renovation projects were carried out in 1442, during the time of the Kangxi emperor (1662-1722) and again after the founding of the People's Republic when the buildings were entirely repainted and redecorated.

Directly inside the front gate stands a hexagonal structure known as the Moon-Watching Tower. Every year at the beginning and ending of the month of fasting (Ramadan), the Imam will ascend the tower to observe the moon's waxing and waning so as to auspiciously fix the exact duration of the fast.

In front of the tower is a memorial archway and a screen wall covered with carved murals which together form the main entrance of the mosque. Beyond it is the main hall where the congregation comes to pray. According to Islamic tradition, a Muslim in prayer must kneel down and prostrate himself in the direction of Mecca (in Beijing, to the west), which explains why the facade of the main hall has an eastern aspect.

To the rear of the main hall is a group of small religious halls and stela pavilions designed in Islamic style. As the teachings of the Koran forbid the portrayal of human or animal forms, the designs and patterns in all of the decorations are composed of Arab letters and geometrical patterns. Directly in the center of this section is the minaret, from which the muezzin calls the faithful for prayers five times a day, beginning at dawn.

In the innermost courtyard of the compound are a number of auxiliary buildings, including classrooms for religious training. In the southern part of the compound there is a very large bath-house used for religious ablutions.

Dongsi Mosque

The Dongsi Mosque takes its name from its location near the Dongsi (Eastern Four) Archways in the East City District of Beijing.

The mosque was first built in 1447 in the Ming dynasty. According to historical records, it was Chen You, a general, who provided the funds for its construction. In 1450, the Ming Jingtai emperor bestowed on it the name Temple of Purity and Truth (Qingzhensi), as all mosques in China are designated.

The main hall is made entirely of wood. The Repository Hall, behind the main hall, is a beamless building whose supporting walls with varicolored motifs are in the style of the Ming dynasty. On the surface of the dome-shaped roof the words of the Koran are engraved in Kufic script, the form of Arabic calligraphy reserved for religious and official purposes.

In 1486, a minaret was built which fell into ruins only in 1908. Today, only the bronze canopy remains, with the words "Cast in 1486" still legible on its surface.

During the past 30 years the mosque has undergone two major renovation efforts. The first took place in 1952 when all the dilapidated buildings were redecorated, and the second was in 1978.

Today, the mosque has three resident Imams who administer the five daily prayers and the Friday Djuma Service. When requested by foreign Muslim residents, they also perform religious ceremonies at births, weddings and funerals.

Lamasery of Harmony and Peace
(Yonghegong)

Situated on the east side of Yonghegong Street in the northeastern corner of the city, the Yonghegong is the largest and best-known Lamaist temple in Beijing. The lamasery's principal components are three exquisite memorial archways and five major halls, all of which stand on a north-south axis. The total area of the compound calculated from the southernmost memorial archway to the temple's northernmost point is 66,400 square meters.

The Yonghegong was originally built by order of the Kangxi emperor in 1694 to serve as a residence for his son and successor to the throne — Yinzhen. The new residence was given the name Yin Beile* Fu — the

---

* Beile — the fifth highest rank in the Manchu nobility.

mansion of the Beile Yin.   When his title was later officially raised to that of prince, the name of the residence was changed to "Residence of Prince Yong." Yinzhen lived here till his ascension to the throne in 1723.

When Yinzhen became the Yongzheng emperor after
his father's death, a section of the residential grounds
was maintained as a temporary palace to be used by
the emperor for short visits, while the other half was
turned over to the Lamaists to serve as a place for the
recitation of scriptures.   Later, the palace section was
razed by fire and in 1725 that section of the compound
occupied by the Lamas was given the name Yonghegong — The Lamasery of Harmony and Peace.

Entering the lamasery compound at the southernmost
gate, the visitor will notice that this first courtyard contains only two screen walls decorated with carved murals
and a single memorial archway.   Passing north through
the gateway, a stone-paved pathway leads through the
center of a rectangular courtyard planted with rows of
pines and cypresses to the Gate of Luminant Peace
(Zhaotaimen).

This gate leads into the third courtyard, where two
stela pavilions and the Drum and Bell Towers typical
of all Buddhist temples may be seen. At the north end
of this courtyard stands the Gate of Harmony and Peace
(Yonghemen), the entrance to the Devaraja Hall (Tianwangdian).   In the center of the hall is a statue of
Maitreya Buddha and, flanking it, four large statues of
the Heavenly Kings.

Behind this hall is a stela pavilion containing a
tall stone tablet inscribed in the Han (Chinese), Manchu, Mongolian and Tibetan languages.   A bypass from

here leads to the largest hall in the lamasery — the Hall of Harmony and Peace.

The hall's pillars and square ceiling panels are painted in brilliant varicolored motifs. In the center is an altar where offerings are made to the Buddhas of the Three Ages — Sakyamuni, Kasyapa and Maitreya. On the side walls are mural paintings of the Eighteen Luohan (Immortals), and in the corners images of Ksitigarbha and Maitreya.

The entrance to the fifth courtyard is known as the Hall of Eternal Blessings (Yongyoudian). This hall and the Hall of Heavenly Kings are almost identical in size. Immediately to the north is the Hall of the Dharmacackra (Wheel of the Dharma) in which stands a 15-meter-high bronze statue of the founder of the Yellow Sect of Tibetan Buddhism, Tsong-kha-pa. Behind the statue is a panoramic sandalwood sculpture of 500 immortals standing in different postures on a hill, known as the Hill of the Luohans. On the walls there are huge mural paintings depicting episodes in the life of the Buddha.

The principal building in the rearmost courtyard and tallest building in the lamasery is the three-story Hall of Infinite Happiness (Wanfuge), also called the Hall of Great Buddha (Dafolou). Flanking it on both sides are two two-story pavilions — the Eternal Health Pavilion (Yongkangge) and the Perpetual Tranquility Pavilion (Yanningge), both connected to the central hall by overhead bridges. A huge statue of the Tathagata Buddha (Rulaifo) stands in the center of the hall. Made from the trunk of a single sandalwood tree, the standing statue is 26 meters in height (beginning 8 meters below the ground floor and towering 18 meters above it) and 8 meters in diameter. It is said that when this statue was first installed it was fitted with a yellow monk's robe made of more than 1,800 meters of satin.

Besides the structures described above, the Yonghe-gong has a number of auxiliary buildings lining the courtyards on the east and west, many of which display exotic Lamaist sculptures and paintings. The buildings set along the central axis rise progressively from south to north, and a visitor entering from the southernmost gate looking north will see a series of roof-ridges rising impressively one above the next.

The lamasery houses a treasury of Buddhist art. To mention a few of the most interesting items: examples of the calligraphy of Qing emperors written on scrolls and inscribed on stelae; bronze lions and incense burners; sculptured images of gods, demons and Buddhas; and Tibetan-style murals known as *tankas*.

Yellow Temple (Huangsi)

The Yellow Temple is situated in the Andingmen (Gate of Peace and Stability) area, about three kilometers north of downtown Beijing.

The temple compound is divided into the East and West Yellow Temples. The walls and gates of the two are identical in construction, though their interiors vary somewhat. Yellow refers to the color of the glazed tiles on the roofs.

The East Yellow Temple, known as the Temple of Universal Purity (Pujingchanlin), was built for the Living Buddha Naomuhan in 1651 during the reign of the Qing Shunzhi emperor.

The West Yellow Temple, called the Temple of
the Dalai Lama (Dalaimiao), was built one year later
as a residence for the Fifth Dalai Lama when he made
a visit to the capital. On the day the Dalai Lama
arrived, the Shunzhi emperor was away on a hunting
excursion in the Nanyuan game reserve, yet he still received the Dalai Lama in informal audience and accepted the Dalai Lama's tribute of horses. The following
day, the Dalai Lama moved into the West Yellow
Temple and remained there until his departure the following year.

In 1780, during the reign of the Qianlong emperor,
the Sixth Panchen Lama came to the capital on an official visit. The emperor designated the West Yellow
Temple — where the Dalai Lama had stayed more than
a century earlier — to serve as the Panchen Lama's
residence.

Entering the first courtyard of the West Yellow
Temple through the main gate, one comes to a large
hall before which stand a Bell Tower and a Drum
Tower. The hall in the second courtyard is larger than
that in the first, and here there are stela pavilions on
the east and west in front of the hall.

In 1723, according to historical records, "Mongol
nobles made donations of bronze Buddhist statues and
pagodas to the temple, and also had the temple renovated."

Another renovation project was carried out in 1771,
when many horizontal plaques inscribed in the Qianlong
emperor's own hand were installed. In 1782, the City of
Complete Purification (Qingjinghuacheng) was built on
the central axis of the compound behind the West

Yellow Temple. This complex contains a white pagoda inscribed with a biography of the Panchen Lama. Thus while the West Yellow Temple is popularly referred to as the Dalai Temple, the City of Complete Purification is called the Panchen Pagoda.

The octagonal Panchen Pagoda is surrounded by a stone balustrade with white stone memorial archways in front and in back. Four small pagodas stand at the corners, and the surface of each pagoda is carved with a series of Buddha images.

Five Pagoda Temple (Wutasi)

The Wutasi (Five Pagoda Temple) is situated about 200 meters to the northwest of Beijing Zoo. Its original name, the Temple of True Awakening (Zhenjuesi), was later changed to the Temple of Great Righteous Awakening (Dazhengjuesi). Today, however, it is popularly referred to as the Five Pagoda Temple.

The structure of the five pagodas is known in Buddhist terminology as the "diamond throne pagoda" style, wherein five small pagodas stand on a large square foundation known as the "throne." This architectural form was introduced to China by an Indian monk in the early 15th century, and the Temple of True Awakening was constructed here in 1473. The entire temple complex, including numerous wooden buildings, was repaired and renovated in 1761, but in the late Qing dynasty it was looted and burned to the ground, first by the British and French Allied Armies in 1860, and again by the Eight-Power Allied Forces in 1900. Today, the only extant relic is the monumental diamond throne pagoda.

The architectural style of the Wutasi is no mere imitation of its Indian prototype, but displays bold innovations: the height of the throne foundation was raised, the height of the pagodas was reduced, and typical Chinese glazed tiles were added.

The square throne foundation is 17 meters high. The five pagodas rise from their rectangular bases on top of this foundation, one in each of the four corners and the fifth in the center. The central pagoda is slightly higher than the others, with 13 eaves, two more than the four others. The entire structure is made of white marble. Today, after more than 500 years of oxidation, the flecks of iron in the stone have given the entire structure a pale orange cast.

The four walls of the foundation are carved with rows of Buddhas (the One Thousand Sagacious Buddhas) as well as bas-reliefs of Buddhist symbols, floral designs and Sanskrit letters. The five pagodas are also covered with similar carvings on a small scale.

A door at the foot of the foundation on the southern side opens into an inner spiral stairway that leads to the top of the foundation.

There are a total of six "diamond throne pagodas" in China. Two others are in temples in Beijing in the Temple of the Azure Clouds (Biyunsi) and the Yellow Temple (Huangsi). One is in Huhehot in Inner Mongolia; another in Kunming in Yunnan Province — the Miaozhansi (the Temple of Profundity); and one is in Zhengding in Hebei Province — the Guanghuisi (the Temple of Universal Beneficence).

Big Bell Temple (Dazhongsi)

The Big Bell Temple is situated in the western section of the North Ringroad, approximately two kilometers east of Haidian Road. When the temple was first built in 1733, it was called the Temple of Righteous Awakening (Zhengjuesi). In 1743, during the reign of the Qianlong emperor, a giant bell was transferred from the Temple of Longevity (Wanshousi) to this temple. From then on, it has commonly been referred to as the Big Bell Temple.

The temple compound contains three rows of halls, one lined up behind the other. In the courtyard in front of the first big hall is an ancient cypress which has an elm branch grafted onto its trunk.

The famous bell hangs in the Bell Tower at the rear of the compound. The tower is 16.7 meters high, with a square base, a circular upper structure and windows on four sides. It is said that the bronze bell was cast by Yao Guangxiao during the Yongle period (1403-24) of the Ming dynasty. The bell is 6.87 meters high, 3.3 meters in diameter, 0.22 meter thick and weighs 46.5 metric tons. Known as the "king of bells," when struck its toll can be heard several kilometers away.

The inner and outer faces of the bell are inscribed with the full text of the *Huayan Sutra*. The 80 chapters of scriptures contain more than 220,000 characters and are written in the regular script (*kaishu*). Because of this, the bell is also known as the "Huayan Bell."

By climbing the spiral stairway to the top of the tower, the visitor will obtain a fine view of the surrounding countryside.

Cypress Grove Temple (Bailinsi)

The Bailinsi (Cypress Grove Temple) is situated in the northeastern part of Beijing's East City District immediately to the east of the Yonghegong Lamasery.

When first built in 1347 during the Yuan dynasty, the Bailinsi was one of the largest Buddhist temples in Dadu. It underwent repair and renovation three times during the Ming and Qing dynasties, the largest of these projects being carried out in 1712 during the reign of the Kangxi emperor, when his son Prince Yinzhen ordered the work to be carried out to commemorate his father's 60th birthday.

The five main structures in the temple compound are laid out on a central axis. Proceeding from the front gate to the rear of the temple, they are as follows: the main gate, the Devaraja Hall (Hall of the Heavenly Kings), the Hall of Attaining Perfection (Yuanjuxingjuedian), the Mahavira Hall (Daxiongbaodian) and the Vimalakirti Hall or Hall of Bodhisattva Purity (Weimoge).

A horizontally inscribed plaque in the hand of the Kangxi emperor which reads "The Everlasting Cypress Grove" (Wangubailin) hangs on the facade of the Mahavira Hall, while inside are found statues of the Buddhas of the Three Worlds. Behind this hall is the Hall of Vimalakirti, containing seven carved and gilded Buddha images dating from the Ming dynasty.

To the east of the main hall is an auxiliary hall containing two large bronze bells 2.6 meters tall cast in 1707.

Their surfaces were cast with bas-reliefs of coiling dragons and the texts of incantations (mantras) intoned after a person's death in the hope of gaining passage to the Pure Land.

Among the valuable relics in the temple is a complete set of printing blocks for the *Tripitaka* (the complete corpus of Buddhist sutras) carved in the early 18th century. The collection is made up of 7,167 volumes with a total of 781,230 separate blocks. Carved of high-grade pear wood, the blocks remain in fine condition today except for some minor cracks. The work of carving took six years to complete, and was begun in 1733 during the reign of the Yongzheng emperor. However, fewer than two hundred copies of the *Tripitaka* were printed during the ensuing 300 years, one reason why the blocks remain in excellent condition.

The blocks were originally stored in the Hall of Military Prowess (Wuyingdian) in the Palace Museum, but were later transferred back to the Bailinsi. They are presently being cared for under the supervision of the Beijing Library.

Temple of the God of Mount Tai (Dongyuemiao)

The Dongyuemiao (Temple of the God of Mount Tai) stands on Shenlu Street in the Chaoyang District. It is said that the temple was built as a place of worship for the Supreme Celestial Emperor of Mount Tai, one of the five sacred mountains of China.

Dongyuemiao was first built in the Yanyou period (1314-20) of the Yuan dynasty at which time it was one

The Temple of the Pool and the Wild Mulberry (Tanzhesi)

Beihai Park

A view of "Autumn Winds on Taiye" in the Central Lake (Zhonghai)

A beach at Beidaihe

View of Kunming Lake in the Summer Palace

Document Storage Cabinet in the Imperial Historical Archives (Huangshicheng)

Biyong Hall in the Imperial College (Guozijian)

A view of Xiangshan Hotel (built in 1982)

The Temple of Universal Peace (Puningsi)

of the largest Daoist temples in the capital, and the first major temple in northern China belonging to the Zhengyi Sect of Daoism founded by Master Zhang Daoling. A glazed tiled memorial archway inscribed with "In Reverence to the God of Mount Tai" stands at the temple's front entrance.

The temple complex is composed of three courtyards. The main courtyard contains three halberd gates (*jimen*), the Hall of the Mount Tai (Daizongbaodian), and the Hall of Moral Cultivation (Yudedian).

In the center of the Hall of the Mount Tai are statues of the God of Mount Tai and his high-ranking attendants. The two corridors in front of the hall house 72 statues of deities, or "Chiefs of Departments," each representing some form of human activity or natural force.

There are more than a hundred stone tablets dating from the Yuan, Ming and Qing dynasties in the temple compound. The most valuable among these is a four-meter-high stela inscribed, "Tablet of the Daoist Master Zhang" in the hand of the Yuan dynasty calligrapher Zhao Mengfu.

The Dongyuemiao burned to the ground in a battle during the last years of the Yuan dynasty and was rebuilt in 1449 during the Ming. The temple buildings standing today date from the Qing, though they retain the style of the Yuan and Ming periods.

Temple of the Emperor's Safety
(Sheng'ansi)

Sheng'ansi (Temple of the Emperor's Safety), popularly known as "Willow Lake Temple," is situated at

the west end of Nanheng Street near the former Xuanwumen Gate (the Gate of Universal Prowess). It is
said that the temple was originally built in the early
12th century for the monks Fo Jue and Hui Tang
by order of the Emperor Taizong of the Jin dynasty
(1115-1234). The temple site was originally inside the
city walls in Willow Lake Village, from which it took
its name.

Following a major repair operation in 1446, the name
of the temple was changed to the Temple of Universal
Salvation (Pujisi). But after another repair in 1776
during the Qianlong period, its former name was restored.

In the center of the front courtyard stands the Mahavira Hall (Daxiongbaodian), which is the main structure
in the temple. The remaining buildings are the Rear
Hall (Houdian), the Auspicious Pavilion (Ruixiangting),
the Hall of the Heavenly Kings (Tianwangdian), and a
pair of auxiliary halls on the east and west.

Many of the buildings and their decorations date from
the Ming dynasty. The statues of the Buddhas of the
Three Worlds, which stand on a large pedestal in the
center of the Mahavira Hall, were made by a sculptural
technique developed in the Ming dynasty. The procedure is as follows: The "skeleton" of the statue is
formed with sticks of rattan and wrapped with several
layers of cloth. Plaster and gold-dust are then molded
onto the surface of the cloth in the required shapes
and patterns. These statues are the only undamaged
examples of this type to be seen in Beijing. They are var-
nished in purplish-red, and their large aureoles decorated
with an outer circle of writhing flames carved in relief

which surrounds an inner ring of three small Buddhas, each seated on a lotus throne.

The murals in the main hall are attributed to the Ming painter Shang Xi. The eight paintings on the eastern, western and northern walls depict a number of episodes from Buddhist legends. Perhaps the most impressive of them all is the group portrait of three serene and chubby-faced Bodhisattvas on the wall behind the aureoles.

The temple grounds are planted with cypresses, willows and a great variety of flowering shrubs, including lilacs and peonies.

Temple of Wisdom Attained (Zhihuasi)

The Temple of Wisdom Attained situated in the Chaoyangmen district of Beijing was built by order of Wang Zhen, the chief eunuch at the court of the Zhengtong emperor (reigned 1436-49 and 1457-64) of the Ming dynasty. Wang Zhen was the first eunuch in the history of the Ming dynasty to make conspicuous use of his power for personal ends.

The temple is one of the largest and finest examples of Buddhist architecture from the period. Beginning from the front gate and extending to the Hall of Ten Thousand Buddhas, a total of seven principal halls comprise the temple complex. The layout is said to have been modeled after a Song dynasty (960-1279) plan known as "the Seven Monastery Buildings." A notable feature of the temple is the glazed tiles which line the roof ridges of the major buildings, augmenting the solemnity of the complex.

The Hall of Ten Thousand Buddhas (Wanfoge) is dedicated to the worship of the Tathagata Buddha (Rulaifo), and is also called the Rulaifo Hall. The 9,000 niches in the walls of the hall each house a small statue of the Buddha. The ceiling panels and lattice windows with their gilding and multicolored decoration are exquisite examples of temple art. The particularly fine octagonal cupola was removed from the temple in the 1930s and is now in the Nelson Museum in Kansas, U.S.A.

The temple contains a fine octagonal "Revolving Scripture Cabinet" (Zhuanlunzang), which is constructed of wood and rests on a marble base. Its relief decorations of birds, goddesses, deities, human figures, lions, and flowers reveal craftsmanship on a very high level.

Although the temple was repaired and rebuilt many times during the Ming and Qing dynasties, the crossbeams and corner brackets in the main halls date back to the 15th century. The scripture cabinets, Buddhist images and decorative carvings preserved in the temple are all in Ming dynasty style, rendering the temple one of the best examples of Ming architecture in Beijing.

The Southern Cathedral (Nantang)

The oldest Catholic church in Beijing, the Southern Cathedral, also known as the Cathedral of the Immaculate Conception, is located at 181 Qianmenxidajie in the Xuanwumen district. It was first erected in the middle of the 16th century on the former site of the lecture hall of the Donglin party, a political clique active in the late Ming dynasty. When the Italian missionary Matteo Ricci came to China during the reign of the Wanli emperor (1573-1619), the emperor provided him with a residence which stood slightly to the west of the cathedral.

The cathedral was rebuilt in 1657 during the reign of the Shunzhi emperor of the Qing dynasty. A stone tablet erected at the time, inscribed with "Cathedral Built by Imperial Order" still stands in the church yard. The cathedral was severely damaged by earthquakes in 1775 and 1900, and was rebuilt in 1904 in its present form.

Old Chinese records describe the style of the cathedral as "a building with a long narrow vaulted corridor with decorative motifs on the walls executed in an alien style." The main components of the 80-year-old building remain unchanged with one exception — its wooden supporting columns have been replaced by brick-and-mortar columns decorated with stone mosaics.

The arrangement in the nave, however, is quite different from what it had been in the past. On the wall behind the pulpit is an oil painting of the Virgin Mary, before which candlesticks and other ritual implements stand on an altar. To the left of the pulpit is a portrait of St. Joseph and on the right one of Jesus of the Sacred Heart. Other paintings portray episodes in the life of Jesus.

After the death of Matteo Ricci, the Catholic Fathers Didaco de Pantoja (in Chinese, Pang Di'e) and Longobardi (Long Huamin) continued to engage in missionary work, though few among the Chinese literati and officials were converted to the faith.

Today the cathedral remains in excellent condition.

Masses conducted by more than ten Chinese Fathers attract an increasing number of Chinese and foreign worshippers every Sunday, and the church is always crowded at Easter and Christmas.

The Beijing Protestant Church

The Beijing Protestant Church is located at 181 North Dongdan Street (Dongdanbeidajie), at the former headquarters of the Y.M.C.A. set up by the American Protestant Church in 1925. The two-storied church, built in traditional Western style, was first known as the Bible Society.

In 1958, more than 60 Protestant denominations were represented in Beijing. In that year, following a series of consultative conferences, four churches were selected to serve as centers for Protestant worship: in the western quarter of the city at Gangwashi; in the southern quarter at Zhushikou; in the northern quarter at Kuanjie; in the eastern quarter at Dongdanbeidajie.

Chapter 7
Scenic Spots in the Outskirts of
Beijing

Cherry Vale Flower Garden
(Yingtaogou Huayuan)

Cherry Vale (Yingtaogou), commonly known as the Zhou Family Flower Garden (Zhoujia Huayuan), is situated at the foot of Shou'an Mountain in Xiangshan Park. Walking west from the Temple of the Reclining Buddha one comes to a narrow, winding path which leads to the Cherry Vale — a quiet, secluded valley ideal for summer visits. During the Ming dynasty, the Temple of Broad Wisdom (Guanghuisi) was built here. In front of and behind the temple were orchards in which cherry trees were especially abundant. Hence the valley obtained its present name.

Entering Cherry Vale, one can hear the rushing water of a small brook bounded on either side by numerous strange rock formations. At several points along the stream, pools have formed which are used for swimming, rearing fish and irrigating the nearby fields. Along the stream towards the northwest, numerous species of wild flowers and fragrant grasses grow.

Along the stream in the direction of the mouth of the valley, the sound of a bubbling spring can be heard.

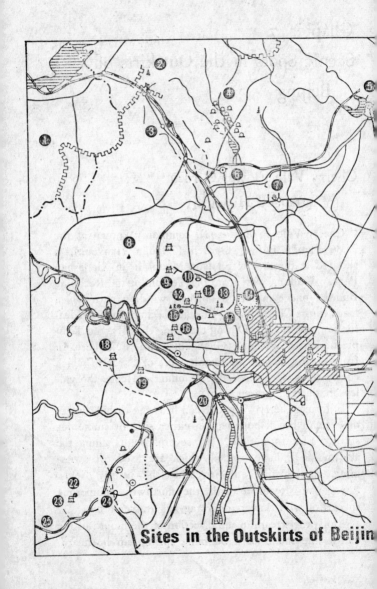

Sites in the Outskirts of Beijin

The clear spring trickles between rocky crevices and forms tiny rivulets that wind their way in and out of strange stone formations. The cascading waters play a continually changing melody as they splash against the rocks.

Dividing the wooded mountains into two parts is a small gully called the "Vale of Retreat" (Tuigu). This is said to have been the hermitage of the Ming scholar Sun Chengze, who enhanced the natural mountain landscape by planting forests of pine and bamboo. Sun is also credited with having built a pavilion here known as the "Old Man's Retreat" (Tuiwengting). He also gave himself the poetic name "The Hermit of the Vale of Retreat."

The pines growing on the slopes beside the source of the spring are particularly attractive. At the "Clear Spring Teahouse" two ancient white-barked pines form lush green parasols overhead. While great forests of pine rise up on the mountain crags all around, the valley floor is planted with luxuriant green bamboos.

Following the small road west and turning north, one will come upon another verdant pine forest. Crossing through the adjoining bamboo grove, one will come to another stone pavilion. On its pillars two lines by the Tang poet Wang Wei have been etched:

> *Stroll to where the waters begin to flow,*
> *And sit and watch the rising clouds.*

On the cliff opposite the pavilion, there is another inscription in ancient seal calligraphy:

> *Here are the traces of the immortal riding upon*
> *   a white deer;*
> *The hermit retires to dwell in the tranquil valley.*

To the west is a finely carved granite bridge transported here from the mansion of Prince Duan in Beijing. By crossing this bridge and following a mountain path, one will come to a large, high stone stairway. At the top of the steps is a small gate inscribed with the words "Deer Crag Lodge." Crossing the threshold, one enters the Cherry Vale Flower Garden. The modern scholar Ji Shui described the garden as follows:

"A stairway providing a series of contrasting vistas rises to the beginning of a narrow, winding trail; there are several small cabins here, half hidden in the shade of the trees. Earthen terraces are faintly visible on the slopes of the stony peak. Lush bamboos bow to the wind and wild flowers bloom in abundance. Early spring welcomes the return of swallows, while the midsummer sky resounds with the cry of the cicada. Here at all places and all seasons one is struck by the purity and freshness of the valley."

The Cypresses of Cuiwei Mountain

Cuiwei Mountain lies in the northern part of the Shijingshan District in Beijing's western suburbs. It is a tranquil, secluded spot of great natural beauty famous for its compact arrangement of temple buildings and many fine trees.

The pines and cypresses of Cuiwei Mountain greatly impressed the Qing scholar and poet Gong Zizhen. In one of his poems, Gong extolled the four "hundred-foot-tall" white-barked cypresses by the spring on the mountainside, and four pine trees at Dengwei Mountain in Suzhou, as "the eight great pines under heaven." Although the four white-barked cypresses in the poem no longer exist, there are still numerous other pines and cypresses on Cuiwei Mountain to be enjoyed.

Among the fine specimens are the two ancient pines in front of the Mahavira Hall (Daxiongbaodian) in the Fahai Temple. The trees stand erect and dignified, rising to a height of nearly one hundred feet. With their trifurcated branches and silvery white bark, they resemble silver dragons guarding the courtyard.

The crescent-shaped grove of ancient cypresses at the southern foot of the mountain is even more impressive. These trees appear all the more luxuriant against a background of the relatively barren mountain slopes of northern China. The cypresses here vary enormously in height and stature; some nearly touching the sky, others standing only a meter high, some with a circumference of 1.5 meters, others as thick as a man's thumb.

The major attraction of Cuiwei Mountain is the Fahai Temple, built in the Ming dynasty at the suggestion of Li Tong, a eunuch in the service of the Zhengtong emperor (reigned 1436-49). Construction of the temple began in 1439 and was completed five years later. The temple buildings include the Mahavira Hall (Daxiongbaodian), the Sangharama Hall, the Devaraja Hall, drum and bell towers, monks' residences and storerooms.

The wall paintings for which the Fahai Temple is famous are found on the north wall behind the platform displaying the Buddha statues; on both sides of the northern wall beside the entrance; and on the two gables behind the statues of the 18 *luohan* (immortals). A total of nine paintings survive to this day. On the northern wall beside the entrance is a diptych entitled "Worshipping the Buddha and Promoting the Faith" made up of the figures of the emperor and empress, eight protective Buddhist spirits, and 36 other celestial beings. The tallest of the figures is 1.6 meters in height. The emperor and empress are elaborately dressed and depicted in a highly poised manner, while the rippling muscles of the protective spirits attest to their strength.

The three paintings behind the Buddha statues portray the three principal Bodhisattvas; Avalokitesvara (Guanyin), Manjusri and Samantabhadra. Of these, the portrait of Avalokitesvara (center) is the most striking. The two paintings behind the statues of the 18 *luohan* contain portraits of the Tathagata Buddha and flying Asparas set off by peonies, Chinese roses, pipals and plantains. The caisson ceiling of the Mahavira

Hall is finely decorated with mandalas. In addition, the temple interior contains a large bronze bell, carved wooden images of the Buddha, an offering table and a set of ritual objects, all fine examples of Ming dynasty craftsmanship.

Miaofeng Mountain and Wild Rose Valley

Miaofeng Mountain, with its towering peaks rising majestically to a height of more than 1,300 meters, is the major peak in the northern range of the Western Hills. Situated at a distance of about 70 kilometers from Beijing, its sheer cliffs, jutting crags and tortuous mountain paths make it one of the most renowned scenic spots in northern China.

Towards the end of the Ming dynasty, it was the custom to hold temple fairs on Miaofeng Mountain every year during the fourth month of the lunar calendar. People from all over northern China would travel great distances to make their pilgrimage to the Temple of Inspiration (Linggangong), known today as the Temple of the God of Mount Tai (Dongyuemiao), and to the Shrine of the Great Goddess of the Blue Sky (Bixiayuanjunci), also called the Temple of Niangniang, both of which are situated on the mountain's summit. These temples are reputed to have been built during the Ming dynasty though the exact dates of construction are unknown.

The Temple of Niangniang was the home of three female deities; the Sacred Goddess of the Heavenly Sages (Tianxian Shengmu), the Sacred Goddess of Brilliant Insight (Yanguang Shengmu) and the Goddess of Sons and Grandsons (Zisun Niangniang). A legend held that the Kangxi emperor dedicated the temple to these female immortals in honor of good deeds they performed on his behalf. As the legend spread, the number of pilgrims to the temple increased.

During temple fairs, tea stalls sprang up in great numbers along the route up the mountain and at nightfall their lamps would shine like a myriad of stars. The faithful pilgrims would nevertheless continue straight up the mountain without a rest in order to pay their respect to the deities.

The local people produced a variety of handicrafts which became renowned as tokens of good luck. For instance, the red painted wooden fish were called "brimming with prosperity," a pun on the words fish (*yu*) and brimming (*yu*), while the paper cutouts of children were called "bounty bringers."

During the War of Resistance Against Japan (1937-45), the Chinese revolutionaries established a guerrilla base on Miaofeng Mountain.

In the gully to the east of Miaofeng Mountain is Beijing's famous Wild Rose Valley. Each year beginning at the end of May, the slopes of this valley are festooned with countless rose blossoms, which form a forest of brilliant green leaves and branches dotted with pale and dark red roses and perfume the air with a strong lingering scent.

Jade Spring Mountain (Yuquanshan)

The Jade Spring Mountain lies approximately 2.5 kilometers west of Longevity Hill (Wanshoushan) in the Summer Palace. In approximately the year 1200, a Hall

of Lotuses (Furongdian) was built on top of the mountain to serve as a traveling lodge for the Jin dynasty
emperors.   During the Yuan and Ming dynasties, the
Temple of Clarity and Conversion (Zhaohuasi) and the
Huayan Temple were built here and similarly served
emperors and empresses as a place of recreation.   The
Pure Heart Garden (Chengxinyuan) was established in
1680 during the reign of the Kangxi emperor.   In 1692
it became the Garden of Light and Tranquility (Jing-
mingyuan), a name which accurately describes its elegant setting and peaceful surroundings.

The Jade Spring Mountain is famous for the clear,
sweet waters of its spring, which were well known in
ancient times.   During the Qing dynasty, the spring
was the source of drinking water for the Imperial
Palace.   On the mountainside, a stone dragon's head
has been placed over the source of the spring. The spring
water foams out from the dragon's mouth with such
force that it is also called the "Snow-Spurting Spring."
In addition, the crystalline water which reflects the myriad colors around it has earned it yet another name, the
Jade Spring Rainbow, and as such the spring was listed
among the Eight Great Sights of Yanjing.   On top of
the cliff there is a stone tablet inscribed: "The Foremost Spring Under Heaven" on its front side, and on
its back "Baotu Spring* in Jade Spring Mountain" in
both Han Chinese and Manchu. Both inscriptions are in
the hand of the Qianlong emperor.

In former times, the Jade Spring Mountain was
the site of numerous traditional buildings.   The largest

---

* Commemorating a famous spring of this name in Shandong
Province.

of them was called by the fanciful name, the "Grand Duke Who Stands Aloof" (Kuoran Dagong). In the middle of the lake to the north of the hall was a pavilion known as "Clear Reflections of Lotus" (Furong Qingzhao) and to the west stood the Dragon King Temple (Longwangmiao). According to local history, "From the Hall of Benevolence to the Cool Shade Under the Blue Clouds there were 16 scenic spots in the Garden of Light and Tranquility. The hall on the mountain-top often disappears in the mist and clouds. Lotuses hide the world beneath the water. The four hundred temples of earlier times were all given their names on fine autumn days." From these descriptions, the scenic magnificence of the area can well be imagined. However, following the plundering by the English and French Allied Armies and the Eight-Power Allied Forces, very few historical relics remain at the Jade Spring Mountain today.

On the peak of the mountain, the Pagoda of Supreme Height (Miaogaota) stands on the Platform of Supreme Height (Miaogaotai). The pagoda is 33 meters high and has nine stories. A spiral staircase inside leads to the roof, where there is a statue of the Buddha in bronze.

Fangshan Mountain and the Ten Crossings

Fangshan County lies in the southwestern corner of the Beijing municipality. The Great Fangshan range winds its way through this county, its undulating peaks stretching far into the distance. Here there are many fine landscapes and places of historic interest, the most famous of which are described below:

Shangfangshan (Upper Square Monutain)

Shangfangshan, known in ancient times as Liupinshan, is a branch of the Great Fangshan range. It is situated some 75 kilometers southwest of Beijing and 20 kilometers from Zhoukoudian, the ancient home of Peking Man.

According to historical records, sometime between 58 and 75 A.D. (Eastern Han dynasty), a Buddhist monk of the Huayan School named Huisheng built a number of pagodas and temples here, designating the area as a center for Buddhist worship. Later, the buildings were renovated and 72 convents were constructed between Shangfangshan's nine grottoes and 12 peaks, with the Tusita Temple (Doushuaisi) at their center. Sixteen of these convents are still standing today.

This area of imposing crags and gullies, and verdant woodland, scattered with fine buildings and temples has been a center of Buddhist activity for more than one thousand years. Its famed beauty has inspired the saying: "In the south are Hangzhou and Suzhou, while in the north there is Shangfangshan." In 1949 the site was in a state of ruin and was overgrown with weeds, but following restoration it has become one of the finest historical sites in the countryside outside Beijing.

Setting out from Zhoukoudian, there are two possible routes to Shangfangshan, both of which pass through Gushankou. One route passes through Louzishui and Bazhaizi, while the other goes through Wajing and Tian-

kaicun. The first route is shorter but steeper, making
it the natural choice for mountain climbers. In June
1980, the Fangshan County authorities completed two
new roads to the east and west of the Yunshui (Clouds
and Rivers) Grotto. The east road is tarred and can
be used by vehicular traffic, while the western route
is a footpath only.

Arriving at Gushankou, one can discern in the distance the uneven line of mist-covered peaks, the winding paths, the crags and sheer cliffs, the steep ravines
and strange shaped summits that form the Great Fangshan range. Closer by is a lush green woodland and the
villages of Shangzhongyuan and Xiazhongyuan, fine
resting places for the hike ahead.

Leaving Gushankou, one follows the Shahe River
to the entrance gate of the Temple of Welcome (Jie-
dai'an), the first of the 72 convents. From here, turn
northward and follow a twisting mountain path leading
to the East and West Pigeon Halls (Donggetang and
Xigetang), where a number of different species of
pigeons reside.

Crossing the Fragrant Water Lake (Xiangshuihu) and
the Stinking Water Lake (Choushuihu), one comes to
the Thunder-Cleaved Rock (Pileishi). According to
local legend, a snake demon named Bare-Tailed Old Li
came to Fangshan and committed many grave misdeeds.
When the old Buddhist monk Huisheng discovered this,
he admonished the snake demon, but it paid no heed and
the two began to fight. The snake demon was no match
for the monk and it fled with all the water in the mountain. The monk chased the demon to the Stairway to the
Clouds and raised his hands, whereupon a tremendous
clap of thunder and lightning split the mountain asunder.

The snake demon was beginning to weaken and when it arrived at Sweating Ridge (Fahanling), lightened its burden by discharging all of the stolen stinking water. The monk continued chasing after it and the snake demon, finding no means of escape, discharged the fragrant water as well. Hence to this day there are two springs, one stinking and one fragrant, which continue to flow all year round. This fairy tale is depicted on a wall in the Hall of the Dipper Spring (Yidouquan).

The path which crosses the Sweating Ridge is flanked by sharp crags and abrupt cliff faces that tower up to a height of over 30 meters. A stairway of over a hundred steps (said to have been constructed by the Ming eunuch Feng Bao) has been cut into the rock, and a steel cable aids climbers in their ascent. At the top of this "Stairway to the Clouds" (Yunti), there is a convent of the same name which was built in the Ming dynasty. The convent contains a fine collection of ancient art and images of the Buddha.

Heading north from the Convent of the Stairway to the Clouds and crossing the Kuanlong Bridge, one will come to another gateway. Nearby, one can visit the Mingled Fragrances Convent (Banxiang'an), the Pagoda Courtyard (Tayuan), the Ten Square Courtyard (Shifangyuan), the Ksitigarbha Hall (Dizangdian), and the Seaview Convent (Wanghaidian), before going on to the Shangfang Temple.

The Pagoda Courtyard contains numerous pagodas said to hold the remains of Buddhist monks. One pagoda, dating from 1070 (Liao dynasty), displays a stone tablet which reads: "Here lies Cao Chang who dwelt on this mountain for thirty years and ordained over two hundred thousand monks. He passed away in 1070."

Heading northwest, one will pass the Convent That Faces the Sun (Chaoyang'an) before coming to the Sea-view Convent (Wanghai'an). In its courtyard is the famous old "King of Cypresses" with a trunk over five meters in circumference. Turning east from here and crossing a lush bamboo thicket, one comes to the Manjusri Hall (Wenshudian), where there are over 20 finely sculpted Buddha images.

The Shangfang Temple, situated near the central peak of the mountain range, is the most important of the 72 convents. It is surrounded by many other buildings — the Abbot's Courtyard (Fangzhangyuan), the Hall of Quiet Return (Qingguidian), the Great Kitchen (Dachu-fang), and the monks' dwellings. The majority of these buildings date from the Ming dynasty. Although many of the wooden beams were repainted in the Qing dynas-ty, the style remains typical of the earlier period.

At the Convent of Retreat (Tuiju'an) and the Hall of the Dipper Spring (Yidouquan), the scenery begins to change. Splendid architecture is no longer to be seen and the sounds of the wind in the pine trees and of birds chirping have disappeared. Instead, one is surrounded by simple buildings constructed in the form of local res-idences. The Hall of the Dipper Spring and the Great Bell Tower (Dazhonglou) complement each other, the former standing at the foot of the steep slope and the latter on the very summit of the crag. Although there is a small natural pathway connecting the two, it is necessary to scramble through trees and vines to get to the top. The large bell in the Bell Tower, still in per-fect condition, weighs some 1,500 kilograms and is 2.5

meters high. How did people in ancient times manage to transport such a huge bell up this mountain? Perhaps by laying a path of ice and sliding the bell along it on skids. Of the nine grottoes of Shangfang-shan, Yunshui Grotto is surely the most exotic; and of the 12 peaks, Tianzhu peak is the steepest and most rugged — to this day, it has never been climbed.

The Yunshui (Clouds and Rivers) Grotto

The Yunshui Grotto lies on the western slopes of Shangfangshan, about eight kilometers from the Tusita Temple. In front of the cave entrance stands the Convent of Great Compassion (Dabei'an), which dates from the Ming dynasty. Its main hall contains a number of Ming wall paintings. The human figures stand 1.6 meters tall and appear vividly lifelike.

The grotto opens onto a natural cavern six meters high, though the height of the ceiling in the rest of the grotto varies greatly. Over many thousands of years, the cave walls have gradually dissolved into strange and wonderful natural shapes, some of which resemble familiar things. These have been given appropriate names, such as "Crouching Tiger Mountain," "Elephant Bearing a Precious Jar," "Watermelon Patch" and "Snowflake Mountain."

Two "dragons" guard the entrance to this grotto. Passing beyond these into the interior, one will come upon a crouching "tiger" which looks ready to pounce at any moment. Further on, one will discover the figure of a "sprightly old gentleman" with long eyebrows hanging down from his forehead, sitting alone on the rocks. "Bell Towers" and "Drum Towers" rise from the floor and hang from the ceiling. When struck, these stalagmites and stalactites produce the sounds of bells, drums and the Buddhist "wooden fish" woodblocks, which are struck to accompany the chanting of scriptures. Proceeding further along amidst the echoes of this strange music, one will arrive at the "Mountain of Gongs," a group of stalactites which vibrate like stone chimes when struck lightly, but which sound like Chinese gongs when struck harder. Hanging from the roof of the cave are large, broad stalactites which resemble the long cloth banners suspended from the ceilings of Buddhist temples. Other forms inside the cave include "The Goddess of Mercy Explaining the Buddhist Canon," "The Precious Snake Jar" and "The Eighteen Buddhist Immortals."

The grotto is a total of 600 meters long and consists of seven consecutive caverns. In February 1980, the Fangshan County government built a road to the grotto, widened the walkway inside the cave and illuminated it with colored lights.

The Mountain of Stone Scriptures (Shijingshan)

It takes approximately three hours to walk along the mountain path that leads from Shangfangshan to the Mountain of Stone Scriptures. It is also possible to go via Tiankaicun and cross Changgou, yet this route is slightly longer.

The Mountain of Stone Scriptures was originally called White Belt Mountain (Baidaishan) and later Little Western Heaven (Xiaoxitian). The "Fangshan Stone Scriptures" found on this mountain is the only complete set of texts of the Buddhist canon carved on stone slabs in China. This outstanding feat of craftsmanship dates back over a thousand years — the earliest of the Fangshan Stone Scriptures are from the Sui dynasty (581-618) and the latest from the Ming dynasty (1368-1644). Rubbings taken from the inscriptions are preserved in the Guangji Temple in Beijing.

The inscribed stone tablets are found in nine caves which face the Cloud Residence Temple (Yunjusi) on the eastern peak, and a number of other tablets are buried underground. The nine caves are situated about half way up the mountain and are on two levels, the upper level containing seven caves and the lower only two. The latter two caves alone contain nearly two thousand tablets. Of these, a small number were carved by the Buddhist priest Jing Wan in the Sui dynasty, while the rest were completed in the Liao dynasty (907-1125). The fifth cave on the upper level is the largest of the nine and its contents are especially rich. Called the "Roar of Thunder Cave" (Leiyindong), it contains four unevenly hewn octagonal stone pillars on which 1,806 statues of the Buddha have been carved. The four walls of the cave are covered with 77 different Buddhist inscriptions, including the *Diamond Sutra* and *Lotus Sutra* which, apart from a few inscriptions carved in the Yuan dynasty (1206-1368), were executed by Jing Wan. In 1956, the Chinese Buddhist Society took a complete set of rubbings of these inscriptions.

On the top of the mountain there stands a single-storied stone pagoda carved with a five-line inscription. Built in the year 898 during the Tang dynasty, both its architecture and the carvings on its walls are particularly fine.

The Ruins of the Cloud Residence Temple (Yunjusi)

The Cloud Residence Temple stands within the walls

of a small cemetery in Shangle People's Commune in Fangshan County. It is perched on the slope of the White Belt Mountain (Baidaishan) at a distance of about 75 kilometers from Beijing. Vermilion Mountain (Zhushan) forms a backdrop to the temple.

According to Tang dynasty records, the Cloud Residence Temple was built in the early seventh century by the Buddhist monk Jing Wan, after a violent flood which brought with it thousands of tree trunks later used in the construction. After the monk's death, his disciples took over the temple. In spite of the damage wrought by wars and strife over the centuries, the temple was rebuilt in the Liao, Jin, Yuan, Ming and Qing dynasties. In 1940, it was severely damaged by Japanese troops, and the Ming and Qing dynasty sections were entirely razed. The Southern Pagoda, dating from the Liao dynasty, was also damaged, along with the fine treasures it contained. Among the ruins of the Cloud Residence Temple there are still, however, many points of interest.

By entering the white marble arched gateway and climbing gradually upward, one can easily imagine the former glory and splendor of the temple buildings. The original temple had five central courtyards and six great halls, with further auxiliary halls, imperial lodges and monks' dwellings adjoining them.

The Cloud Residence Temple was designated as a holy Buddhist shrine for the Hebei Province area. At its height, the temple was occupied by as many as one hundred monks. Apart from the fame of the carved stone scriptures, the temple was also famous for its magnificent pagodas, in particular two that still stand to the north and south of the temple. The Southern Pagoda is octagonal with 11 stories and pointed eaves, and is constructed of brick. Buried under the pagoda is a depository of Buddhist scriptures. Hence the pagoda is also known as the "Pagoda that Covers the Scriptures." It was built in the Liao dynasty in 1117.

The Northern Pagoda, also built in the Liao dynasty, was originally called the Sheli Pagoda, but was later named the Immortals' Pagoda (Luohanta). Because the pagoda is painted red, it is also known locally as the Red Pagoda. The bottom half of the pagoda is octagonal with bracketed eaves and carved niches. On its four sides are arched entrances and false windows. The upper half of the pagoda is cone-shaped and decorated with nine circular bands. It is surrounded by smaller stone pagodas dating from the Tang dynasty, several of which resemble the Small Wild Goose Pagoda in Xi'an. There are fine carved inscriptions on both sides of the pagoda doors.

After the founding of the People's Republic, extensive excavation and restoration work was carried out on the stone tablets inscribed with Buddhist scriptures in the Cloud Residence Temple. Today, a total of 1,277 texts are distributed among the nine caves on the Mountain of Stone Scriptures and the depository at the temple.

In 1961, the State Council classified the ruins of the Cloud Residence Temple, the Liao and Tang pagodas and the Buddhist scripture caves as national historic sites. The Liao dynasty Northern Pagoda was repaired and a depository to preserve the stone scriptures was built.

The Stone Buddha Cave (Shifodong)

The Stone Buddha Cave is a cavern of karst rock situated at the foot of Danan Mountain near South Cheyingcun in the Hebei People's Commune. It is over 700 meters in length and, according to legend, once contained ten stone statues of the Buddha from which it acquired its name. The cave contains many strange and varied rock formations that rival in beauty those of the Yunshui (Clouds and Rivers) Grotto.

Though the question as to whether or not stone Buddhas ever stood in the cave remains unanswered, the cave does have an enchanting fairy tale attached to it: Once upon a time, there was a black dragon which lived in the Black Dragon Pass (Fangshan County). This dragon took a beautiful local village girl to be his wife and they lived a contented life together. Some time later, however, a white dragon crossing through the Black Dragon Pass took an interest in the fine land here and decided to claim some of it for himself. Of course, the black dragon would not concede his land and entered into a terrible battle with the impostor. The black dragon's father-in-law, realizing that the black dragon could not defeat his opponent, shot an arrow and injured the white dragon. The latter made a terrible cry, leaped into the air and then fled into the Stone Buddha Cave.

The Stone Buddha Cave contains six different caverns. To gain access to the cave, one must first walk through a tunnel 20 meters long, the entrance of which is guarded by a stone lion. Following along the tunnel, the route gradually widens into a large cavern with a high domed roof and a smooth floor, filled with a veritable forest of fantastically shaped stalactites and stalagmites. In the lamplight, the rocks take on a rosy tint and their variegated contours become apparent — one can easily imagine oneself among a bevy of dancing fairies.

To get to the second cavern it is necessary to slip through a narrow crevice which leads to a flat, raised platform and a much larger flat area beneath it. This cavern contains many strange jagged rock formations and a group of stalactites with countless cascading forms which resemble a waterfall.

By turning left on the raised platform and walking around a deep underground spring, one comes to the third cavern. At the cavern entrance there are two large rocks, one hanging down from the roof and shaped like candied cherries-on-a-stick, and the other a formation of two contiguous rocks, one resembling a dragon's claw and the other the crest of a wave which is called "The Dragon Entering the Sea." To the right, there are numerous flat-topped stone pillars of many different sizes and on the left wall of the cavern, a pillar over ten meters high which appears like a great glacier inching its way downward. This is appropriately named "The Tianshan Glacier." On the opposite side of the cave is a grotto before which stalactites hang suspended like a watery screen. Between these two major formations, four gigantic pillars are arranged in line like the four great warrior attendants of the Buddha (Devarajas). Leaving through a narrow passageway, one comes to the fourth cavern.

Here one will notice a narrow underground "chimney" 40 meters long, through which the legendary white dragon is reputed to have entered the cave. The hollow at the bottom of the chimney is even larger than the Stone Buddha Cave and it too contains many fantastically shaped stalagmites and stalactites. However, since the "chimney" is extremely steep, few visitors are able to descend through it.

To the left of the "chimney" there is a sloping area. By climbing up this and passing through a narrow chink, one will discover the fifth cavern which resembles a small mountain slope. The rocks on the slope have been worn smooth by running water, which has created small gullies in the stone. The slope is known as the "Ox Trough."

Climbing to the top of the slope will take you to the sixth cavern. The roof and floor of this cavern contain several dozen hollows which have small mouths but which are spacious inside. Their resemblance to earthenware jugs has given them the name, "Jugs of Heaven and Earth." The countless stalactites hanging from the ceiling of these hollows resemble mountain peaks reflected on the surface of a lake.

"Ten Crossings" (Shidu)

The "Ten Crossings" are situated about 100 kilometers to the southwest of Beijing on the upper reaches of the Juma River. To get from Zhangfang to "Ten Crossings" Village it is necessary to cross the Juma River ten times, which is how the spot acquired its name.

The Juma River flows out of the mountains at the village of Zhangfang, 20 kilometers from Zhoukoudian. The entire valley, which begins at the village, is filled with sparkling streams, for apart from the Juma River itself which serpents its way through the valley, the marshy swampland of the valley floor is also traversed by brimming tributary streams and gushing springs which descend from the mountainside.

One makes the first of the "Ten Crossings" upon entering the river valley and crossing the bridge. By following the path that winds around the mountains, one will come to the second bridge. The path continues to meander in this manner, crossing the stream a total of ten times.

Tangshan Hot Springs

The Tangshan Hot Springs are situated about 30 kilometers north of Beijing on the road leading to the eastern range of the Western Hills. The springs can be reached by regional bus from Beijing.

Tangshan Mountain is made up of two solitary towering peaks with scree-covered slopes: Greater Tangshan, with its needle-like crags; and Lesser Tangshan, with its peculiar rock formations. Both are famed for their hot mineral springs.

To the east of Lesser Tangshan is a park shaded by luxuriant green trees and dotted with pavilions. Flowers and plants flourish in this ideal spot for rest and relaxation. To the south of Lesser Tangshan there are two hot springs. The eastern source bubbles out of the earth at extremely high temperatures and is called Boiling Spring (Feiquan), while the western source, the Warm Spring (Wenquan), is more suited for bathing. Although the two springs are only three meters apart, their water temperatures vary as greatly as their names suggest. The spring waters are rich in minerals useful in the treatment of skin diseases.

In the Qing dynasty, during the reign of the Kangxi emperor (1662-1722), a square pool three meters deep surrounded by a carved stone balustrade was built at the spring source. The crystal clear waters of both springs flow into this pool, and small pearl-like air bubbles burst continually from the water surface.

To the north of the pool is an imperial lodge built up by the Qianlong emperor (reigned 1736-96). Graceful pavilions, villas, temples and a large lotus pond, all enclosed by a long protective wall, form a haven of tranquility and seclusion at the foot of the mountain. Carved on the cliff face of the northern summit is the inscription, "Sharing the Refinement of Jiuhua Mountain" in Qianlong's own hand.

Behind the imperial lodge is a lake fed from mountain springs. The lake is surrounded by a stone wall and maple trees. The maple leaves turn a rich red in autumn, forming a vivid contrast with the dark green cypresses.

Glacial Vestiges

On the slopes of Cuiwei Mountain near the Fahai Temple, a number of vestiges of the Ice Age can be seen. First discovered in 1954 by the geologist Li Jie, this important geological landmark was listed alongside the "Eight Great Sites of Yanjing" by Li Xianyue, head of the Beijing Museum of Natural History.

These ancient remains date from the Quaternary Period, some 2.5 million years ago. Several hundred million years earlier, however, the Beijing area was engulfed several times by the sea. The Western Hills, for example, came into being a mere 100 million years ago as the result of a movement of the earth's crust. During this period, the Beijing area was covered with a mantle of ice and snow and populated by hairly rhinoceri, mammoths, cave bears and other creatures now long extinct. Due to climatic variations, the glaciers alternately advanced and receded, carrying with them large quantities of rock which continually scraped away at the earth's surface, leaving traces of their movements in the brown base rock.

The Beijing Bureau for the Preservation of Cultural Relics has set up railings to protect these vestiges. When visiting this site, it is likely that at first one will be unable to discern anything at all. But by using the method developed by the geologist Li Siguang, one will be able to discover the traces of the glacial period: Sprinkle water onto the brown base rock along the mountain slope, and the marks of the glacial abrasion will gradually come into view.

The Charm of the Flower District

Flower cultivation in China has a history of over 2,700 years. From the earliest times, flowers have been cultivated that blossom throughout the year — numerous species in the springtime, lotus flowers in the summertime, frost-defying chrysanthemums in autumn and wintersweets in winter.

As in the rest of China, flower cultivation in Beijing has a long history, having begun in the Yuan dynasty, more than 700 years ago. The principal flower-raising area was known as the "eighteen villages of Fengtai," located around Caoqiao (Grass Bridge), Huangtugang (Yellow Earth Hill) and the Fan Family Village in the Fengtai District

By the late Yuan, flower cultivation was highly developed, and during the Ming and Qing dynasties there was not a single imperial palace, prince's mansion, official's residence, villa or park in Beijing where flowers were not grown. At this time, the area around Fengtai and Caoqiao thrived. According to historical records, "Lotus ponds scented the air for miles around." Flower merchants "by the hundreds and thousands streamed through the city gates every morning."

The nursery district has always provided a wide variety of flowers throughout the year. The *Yanjing Annals* records the cultivation of 300 types of chrysanthemums alone, and it is said that the flower growers would build a "mountain of chrysanthemums" when displaying the potted flowers to the public.

Beijing's horticulturalists possessed considerable technical skill and developed techniques for forcing flowers and shrubs out of season. Peonies were blossoming at the Temple of Heaven and at the Fangshan Mountain Temple as early as March. Nurserymen in the Caoqiao region forced peonies with the warmth of their heated brick beds to supply the imperial palaces with fine specimens in the middle of November. From December to February, the imperial family enjoyed flowers of all seasons — peonies, plum blossoms, red peach blossoms, osmanthus and primulas.

Since 1949, horticulture has developed very rapidly. The Huangtugang Commune now manages 120 hectares of flowerbeds and over 2,800 hothouses cultivating nearly 2,000 varieties of flowers and ornamental trees. The area not only supplies Beijing, but also sends flowers to the northwest and northeast of China. In 1949, annual sales totaled 300,000 potted flowers and 500,000 cut flowers. To celebrate the 10th anniversary of the founding of the People's Republic in 1959, nurserymen supplied 100,000 pots of flowering roses and chrysanthemums to decorate Tian'anmen Square and East and West Chang'an Boulevards. By 1969, the flower district had under cultivation over 13 hectares of rosebeds alone, 10,000 pots of osmanthus, 50,000 pots of magnolias, camellias and jasmine and several hundred thousand pots of chrysanthemums, as well as thousands of pine, pomegranate and iron trees.

In recent years, the Huangtugang Commune has intensified its drive to develop the quality and quantity of its flower cultivation. According to its latest five-year plan, it will further increase the cultivation of peonies, amaryllis, magnolias and roses, with an end to turning the flower district into a scenic area of "one hundred varieties of exquisite flowers every ten *li*."

The Eight Great Sights of Yanjing

Yanjing (Capital of Yan) is an alternative name for the city of Beijing which was first used in the Liao (907-1125) and Yuan (1206-1368) dynasties. The Eight Great Sights of Yanjing are places of historic interest and scenic beauty in and around Beijing. Each of them has a name in which their particular qualities are summarized in lyrical four-character phrases, which may be translated as follows: "The Great Wall Surrounded by Lush

Greenery at the Juyong Pass"; "Trees Enveloped in Mist at the Ancient City of Jizhou"; "The Moon over the Lugou Bridge at Dawn"; "The Rainbow Floating over the Jade Spring"; "The Western Hills Shimmering in Snow"; "Jade Islet in Shady Springtime"; "Autumn Winds on Taiye"; and "The Golden Terrace in the Glow of the Setting Sun." They are introduced individually below:

The Great Wall Surrounded by Lush Greenery at the Juyong Pass (Juyongdiecui)

The first and finest of the "Eight Great Sights of Yanjing" is the "Great Wall Surrounded by Lush Greenery at the Juyong Pass." This comprises a small river valley approximately 15 kilometers long which is crossed by the Great Wall and surrounded on either side by lofty peaks and lush mountain vegetation. The undulating series of mountaintops stretches into the distance like leaping ocean waves, creating a scene of outstanding natural beauty. As early as the Jin dynasty (1115-1234), this spot was known by its present title.

In some places, the valley is extremely narrow with only a small passage through which the stream water can flow. At these points the mountains loom overhead as if about to cave in. Visitors are then tempted to turn back at this point, since the valley looks quite impassible. If they do, however, they will miss the experience of wonder that these imposing rock formations inspire. Trees also abound in this area, their red and white blossoms decorating the valley with bright splashes of color against a background of lush green leaves.

Trees Enveloped in Mist at the Ancient City of Jizhou (*Jimenyanshu*)

This spot is reputedly the site of the ancient city of Jizhou, also called Jiqiu and popularly named the "Earthen Walls" (Tucheng). The remains date from the Liao and Yuan dynasties and are situated about four kilometers northwest of the Deshengmen. The ancient city walls and buildings of Jizhou have all disappeared, and all that remain are two long stretches of earthen mounds that marked the former gateway into the city. From the Ming dynasty onwards this spot has often been extolled in poetry, and on the site itself there is a stone tablet inscribed in the calligraphy of the Qing Qianlong emperor with the four-character phrase which gives the place its title.

The Moon over the Lugou (Marco Polo) Bridge at Dawn (Lugouxiaoyue)

Ever since the Zhangzong emperor of the Jin dynasty (reigned 1190-1208) penned the phrase "The Moon over the Lugou Bridge at Dawn," this site has been known by this poetic name. The title was adopted once more in the Qing dynasty by the Qianlong emperor (reigned 1736-1796), who inscribed it upon a commemorative tablet at the site, hence further spreading its renown. In those days, the scenery comprised only "a pale moon over a river bridge" with a few "scattered clouds" floating occasionally overhead. However, it attracted "so many travelers passing by this spot that by early dawn the air was filled with the clattering of horses' hooves."

At daybreak nowadays, the lamps suspended on the bridge and the stars gleam through the early morning mists, sparkling on the clear waters of the river. A light wind sends silvery ripples running across the water, making the pale reflection of the moon on its surface quiver and dissolve — a scene of truly poetic beauty. But as one strolls along the bridge, stopping to lean over its parapet and gaze into the distance, one will notice the first colors of early morning appear on the horizon. Mountain peaks, treetops and tall buildings are bathed in the rosy glow of the sun.

The Rainbow Floating over the Jade Spring (Yuquanchuihong)

The Jade Spring was originally called the Baotu Spring in Jade Spring Mountain (after a famous spring in Shandong Province). However, when the Qing Qianlong emperor wrote the phrase "Rainbow Floating over the Jade Spring" and a stone tablet bearing this inscription was erected on the spot, the site was henceforth known by this name.

The Jade Spring is famous for its pure cool waters which flow in abundant supply from its underground source, spurting from the dragon-head-shaped stone fountain head in a fine spray that resembles snowflakes. For this reason it is also known as the "Snowflake Spring." In the Qing dynasty, the spring was praised as the "Finest Spring Under Heaven," a description which seems fully deserved when one witnesses it in its wonderful natural setting. This mountain source flows down the mountain and feeds Kunming Lake in the Summer Palace and a number of the other lakes in the city.

The Western Hills Shimmering in Snow (Xishanqingxue)

To find the spot known as "The Western Hills Shimmering in Snow" in the Fragrant Hills, one must turn northwards after reaching the Halfway Pavilion and then climb upwards past the Cave Facing the Sun (Chaoyangdong). The spot was originally one of the "Twenty-eight Scenic Beauties of Xiangshan" and known as the "Grotto of Fragrant Mists" (Xiangwuku). The stone pillar on which the four characters "Western Hills Shimmering in Snow" are inscribed in the calligraphy of the Qianlong emperor stands on the rocky slope to the north of the grotto. Here on a winter day, as the weather clears after a fresh snowfall, the glittering silver mantle covering the numerous jutting peaks seems to stretch away boundlessly, offering a spectacle of great beauty.

Today there are differing opinions as to the true meaning of the words "shimmering snow." Some believe that the "snow" is in fact peach blossoms. Others maintain that it is simply snow. Adherents of the latter interpretation cite a verse from a Qing dynasty anthology to back their claim: "In the depths of winter, the sky clears after a fresh fall of snow. A traveler gazes away into the distance at the cold crispness of this winter scene. The trees and villages are transformed and the gods have sprinkled the beautiful woodlands of the Western Hills with white jade, so that from afar they look like silver. This silver blanket smothers the rugged slopes and misty peaks so that they resemble an expanse of plum blossoms, and sheer cliffs rise up like screens, touching the sky. The light of dusk bathes the distant hills and scattered clouds weave about the dark green pines. A solitary woodcutter trudges his way home along the narrow mountain path with only his broad rimmed hat visible through the trees. . . ."

Jade Islet in Shady Springtime (Qiongdaochunyin)

The site known as "Jade Islet in Shady Springtime" is located on the eastern slope of Jade Islet (Qiongdao) in Beihai Park. Here, the buildings are few while trees abound, creating an air of tranquility and solitude. In 1751, the Qianlong emperor was so moved by the scene that he had a stone tablet inscribed with the name of the site erected in the shade of the trees. Two winding paths lead up from the tablet to the Spring View Pavilion (Jianchunting) and the Corridor for Viewing Paintings (Kanhualang). As you meander through the corridor, the view closely resembles a landscape painting.

Autumn Winds on Taiye (Taiyeqiufeng)

A stone tablet in the Pavilion of Clouds on the Water (Shuiyunxie) in the Central Lake (Zhonghai) bears an inscription in the hand of the Qianlong emperor which permanently records the name of the site. Taiye, or the "Great Secretion," is the name the lake was known by in the Qing dynasty. The open air pavilion stands on an island in the lake amidst the loveliest surroundings: bright white clouds are reflected on the water; the pavilion rests on the lake like a lotus blossom; and in summer, the scent of lotus blossoms permeates the air. This fine scene is lyrically described in the poem "The Pavilion of Clouds on the Water in Early

Autumn" by the Qing poet Zhu Yizun: "In the blazing heat of autumn, a cool breeze at noon stirs the air. The lotus leaves bob in the ripples and sweet pea flowers bloom after fresh rains. The bridge casts gentle shadows in the clear cool river. In the evening light, the mountains take on added beauty as blue and gold reflections from the palace swell on the water's surface."

Previously, a ferry boat stationed to the right of the pavilion connected the pavilion to the Hall of Benevolence (Jurentang), the Hall of Diligent Government (Qinzhengdian) and to the Golden Turtle and Jade Rainbow Bridge.

The Golden Terrace in the Glow of the Setting Sun (Jintaixizhao)

"The Golden Terrace in the Glow of the Setting Sun" is situated at the former Miao Family Estate near the Altar of the Sun (Ritan). In the Qing dynasty, this area originally served as drill grounds for the Manchurian and Mongolian troops of the Emblazoned White Banner. It is said that there was once a tall platform called the "Golden Terrace" within the grounds, and that on spring and autumn evenings, the sunlight would continue to fall on this terrace for a few moments after the sun had set. This was, of course, a natural phenomenon, but when the Qianlong emperor came here once on an inspection tour, he was disturbed by the strange spectacle. Enquiring after the name of the place, the emperor became worried that a site so well endowed by nature would bring its owners inordinate good fortune and feared that this would threaten the supremacy of the Qing court. He therefore ordered the name "Miao Family Estate" (Miaojiadi) changed to "The

Golden Terrace in the Glow of the Setting Sun," and erected a stone tablet to record this. In this manner the last of the "Eight Great Sights" acquired its present name. The original inscription on the stone tablet in the drill ground conveyed the emperor's wish that the Manchus and Mongols should unite in assuring the prosperity of China.

Chapter 8
Historical Sites

Zhoukoudian (The Cave of Peking Man)

Zhoukoudian, situated 50 kilometers to the southwest of Beijing, is the former residence of Peking Man, who lived here approximately 200,000 to 500,000 years ago. Since the discovery of a complete skull on December 2, 1929, Zhoukoudian, which had more recently been noted for its production of lime, became world-famous as the "home of the Chinese apeman." After the establishment of the People's Republic, the number of sightseers and scientists increased rapidly, and Zhoukoudian has become a great tourist attraction.

Peking Man chose Zhoukoudian as his residence because the limestone caves and crevices in the area provided an excellent habitat. The northern face of Dragon Bone Hill (Longgushan), which stands to the east of the Zhoukoudian train station, is the site of the caves occupied by Peking Man; in fact, a total of four early residential sites have been discovered on this hill. Besides those belonging to Peking Man, the remains of a site occupied by Hilltop Caveman are the most representative.

At present, Zhoukoudian's Dragon Bone Hill has an exhibition hall which is divided into seven rooms. The first room exhibits fossil remains of Peking Man, stone tools, and evidence of Peking Man's use of fire. These

327

exhibits also depict Peking Man's external appearance and general living conditions.

The second room exhibits hilltop caveman's fossils, stone tools, bone needles, decorative objects and animal fossils.

The second room exhibits Hilltop Caveman's fossils, various parts of China, such as Dingcun Man, Hetao Man, Ziyang Man, Zhalainuoer Man and other fossil copies. For comparative purposes, there are also fossil copies of the ancient jungle ape, southern ancient ape, Java Man, Neanderthal Man and Cro-Magnon Man that provide an overall understanding of human evolutionary development.

The fourth room introduces the geological history of Peking Man's residence site and displays the process of human and animal evolution through different geological periods.

The fifth and sixth rooms exhibit vertebrate fossils discovered in other locations around Zhoukoudian, including a display of fish fossils.

The seventh room contains the fossils of some of the animals hunted by Peking Man. Among them, the tiger and bear were considered Peking Man's enemies. The discovery of elephant and rhinoceros fossils at the site demonstrates that the climate during the time of Peking Man was far warmer than it is today.

In addition, one can see the actual caves in which Peking Man and Hilltop Caveman lived. The cave at site No. 1 originally measured 140 meters from east to west. Its width was irregular and it had a height of more than 40 meters. The cave was first occupied approximately 500,000 years ago, and it is estimated that Peking Man maintained this residence over the course of a quarter of a million years.

The bones of Peking Man discovered in the cave in the hill's north face include six complete or relatively complete skulls, eight skull fragments, six pieces of facial bone, fifteen mandibles, 153 teeth, seven sections of broken femur, one broken shinbone, three pieces of upper arm bone, one clavicle and one wrist bone belonging to more than 40 individuals of different ages and sexes. Although the materials are fragmentary, they make up one of the most complete collections of human fossil remains from this particular stage of human development.

In addition, 118 animal fossils have been found in the north face cave. It should be noted that with the exception of five teeth, one upper arm bone and one leg bone, all the original Peking Man fossil remains, together with those of Hilltop Caveman, disappeared during World War II and have never been recovered.

The Great Wall

According to legend, the Great Wall was built by the first emperor of the Qin dynasty, Qin Shi Huang (reigned 221-210 B.C.), though historical records trace the true origin of the wall to defensive fortifications built in the fifth century B.C. From the statement "Square walls surround the Kingdom of Chu," we can trace walls with a total length of 500 kilometers in what is now Henan Province dating back to the Eastern Zhou dynasty (770-256 B.C.). In addition to Chu, the kingdoms of Qin, Qi, Wei, Zhao, Han and Yan all had their own separate defensive walls spread about through the Yellow and Yangtze River basins, running in different directions and beginning and ending abruptly. The walls of this period bear little relationship to the wall of today with its predominantly east-west configuration.

In 221 B.C., the armies of Qin conquered the above-mentioned six kingdoms and unified China. Qin Shi Huang ordered the demolition of the walls separating these kingdoms and rebuilt a new "Great Wall," based on the walls protecting the northern frontiers of Yan, Zhao and Qin. According to the *Records of the Historian (Shiji)*, written approximately 100 B.C., "General Meng Tian mobilized three hundred thousand laborers . . . and built a great wall which followed the contour of the land, taking advantage of natural defenses." This wall extended more than 6,000 kilometers from Lintiao (in Gansu Province) to Liaodong. Thus the general plan of today's Great Wall was laid down during the Qin dynasty (221-206 B.C.).

During the Han dynasty (206 B.C.-220 A.D.) which followed the Qin, in addition to making improvements in the Qin wall, the Han emperors constructed a separate outer wall north of the Yinshan range with a total length of 10,000 kilometers. This was the longest single wall built in ancient China. After the fall of the Han dynasty, the wall gradually decayed into ruins. In 1368, the founding year of the Ming dynasty, Emperor Taizu commanded his general Xu Da to direct the reconstruction of the Great Wall. Beginning at the Juyong Pass, the work went on for more than one hundred years. Based on the general dimensions of the Qin wall, the Ming wall stretched from its westernmost point at the Jiayu Pass more than 6,000 kilometers east to the Yalu River. The section which lies between the Jiayu and Shanhai passes remains in good condition today and is known throughout the world as the Great Wall of China.

Setting out from Beijing, the most popular destination for visiting the Great Wall is Badaling. Both trains and buses go to the Juyong Pass, which lies about 60 kilometers to the northwest of the city in a deep mountain-flanked gully 15 kilometers long. In summer, the peaks here are covered with brilliant stretches of leaves and luxuriant flowers. As early as the 13th century, the area was known for its beauty, and was listed as one of the "Eight Great Sights of Yanjing." (See page 320.) The name "Juyong" first appeared in the *Huainanzi*, a philosophical work from the second century B.C., in the following annotation: "The Juyong Pass is one of the nine great passes in the country."

To the west of the Juyong Pass is a white marble structure called the Cloud Platform (Yuntai), which was built in 1345 to serve as the foundation for a set of three stone pagodas built at the command of Emperor Huizong, the last ruler of the Yuan dynasty. At this time, the structure was known as the Pagoda Bridge (Guojieta). After the pagodas were destroyed some time around the fall of the Yuan dynasty (1368), a Great Peace Temple (Tai'ansi) was built to replace them. But this burned down in 1702, during the reign of the Kangxi emperor.

The Cloud Platform is pierced by a hexagonal arched gateway, a great rarity in traditional Chinese architecture. Both the ceiling and facades are covered with Buddhist carvings, including depictions of the Four

Heavenly Kings in relief executed with great detail and expressiveness. Texts of Dharani sutras and an inscription entitled "A Record of Charitable and Pious Pagoda Building" carved in six languages — Lantsha (Nepalese Sanskrit), Tibetan, Phags-pa Mongolian, Uygur, Xi-Xia and Han — are valuable for the study of philology. The inner roof of the arch is covered with mandala patterns and Buddha images surrounded by flowers, all fine examples of Yuan dynasty craftsmanship.

The Juyong Pass area contains many relics associated with popular legends. One of these relics, dating back to the Northern Song dynasty (960-1127), is the Five Heroes Temple, which commemorates the ostensible digging of the gully by five men of unusual strength. The fanciful name of the Playing the Zither Gorge (Tanqinxia) is derived from the clear and melodious sounds of the river flowing through it.

Continuing on from the Juyong Pass, one will arrive at Badaling, the highest point along the entire length of the Great Wall. Between Badaling and Juyong Pass, the words "Natural Barrier" (Tianxian) are carved into a steep and imposing cliff. During the Ming dynasty, two fortifications were built in this area, the Northern Gate Pass on the west and the Juyong Garrison on the east. By climbing up through the pass and looking westwards, one will be able to see a chain of mountains stretching away to the horizon with a single defile leading through them. To the north of the ridges near the wall is the Platform for Viewing the Capital (Wangjingtai) and on clear days the White Dagoba in Beihai Park can be seen from here. By climbing over another slope and following a flight of stone steps up to the highest point of the southern section of the wall, one can see the dragon-like Great Wall making its way over the mountains.

Strategic platforms were built every three to five hundred meters along the wall. These platforms served a variety of purposes: for posting patrols and sentries; to serve as observation posts; and as battle platforms for offensive actions and weapon storage. Here there are also reinforcing walls built alongside the wall proper and beacon towers for transmitting military information.

The section of the Great Wall at Badaling most frequented by visitors dates from the Ming dynasty. Constructed of large blocks of granite and bricks, the wall at this point is 6.6 meters high and 6.5 meters wide at its base, narrowing to 5.5 meters on the rampart. It is wide enough to permit five or six horses to stand side by side.

In recent years, the Chinese government has carried out restoration work on the sections of the wall which have collapsed or been eroded by wind and sand. Despite this, the great increase in tourists at the Great Wall in recent years has led experts to suggest the opening of a "second Badaling" to accommodate the great number of visitors. The "second Badaling" is located to the northeast of Beijing proper and can be reached by bus from the city in approximately two hours. Built on the Great and Lesser Gold Mountains (Jinshan), this section is also called the Gold Mountain Great Wall. According to historical records, the construction of this part of the wall was begun in 1571, and is part of the 1,000-kilometer-long section of the wall between the Shanhai Pass in the east and Changping County in the west which was the result of cooperation between two famous Ming generals, Qi Jiguang and Tan Lun. In terms of construction it is in no way inferior to the wall at Badaling.

The Great Wall at the Gold Mountain is 7 meters high, 6 meters wide, and built of rectangular slabs of stone. The brick-paved walkway along the top of the wall is 4 meters wide and provided with crenellated openings two meters wide. In the merlons (the solid intervals between the crenels) there are small holes for observation and shooting arrows. There are also special openings between the crenels to insert flags for display or signal transmission.

The 158 battle platforms in the Gold Mountain section of the Great Wall were designed in a great variety of shapes — square, circular, oval and multi-cornered. Their interiors are constructed of wood or brick and their roofs are flat, domed or barrel-vaulted. There are also variations in the shape of the archways which give access to the battle platforms.

To the north of Tiger Mountain is a huge solitary piece of rock which has in it an indentation one meter in diameter and 20 cm. deep called the Spring of Heaven. The water from this spring flows continuously in both the rainy and dry seasons. Near the spring is a defense tower called the Five Eyes Tower. Unique in design, the body of the tower is made of rectangular stone blocks and the roof of polished bricks. Inside there are two large barrel-vaulted ceilings, three corridors, ten arched openings and a central octagonal dome supported by four brick columns arranged in a square. The stone columns are decorated with relief carvings of flowers which add a touch of elegance to this otherwise austere building. Standing atop this

tower, one can see the Great Wall winding its way along
the contours of the mountains. From this vantage point,
the wall appears like a ribbon of jade linking the Wuling
Mountain (the highest peak of the Yanshan range) with
the Sleeping Tiger range near Gubeikou.

Leaving the Five Eyes Tower and proceeding along
the wall, one comes to the Tower for Viewing the Capital (Wangjinglou) which sits at a strategic point in
Tiger Mouth Peak. The tower commands a panoramic
view of the surrounding countryside. Off to the southwest, the mirror-like surface of Miyun Reservoir appears
to be floating in space. According to local residents,
the outline of Beijing can be seen in the early morning
and the city lights become visible at night.

The Ming Tombs (Shisanling)

Although Beijing has been the capital of China for
five dynasties, the only imperial mausoleums in the immediate vicinity of the city today are those of the Ming
dynasty. The tombs of the Liao (907-1125) and Qing
(1644-1911) emperors are in the northeast China and in
Hebei Province respectively. The tombs from the Jin
dynasty (1115-1234) were destroyed at the end of the
Ming dynasty, and since the Mongol rulers of the Yuan
dynasty (1206-1368) had no specific funeral rituals, there
are no extant burial sites from this period.

The Ming tombs lie in a broad valley to the south
of Tianshou (Longevity of Heaven) Mountain in Changping County, about 50 kilometers northwest of Beijing.
To the southwest of this valley, a branch of the Yanshan range suddenly breaks off and forms a natural

gateway to the 40-square-kilometer basin in which the
tombs have been erected. This gateway is "defended"
on each side by the Dragon and Tiger Hills, which are
said to protect this sacred area from winds carrying evil
influences. Thirteen out of the sixteen Ming emperors
are buried in this peaceful valley.

Visitors first pass by an elegant, 5-arched white
marble memorial archway (*pailou*). Built in 1540, this
29-meter-wide and 14-meter-high structure, with its deli-
cate bas-relief carvings of lions, dragons and lotuses,
is still in near-perfect condition. About one kilometer
to the northeast of this archway stands the Great Red
Gate (Dahongmen), the outermost gate of the entire
mortuary complex.

The Great Red Gate marks the beginning of the 7-
kilometer-long Sacred Way (Shendao) which leads to
the entrance of the Changling, the tomb of the Yongle
emperor. Continuing on, one comes to a tall square stela
pavilion (*beiting*), with a tall white stone ornamental
column (*huabiao*) set at each of its four corners, standing boldly in the center of the Sacred Way. The pavilion
houses a huge stone tortoise with a tall stela mounted
on its back. This is followed by the famous Avenue of
the Animals, where pairs of lions, elephants, camels,
horses and a number of mythological beasts line the
road. There are 24 stone creatures in all. These beasts
are followed in turn by a group of 12 stone human
figures which represent the funeral cortege of the deceased emperors. Carved in 1540, this group is made
up of military, civil and meritorious officials. Immediately beyond these human figures is the Dragon
and Phoenix Gate (Longfengmen), which is pierced with
three archways.

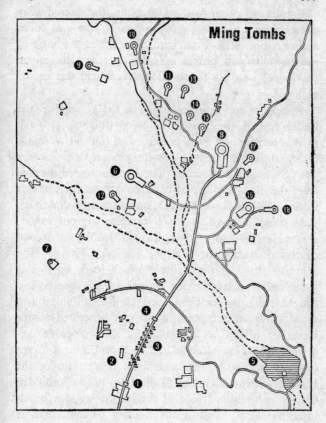

1. Great Red Gate
2. Stela Pavilion
3. Stone Sculptures
4. Dragon and Phoenix Gate
5. Ming Tombs Reservoir
6. Dingling
7. Siling
8. Changling
9. Kangling
10. Tailing
11. Maoling
12. Zhaoling
13. Yuling
14. Qingling
15. Xianling
16. Yongling
17. Jingling
18. Deling

Continuing north to the Changling, the Sacred Way passes over a river via two bridges of five and seven arches respectively. From here, all 13 tombs can be seen; the foothills and groves of trees dotted with golden yellow roofs stretch for 19 kilometers across this sacred valley.

Compared to the other 12 tombs the Changling, the burial site of the Yongle emperor (reigned 1403-24), is the largest and best preserved. Built on a south-facing slope, the Changling's three courtyards are entirely surrounded by walls. The first courtyard extends from the massive 3-arched entrance gate to the Gate of Eminent Favor (Long'enmen); on the east of this courtyard stands a pavilion which contains a stone tablet, a stone camel and a stone dragon. Inside the second courtyard stands the Hall of Eminent Favor. The central portion of the stairway which leads up to this great hall is carved with designs of sea beasts and dragons. To the east and west of the hall stand two ritual stoves where bolts of silk and inscribed scrolls were set aflame as offerings to the emperor's ancestors. The dimensions of the Hall of Eminent Favor (67 × 29 meters) closely match the dimensions of the Hall of Supreme Harmony (Taihedian) in the Forbidden City, which makes it one of the largest wooden buildings in China. Four giant wooden columns and 28 smaller pillars support this structure. The four large columns are 14.3 meters high and 1.17 meters in diameter, and are extraordinary for the fact that they are each a single trunk of Phoebe nanmu.

Inside the third and final courtyard is a square stone rampart topped with a stela tower (*minglou*), in front of which stand incense burners and other ritual objects

known as the "Nine Stone Feast Implements." A staircase leads up through the 15-meter-high rampart to the
tower, which contains a stela bearing the words "The
Mausoleum of Emperor Chengzu" (the temple name of
the Yongle emperor). A circular wall one kilometer in
circumference commonly called the "Precious City"
(Baocheng) surrounds the 31-meter-long, 28-meter-wide
burial mound. To the east and west of the great mausoleum are the tombs of imperial concubines. Sixteen
concubines were "rewarded" with death and buried
alive here to serve their emperor in the underworld.
(Such sacrifices were not abolished until the time of
the Zhengtong emperor, who reigned 1436-49 and 1457-
64).

The tomb of the Wanli emperor (reigned 1573-1619)
and its underground palace are located at the foot of
Dayu Mountain southwest of the Changling. The Wanli
emperor was buried here in 1620 with two of his wives,
Xiao Duan and Xiao Jing. The labor of more than
30,000 workers and 8 million taels of silver (equal to
two years of national land tax revenues during the first
years of Wanli's reign) were spent on the project. It
was completed in six years (1584-90).

The tomb, known as the Dingling, occupies a total
area of 1,195 square meters and is located directly behind
the stela tower. A 40-meter-long tunnel leads to the first
massive door, which is 7.3 meters below the ground. The
underground palace consists of five rooms with giant
marble archways and a floor paved with huge polished
stone known as "gold bricks." Fifty thousand of these
were produced in Suzhou over the course of three years
and transported some 1,400 kilometers to the north.

Descending to the level of the burial chambers, one comes first to the unfurnished front hall. This hall connects to the central hall, where three marble imperial thrones, one for the emperor and two for his consorts, are located. Here also are "eternal lamps" (oil lamps with a floating wick) and a set of the "five offerings" — an incense burner, two candlesticks and two vases, all of yellow glazed pottery. Adjacent to the middle hall are two side chambers, each containing a marble coffin platform 17.4 meters long and 3.7 meters wide. Known as "gold wells," each of these platforms is topped with "gold bricks" and has a small area in its center which is filled with yellow soil. No coffins, however, were found in these chambers.

The rear hall is the largest (9.5 meters high, 30.1 meters long and 9.1 meters wide) and most important hall in the underground palace. In the center of the hall are the three platforms used to support the coffins of the Wanli emperor and his empresses. Twenty-six red lacquer chests, containing crowns, pitchers and wine vessels of gold, pitchers, cups, bowls and earrings of jade, and porcelain vases and bowls were placed around the coffins. In addition, sacred objects of jade and blue-and-white porcelain vases were placed alongside the chests. Among the more than 3,000 objects which have been unearthed from the underground palace is an extremely fine crown made of gold filigree decorated with two miniature dragons playing with a pearl. This, along with an exquisite embroidery of 100 children playing and other exhibits of historical interest, can be viewed in two exhibition halls located within the Dingling complex.

Marco Polo Bridge (Lugouqiao)

"Over this river there is a very fine stone bridge, so fine indeed, that it has very few equals in the world."

The Diary of Marco Polo

The Marco Polo Bridge is located 15 kilometers southwest of Beijing. Known also as the Guangli Bridge, it spans the banks of the Yongding River. According to historical records, the "Lugou River is also called the Heishui (Black Water) River." In the local dialect in ancient times, *lu* (reed) meant black; thus the Heishui River became known as the Lugou River, and the bridge was accordingly given the same name.

Historical records also inform us that the Lugou River was "violent and flowed extraordinarily rapidly." With the post-1949 construction of the Guanting Reservoir upstream from the bridge, a multitude of trees were planted on the river banks and the formerly muddy water became clear. The river's willful disposition was also tamed, no longer presenting the constant danger of floods. The Lugou River was also known as the Wuding (Lacking Stability) River, and despite the fact that the Kangxi emperor had the auspicious name Yongding (Eternal Stability) bestowed upon it, it was only after the founding of the People's Republic that the river truly became "eternally stable." After seven centuries, however, the river water remains as swift as ever. Owing, however, to the extraordinarily durable construction of the bridge's foundation, the endless battering of the torrential current has left no mark on it.

The Lugou Bridge is situated at a strategic point on the one overland route to the capital from the south.

Bridge construction was begun in 1189 and completed four years later. The bridge is 235 meters long, eight meters wide, and is constructed entirely of white marble. It has 11 arches and as many broad piers. At the extremes of the bridge there are two stone stelae, one recording the history of the renovation work carried out in the Kangxi reign (1662-1722), and the other bearing the inscription "The Moon over the Lugou Bridge at Dawn" in the handwriting of the Qianlong emperor. (See page 319, "The Eight Great Sights of Yanjing.")

Lining the bridge are two rows of carved white marble balustrades topped by posts carved with figures of lions. The people of Beijing have a saying to the effect that "The lions of the Lugou Bridge are too numerous to count," which is explained by the fact that the lions are carved in a great variety of aspects and distributed unequally among the 280 white marble posts. A pair of vividly carved reclining stone elephants and a number of other animal figures guard each end of the bridge.

On July 7, 1937, the first shot of the War of Resistance Against Japan rang out beside the Lugou Bridge. But now all signs of the war have long since disappeared. As the sun sets, the furnaces of nearby Shijingshan Steel Mill cast a red glow across the sky, lighting up the bridge in fiery splendor.

The Ruins of the Yuanmingyuan
(The Garden of Perfection and Light)

In a quiet section of the suburbs of Beijing to the north of Qinghua University, there once stood a complex of gardens known as the Yuanmingyuan. Built during the early and middle years of the Qing dynasty, this "garden of gardens" was made up of the Garden of Perfection and Light (Yuanmingyuan), the Garden of Eternal Spring (Changchunyuan), and the Garden of Ten Thousand Springtimes (Wanchunyuan).

The work of building the garden went on over a period of one hundred and fifty years, beginning in around 1700. The grounds had a circumference of ten kilometers and occupied an area of more than 800 acres. Of the hundreds of large and small buildings which once stood here, all that remains are a few ruins in stone, a sorry reminder of past greatness.

On October 5, 1860, the English and French Allied Armies occupied the town of Haidian in the northwest suburbs of the capital, and on October 7 the mad plunder of the garden began. Finally, Lord Elgin's cavalry set the gardens on fire, leaving them to burn for three days and three nights. After their retreat, repairs were begun, but in 1900 further destruction was brought upon the garden by the Eight-Power Allied Forces, leaving it in complete ruin. Before long, whatever could be made use of from out of the rubble, be it wood, stones, bricks or tiles, was taken away by members of the imperial household and the warlords of the early Republican period.

Visitors can now stroll about the ruins and view the remains of the following sites: (1) the "Vista of the Square Teapot" on the northeast bank of the Sea of Fortune (Fuhai); (2) the Green Mountain Hut near the northwestern gate; (3) the Jade Isle of Sages in the middle of the Sea of Fortune; (4) the Magnanimity of the Seas and Hills in the West Lake of the Garden of

Eternal Spring; (5) Sravasti City, modeled after the capital of the ancient Indian state of Kosala, which was a repository for statues of the Buddha. The ruins of the high walls of this "City" can still be traced today; and (6) the Source of Culture Pavilion (Wenyuange), which housed the collection of books known as the *Complete Library of the Four Branches of Literature*. Besides the remains of the pavilion, one will also notice numerous specimens of Lake Taihu stone lying abandoned in a pool in its courtyard. In addition, other scattered stone fragments and the flagstones from stone paths can be found in various spots throughout the surrounding hills and meandering streams.

The most striking ruin in the whole garden is the complex of Western-style buildings, the construction of which began in the tenth year of Emperor Qianlong's reign (1746). Situated near the northern wall of the Garden of Eternal Spring, these buildings were designed by the Jesuits Castiglione and Benoit. They included the Observatory and Hall of Tranquility which were decorated with fine fountains and pools in the style of Versailles. In addition, their roofs and walls were embellished with glazed tiles in brilliant colors.

It is hoped that before long the splendor of the garden will be restored and that this exquisite cultural relic, once the private playground of emperors, will be open to visitors from all over the world.

In 1977, the municipality of Beijing established a committee to undertake the renovation of the Yuanmingyuan Garden, the first organization of its kind to be set up since the destruction of the garden. Some of the stone carvings removed from the garden are now being returned from places such as Beijing University.

The Drum Tower and the Bell Tower

The Drum and Bell Towers are situated at the northern end of the central axis of the Beijing Inner City to the north of Di'anmen Dajie (Gate of Earthly Peace Road).

The Drum Tower was built in 1272 during the reign of Kublai Khan, at which time it stood at the very heart of the Yuan capital Dadu. At that time it was known as the Tower of Orderly Administration (Qizhenglou). In 1420, under the Ming Yongle emperor, the building was reconstructed to the east of the original site and in 1800 under the Qing Jiaqing emperor, large-scale renovations were carried out. In 1924, the name of the building was changed to the Tower of Realizing Shamefulness (Mingchilou) and objects related to the Eight-Power Allied Forces' invasion of Beijing and later the May 30th Massacre of 1925 were put on display. Nowadays, the upper story of the building serves as the East City District People's Cultural Hall.

The first level of the Drum Tower is a solid square terrace four meters high, 55.6 meters long and 30 meters wide. The front and rear of the terrace are pierced with three arched openings and the two sides with one opening each. The broad, squat multi-eaved wooden structure built atop the terrace is impressive with its red wall and yellow glazed roof tiles. In ancient days the Drum Tower was the time keeping center for the whole city and was equipped with bronze clepsydras (water clocks) and drums that were beaten to mark the hours.

The four bronze clepsydras which once functioned in the Drum Tower were reputed to date from the Song dynasty (960-1279). Set between these four devices was a large bronze gong, which through a series of mechanical devices was linked to the water clocks and sounded each quarter of an hour. When the system of telling time with incense coils which burned for two hours was introduced, the clepsydras fell into disuse.

In ancient times the upper story of the building housed 24 drums, of which only one survives. Its head is made of an entire ox hide and is 1.5 meters in diameter. A sword score on the side of the drum is a souvenir of the Eight-Power Allied Forces' invasion of Beijing in 1900.

In the Qing dynasty, the hours were marked at night beginning at 7:00 p.m., a procedure that was popularly called "setting the watch." At this hour, the drums were sounded 13 times. After the watch had been "set" in this fashion, each subsequent two-hour interval was marked by a single drum beat. Civil and military officials oriented their lives around these time signals. At the sounding of the third watch (1:00 a.m.) officials attending the morning court audience rose from their beds and at the fourth (3:00 a.m.) assembled outside the Meridian Gate (Wumen). At the sounding of the fifth watch (5:00 a.m.) they entered the Imperial Palace and knelt on the Sea of Flagstones (Haiman) before the Hall of Supreme Harmony (Taihedian) to await instructions from the emperor.

Close behind the Drum Tower stands the Bell Tower, a 33-meter-high edifice with gray walls and a green glazed tile roof. Each face of the base of the building is pierced with an arched opening and each side of the Bell Pavilion, which stands on the platform, has an arched gateway as well. The Bell Tower first came into use during the reign of the Ming Yongle emperor (1403-

24) when it was converted from the main hall of the former Temple of Eternal Peace (Wanningsi), which had been built during the Yuan dynasty. The new Bell Tower was destroyed by fire after only a brief existence and it was not until 1747 that the Qianlong emperor undertook the reconstruction of an attractive durable stone structure. This building was so sturdy that the only damage that it suffered during the Tangshan earthquake of 1976 was the loss of a single stone animal head decorating the roof.

The Bell Tower originally housed a huge iron bell. But because its tolling was not loud enough, this was replaced by a massive cast bronze bell over 10 inches thick that survives in perfect condition today. The iron bell was moved to the back of the Drum Tower where it has remained for over 500 years. As recently as 1924, the bronze bell could be heard ringing out the 7:00 p.m. chime from a distance of over 20 kilometers.

According to legend, an official named Deng tried unsuccessfully for over a year to cast the bell. On the eve of the final casting, his daughter, fearing that further delays and loss of working time would bring blame on her father, decided to sacrifice her life in order to move the gods to bring about a perfect casting, and threw herself into the molten bronze. Her panic-stricken father could only recover a single embroidered slipper from the flames. The casting was a success and the emperor, moved by the young girl's spirit of sacrifice, named her the "Goddess of the Golden Furnace" and built a temple in her honor near the foundry. By the ordinary people she was remembered as the "Goddess Who Cast the Bell."

After the bell was installed, the chimes could be heard clearly and resonantly all across the city. But on stormy evenings, the bell would emit a desolate moaning sound similar to the word *xie,* which means "shoe" in Chinese. Recalling the old legend, mothers would comfort their children with: "Go to sleep! The Bell Tower is tolling. The Goddess Who Cast the Bell wants her embroidered slipper back."

Chapter 9
Famous Sites Within One Day's Journey from Beijing

The Imperial Touring Lodge at Chengde (Rehe Xinggong)

The Imperial Touring Lodge, also known as the Chengde Lodge (Chengde Ligong), derives its name from the Warm Spring (Requan)* located in the northeast of the complex. The area is also known as Bishushanzhuang (Mountain Manor for Avoiding the Summer Heat) due to its location among lush, tree-covered mountains, and its pleasant temperatures in summer, which average 19.3°C in the hottest months of the year.

In the early Qing dynasty, a palace complex and a park were built here to provide a holiday resort for the emperor and fulfill some key political demands. According to historical records, the lodge was built as "conciliatory gestures to the national minorities, and to provide a place to practice military skills and to receive important guests." From the reign of the Kangxi emperor (1662-1722) through that of the Qianlong emperor (1736-96), nobles and important personages from every

---

* The city of Chengde was previously known as Jehol (Rehe), literally "warm river."

minority of China were invited here to take part in con-
tests of strength, horse racing and hunting, all of which
served to draw the minority leaders closer to the throne.
Between Beijing and Chengde as many as 20 traveling
lodges were constructed to serve as resting places for
the emperors on their sojourns and for the storage of
various imperial belongings. The lodge at Chengde was
the largest and most important of these and had
administrative control over all the lodges beyond the
Gubeikou Pass. After the Chengde Lodge was constructed, the Kangxi emperor and his grandson, the
Qianlong emperor, entertained Mongolian princes and
nobles and the upper classes of the Tibetan, Kazak,
Uygur and Kirgiz minorities here in an effort to consolidate Qing rule and unite the empire by gaining the
allegiance of regional rulers through bestowing favors
upon them.

Political factors were an important consideration
when the lodge was being built. Behind the emperor's
bed in his sleeping quarters, the Hall of Cool Mists and
Ripples (Yanbozhishuangdian), a concealed door was
installed offering the emperor a means of escape in time
of danger. In addition, the Pavilion of the Wind in the
Pines of Ten Thousand River Valleys (Wanhesongfeng-
dian) was constructed especially for the Kangxi emperor to receive officials and peruse memorials to the
throne.

Despite these provisions, a large number of political
incidents occurred here. In 1860, when the Xianfeng
emperor yielded to the pressure of the foreign powers,
the "Beijing Treaty," concluded in Beijing by Prince
Gong (Yi Xin, Xianfeng's younger brother) with France,

Germany and Russia, was ratified while the emperor was residing in his mountain retreat.

On July 17, 1861, the Xianfeng emperor, sensing his vitality draining away, called his most trusted ministers to his sleeping quarters in the West Warm Pavilion (Xinuange) and entrusted them to oversee his five-year-old son (by the Empress Dowager Cixi), Zai Chun (later the Tongzhi emperor), in running the country until he attained maturity. Xianfeng presented a precious stone seal engraved with "Yushang" (Imperial Award) to Empress Ci'an and another engraved "Tongdaotang" (Hall of Accord with the Way) to Zai Chun with the instructions that the eight ministers were to assist him in state affairs and to take responsibility for drafting and issuing official decrees. Xianfeng also stipulated that these decrees had to be marked at the beginning and end with the two newly presented seals to prove their validity.

Unknown to them, the ambitious Imperial Concubine Cixi had crept into the room via the secret passage and hid herself behind the emperor's bed. On the day the emperor died, she took immediate action and issued an imperial decree in the name of Zai Chun declaring that she, as the emperor's mother, would become the Empress Dowager in both title and fact. Originally, the Imperial Concubine's position was much lower than that of the empress, but Cixi raised her position to the equal of Empress Ci'an. Later, she gained possession of the "Tongdaotang" seal and personally ratified imperial edicts in her son's name. This paved the way for her subsequent large-scale manipulation of state affairs.

In addition to being the most important political center after Beijing of the early Qing period, the

Chengde Imperial Lodge was equally famous as a summer retreat. The Manchu nobles who ruled at the beginning of the Qing dynasty could not accustom themselves to Beijing's hot dry summers and sought relief by traveling north of the Great Wall. In 1650, under the Shunzhi emperor, the Prince Regent Dorgon made plans to build an imperial retreat in the suburbs of Chengde, but the project was abandoned when he died that year. When the Kangxi emperor ascended the throne he made it a habit to head north whenever he needed to recuperate from an illness. Kangxi wrote that touring to the area in the summer strengthened his spirit by contact with the fine Mongolian landscape and comfortable climate. In 1702, Kangxi settled on a site which combined the "elegance of southern China with the grandeur of the north" and began to construct a large-scale palace.

The Imperial Touring Lodge is the largest imperial park in China, occupying an area of over 5.6 square kilometers. It is surrounded by a high stone wall some 10 kilometers in length. The park is twice the size of Beijing's Summer Palace (Yiheyuan), eight times larger than Beihai Park and larger even than the Yuanmingyuan Garden which, incidentally, was constructed contemporaneously with the Lodge. The park includes lakes, mountains, plains and palace halls, and besides the total of 72 scenic spots designated by the Kangxi and Qianlong emperors, there are more than 20 other building complexes scattered throughout the park, consisting of over 100 individual halls, pavilions, studios, pagodas and terraces. Each of these complexes has its own poetic name, such as the Island of Moonlight and the Sound of the River (Yuesejiangshengdao), the Mountain Pavilion of Tranquil Repose (Jingshanfang) and the Lion Forest (Shizilin) in the Literary Garden (Wenyuan).

The buildings in which the emperor handled court affairs, held celebrations and rested from the summer heat stand in the southern part of the palace area. Altogether there were three groups of palace halls — the Main Palace (Zhenggong) to the west, the Pine and Crane Studio (Songhezhai) slightly to the north of the center, and the Eastern Palace (Donggong) to the east. The Main Palace served as the principal living quarters of the emperor and was designed with nine courtyards to represent the nine divisions of the celestial sphere symbolizing the emperor's heavenly mandate. The main gate, the Lizhengmen (Beautiful Upright Gate) stands to the south, with the Inner and Outer Meridian Gates behind it. The Inner Meridian Gate (Neiwumen) was also called the Yueshemen (Gate for Reviewing the Archers). Above the gate hangs the famous horizontal tablet inscribed "Bishushanzhuang" (Mountain Manor for Avoiding the Summer Heat) in the calligraphy of the Kangxi emperor. Before the gate stand two exquisitely crafted bronze lions.

Through the three palace gates lies the main hall of the main palace: the Hall of Rectitude and Sincerity (Danbojingchengdian), more commonly called the Phoebe Nanmu Hall (Nanmudian). The entire building is constructed of Phoebe nanmu wood and gives off an unusual scent reputed to repel mosquitos in the summer. This hall was the setting for the most solemn ceremonies. When the Sixth Panchen Lama arrived at Chengde from Tibet in 1780, he came here first to pay his respects to the emperor.

To the north of the hall is the Great Hall by the Lake (Yihukuangdian) which contains an inscription by the Qianlong emperor "Sizhishuwu" (Library of the Four "Knows")*. The emperor would rest here before and after holding ceremonies, and only the most important members of the court were permitted to come to have audience with him. In the courtyard outside, ancient cypresses still flourish.

The third major hall is the Hall of Cool Mists and Ripples which along with the Hall of the Panorama of Cloud-Covered Mountains (Yunshanshengdi) and several other halls served as the imperial living quarters and the main office from which the emperor ran court affairs. The Pine and Crane Studio to the east of the main palace was originally the living quarters of the Empress Dowager Cixi while to the north stands the Pavilion of the Wind in the Pines of Ten Thousand River Valleys, so named because the wind blowing through the river valley was said to resemble the sound of pipes and bells. When the Qianlong emperor was a child, he would come here with his grandfather Kangxi to read. Qianlong later renamed the building the Hall for Remembering Kindness (Ji'entang) to commemorate his study sessions here with Kangxi.

The Eastern Palace originally included the Qinzheng (Earnest Government) Hall and the Qingyin (Clear Sounds) Pavilion, where the Qing emperors handled the daily affairs of the court and gave audience to the nobles of the national minorities and to foreign envoys.

---

* The Four "Knows" — Heaven knows, the gods know, I know and you know — refers to the upright behavior of an official in the Han dynasty.

By following a stone pathway which leads north from the palace, one will come to an area of lakes known collectively as the Frontier (Sai) Lakes. The area is made up of the Clear Lake, Ruyi* Lake, Upper Lake, Lower Lake, Silver Lake and Mirror Lake, as well as a number of small islands and dikes. In the center of the area is a scenic path known as the Magic Mushroom Path and Cloud Dike (Zhijingyundi). Twisting and turning through the lake district, the path provides a series of wonderfully varied views.

Ruyi Islet is one of the largest islands in the lake area. Its southernmost building, the Cool Refreshing Hall (Wushuqingliangdian), is bright and spacious, and in the morning provides an ideal retreat from the summer heat. In the center of the islet is its principal structure, the Extended Fragrance Mountain Hall (Yanxunshanguan), a simple unadorned building tastefully laid out and so situated that fresh breezes cool it from the north. When grand ceremonies were held at the touring lodge, feasts were held here for the princes, nobles and government ministers.

Northwest of Ruyi Islet, a small bridge leads to Green Lotus Island (Qinglian), on which stands the Tower of Mist and Rain (Yanyulou), built by the Qianlong emperor on the model of a similarly named structure on South Lake at Jiaxing in Zhejiang Province. When it rains, the building becomes clouded in mist and reminds one of the scenery south of the lower Yangtze River. A second path leads east from the Lower Lake past the Juan'e Scenic Spot (named after a place re-

---

* Ruyi: literally "as you please." A *ruyi* is a scepter designed in the shape of a medicinal fungus.

corded in the *Book of Songs**) to the Pavilion in the
Heart of the Waters (Shuixinxie). There were 16 scenic
spots here, but now only a single tumbledown rockery
hill remains.

North of the pavilion, surrounded by Clear Lake,
Upper Lake and Lower Lake, is a large flat island where
a group of buildings peep out from among the trees.
Above the main entrance hangs an inscription "Moonlight and the Sound of the River." The buildings are
laid out around a square courtyard in the typical style
of northern China, each hall connected to the next by
a roofed corridor. Within the courtyard are ancient
pines and an artificial hill made of stones. It was here
that the emperor came to read, fish or listen to music.

North from here next to Clear Lake is a small, rocky
island on which a model of the Gold Mountain Temple
(Jinshansi) at Zhenjiang, in Jiangsu Province has been
built. At the island's summit stands the Pavilion of the
Supreme Emperor (Shangdige), a three-story hexagonal
building which originally served as a temple for the
worship of the Zhenwu Emperor and the Jade Emperor,
two Daoist gods. This is the highest point in the lake
area and a climb to the top gives a wonderful view of
the beautiful lakeside scenery.

The Rehe Spring (Warm River Spring) stands on the
eastern shore of Clear Lake. Starting out from here and
heading to the northwest, the five pavilions on the lake's
northwestern bank can be explored. North of the pavilions lies a stretch of open plain which the Qianlong
emperor called the Park of Ten Thousand Trees (Wan-

* *Book of Songs* (*Shijing*): An anthology of poetry of the Zhou
dynasty.

shuyuan). Here numerous species of birds as well as deer, wild rabbits and squirrels thrive. This was also where the emperor held Great Mongolian Yurt Banquet, watched fireworks displays and received the chiefs of various national minorities and foreign envoys from a throne set inside a huge Mongolian yurt.

To the west of the Park of Ten Thousand Trees is a group of buildings called the Literary Nourishment Pavilion (Wenjinge) which served the emperors as a library. Here was stored one of the four handwritten sets of the *Complete Library of the Four Branches of Literature,* compiled over the course of ten years by more than 500 scholars.

The mountainous area which lies to the northwest of the Touring Lodge occupies some 80 per cent of the park's total grounds. Rising as high as 180 meters above the lakes and plains, these hills provide a majestic backdrop to the lakeside scenery. The hills were originally dotted with numerous buildings, most of which were destroyed before 1949. Of the four hilltop pavilions once standing, only the Snow-Capped Southern Mountain Pavilion (Nanshanjixue) remains. Four deep gullies — the Pine Cloud Gorge, Pear Tree Valley, Pine Grove Gorge and Hazel Gorge — run east and west between the mountains, forming natural scenic paths enhanced by springs which serve as the source of small streams.

The most northerly of the gorges is the Pine Cloud Gorge, where ancient pines line the ruins of the old stone-paved imperial road. The mountains, rich with their green foliage, present a scene of great natural beauty. A poet once described the gorge as follows:

"As in a dream, a boundless expanse of whispering pines waves in the breeze. The splendor fills my heart with irrepressible resolution."

Running north and south between the gorges are several small gullies. Here small paths mingle with winding streams as they meander between hillsides abounding in avian life. Describing this area, the Qianlong emperor wrote: "In the rain, the green hue of the foliage deepens and the remote peaks become more tranquil. Stone steps wind down between pine trees and trailing vines; here and there patches of sunlight filter through the dense dark forest."

Walking west from the Pine Cloud Gorge and up a mountain path, one will come to the highest pavilion in the entire park, the Pavilion Surrounded by Cloud-Covered Mountains (Simianyunshan). Beyond this lies the recently restored Pavilion of the Hammer Peak in the Glow of the Setting Sun (Chuifengluozhao). Hammer (Bangchui) Mountain was recorded by name as early as 1,500 years ago by Li Daoyuan in his famous survey of China's rivers and waterways, the *Water Classic* (*Shuijingzhu*). The Kangxi emperor renamed it Qingchui Peak because of its resemblance to a stone chime, and had the poetically named pavilion erected on the west face of the mountain opposite the peak for the sole purpose of admiring the fine sunset.

Summer is the best season to visit Chengde, though it is well worth a visit at any time of the year. Located about 250 kilometers from Beijing, Chengde can be reached by direct train from the capital in less than five hours.

The Temples of Chengde

Outside the walls of the Chengde Imperial Touring Lodge, temples in the Tibetan, Han and Mongolian styles are found scattered among the nearby hills. Built on a larger scale than any of the temples of Beijing, they are collectively known as the Waibamiao (Eight Temples Beyond the Great Wall). In actual fact, there were originally 11 temples, of which only seven now remain.

The temples were built between the years 1713 and 1780 under the Kangxi and Qianlong emperors, and are clustered along the northern and eastern sides of the Touring Lodge. Apart from the Purensi (Temple of Universal Benevolence) and the Pushansi (Temple of Universal Goodness), built under the Kangxi emperor, all the other temples, built during the Qianlong reign, are so designed that their main gates face the Imperial Lodge. The significance of this is obvious — the Eight Temples symbolize the various nationalities from all parts of China directing their loyalty towards the center of authority. The Qianlong emperor expressed this concept in his poem "One Hundred Rhymes from the Mountain Manor for Avoiding the Summer Heat": "These buildings embody the successful uniting of the hearts of the people of the inner and outer lands." Following this belief, the palaces, halls and gardens erected under Qianlong's direction stress the use of architecture to embody the theme of national unity.

A climb to the Nanshanjixue (Snow-Capped Southern Mountain) Pavilion offers a fine view of the entire temple complex. Here can be found duplicates of the three temples to Maya (the mother of Buddha), the Potala, the Tashilunpo Temple in Tibet and the Gu'erzha Temple in Xinjiang. These represent China's Northwest and Southwest. The Temple of the Image of Manjusri (Shuxiangsi) of Wutai Mountain in Shanxi, and the Hall of the Immortals in the Temple of National Peace (Anguosi) in Haining in Zhejiang have also been duplicated and represent the North and South.

Although each of the buildings has its own individual style, the overall pattern is one of harmony and unity, and whether we view the temples from the angle of overall layout or from that of the structure of the individual buildings, the Waibamiao are models of architectural excellence. The four principal temples are described below:

1. Xumifushoumiao (The Temple of Sumeru Happiness and Longevity). This temple was built by the Qianlong emperor in 1780 after the model of the Tibetan Tashilunpo Temple at Xigaze, and its name is a direct translation of the Tibetan name "Temple of Complete Happiness and Longevity." The year 1780 was the 70th birthday of the Qianlong emperor, so the celebrations were held on a larger scale than usual. In addition to the Mongolian nobles and princes, imperial ministers and their retainers, and foreign envoys who attended the celebrations, the Sixth Panchen Lama Erdeni also came from Tibet to pay his respects. To receive his distinguished guest in style, the Qianlong emperor had the temple especially constructed.

The halls and pavilions built on the massive Great Red Terrace (Dahongtai) are the temple's most important buildings, and are well preserved up to the present day. From the top of the Great Red Terrace, the gilded bronze tile roof of the Main Hall can be viewed from close quarters and the exquisite craftsmanship of the eight gilded dragons standing on the roof ridges can be appreciated in all their splendor.

The Great Red Terrace is comprised of buildings on three levels with the square-shaped Miaogaozhuangyan-dian (Exalted and Dignified Hall) in the central position. The Main Hall (Dadian) is constructed in three stories, each decorated with images of the Buddha. Inside the narrow courtyard which separates the towering buildings, one enters what seems like a new world, and inside the Main Hall the refined atmosphere is most appropriate for the worship of the Buddha. According to tradition, when the Panchen Lama recited scriptures here in 1780, the emperor was present and every single priest and official prostrated himself to avoid setting eyes on the emperor. The Main Hall was absolutely silent save for the quiet incantations of the Panchen Lama.

While the Panchen Lama was in Chengde, the Qian-long emperor treated him with the utmost of politeness and cordiality and the story of their meeting has been handed down through the centuries. In the first month of 1779, the Panchen Lama set out from Lhasa leading a party of three *kanbu* (high priest-officials) and over 100 priests. The Qianlong emperor sent his sixth son and a Mongolian Living Buddha, Zhang Jia, to meet the Sixth Panchen Lama, who traveled to the Imperial Touring Lodge in a large yellow sedan chair.

Qianlong received the Panchen Lama in the Hall of Rectitude and Sincerity (Danbojingchengdian) and after presenting the emperor with a welcome gift of a silk *hada* cloth, the Lama knelt down before him. But

Qianlong immediately left his throne and hurried to
raise the Buddhist leader to his feet, and in his best
newly learned Tibetan, asked the Lama if the long trip
had been very arduous for him. The Lama replied that
with His Majesty's grace reaching out to him from afar,
his journey had been peaceful and pleasant from beginning to end. After the formal greeting ceremonies, the
emperor had a private audience with the Panchen Lama
in the Library of the Four "Knows" (Sizhishuwu), and
entertained him with a feast of tea and fruits. After
the feast the Qianlong emperor once more broke court
convention by personally inviting the Panchen Lama into
the rear palaces to visit the Hall of Cool Mists and
Ripples (Yanbozhishuang) — the emperor's sleeping
quarters, the Hall of the Panorama of Cloud-Covered
Mountains (Yunshanshengdidian) and so on. Afterwards the Buddhist leader left the palace via the Hill
Cloud Gate (Xiuyunmen), and riding in a yellow-
topped sedan chair presented to him by the emperor,
toured the emperor's garden, stopping briefly on the
Ruyi Islet — an island in the garden lake — before proceeding to his lodgings in the Auspicious Hall of the
Buddhist Doctrine (Jixiangfaxidian) in the Xumifushou
Temple.

On the emperor's 70th birthday, the Panchen Lama
and the Living Buddha Zhang Jia led the *kanbu* lamas
to the Hall of Rectitude and Sincerity. Here the Qianlong emperor joined hands with the Panchen Lama and
they walked together to the throne, where Erdeni presented the emperor with a set of Buddhist sacramental
objects and a birthday portrait as well as offered a
congratulatory speech. The highlight of the celebration

was when the *kanbu* rose together and sang in praise of the emperor's long life.

During the Panchen Lama's stay in Chengde, the Qianlong emperor presented him with a golden book and a golden seal. The seal, carved with Han, Manchu, Mongolian and Tibetan scripts, was inscribed "Seal presented to the Panchen Erdeni." However, the written character used for the second syllable of Panchen was "chen," meaning subject or vassal, rather than the character used traditionally. This switch was an expression of the fact that Tibet was under the central political authority of the Qing dynasty.

2. Putuozongshengmiao. Located directly north of Bishushanzhuang (Mountain Manor for Avoiding the Summer Heat), it is the largest temple of the Waibamiao, occupying an area of 220,000 square meters. Construction was begun in 1767 and completed almost four years later. It is modeled on the great Potala Monastery in Lhasa and is thus also known as the Little Potala. The buildings are a synthesis of Han and Tibetan styles.

The temple has a tall and imposing entrance gate similar in design to a city gate tower. Inside the gate is a pavilion housing three stelae, the largest one inscribed with "The Record of the Putuozongshengmiao" in Han, Manchu, Mongolian and Tibetan characters. The stela to the east is inscribed with "The Record of the Turgot Tribe Pledging Their Allegiance" and that to the west is inscribed with "The Record of Offering Assistance to the Turgot People," both in the four languages found on the main stela. The stories behind the two smaller stelae are as follows:

The Turgots were a Mongol tribe living in the present area of the Xinjiang Uygur Autonomous Region. At the beginning of the 17th century, the tribal chieftain came into conflict with the leaders of other tribes, and in the third year of the Chongzhen emperor's reign (1630) led his people and herds on a long trek to the Volga River. Before long, the government of tsarist Russia began to oppress the Turgot people by levying burdensome taxes and conscripting their young men until they could no longer suffer the humiliation. Under a young leader, 33,000 households, totaling some 169,000 people, broke through the encirclement of the pursuing tsarist army and in June 1771, after traveling over 5,000 kilometers in eight months, reached their native land. On arriving at Ili, they presented the Qing government with the jade seal which the Yongle emperor had bestowed on their forefathers in 1411, thereby indicating their desire to once more become part of China.

The western stela tells how the Qing government appointed officials to select good land for the Turgot tribe to settle on, and sent them cattle, sheep, grain, clothing and tents worth 200,000 taels of silver. In addition, the newly returned tribesmen were given the right to herd their cattle throughout the Ili River basin.

Just to the north of the stela pavilion is the Five Pagoda Gate, and beyond this a glazed tile memorial archway. Dotting the hillside there are white terraces and Lamaist pagodas, and behind these, standing on the highest point of the mountain slope, towers the awe-inspiring Great Red Terrace (Dahongtai). From the top of the terrace, the precipitous mountains take on the appearance of an immense jade screen.

The Great Red Terrace, built on the top of a huge
17-meter-high white terrace, is constructed of granite
blocks and bricks, and although from the outside it appears to contain seven stories, inside it is in fact only
three stories high. The outer faces of the terrace are
painted a plain red and the walls of the middle and
top sections are decorated with colored glazed figures
of Buddhas seated in arched niches.

In the central section of the Red Terrace there is a
square hall known as the "Hall Where Ten Thousand
Laws Are Reduced to One" (Wanfaguiyidian) which is
roofed with gilded tiles. Inside the hall are large numbers of images of the Amitayus and other bodhisattvas.
Here also is a statue of a goddess riding a demonic beast
with the figures of two children, part demon, part
human, in front and in back. According to legend, after
this beautiful goddess became a Buddha, she heard that
the Eastern Sea was being ravaged by a man-eating demon with an insatiable appetite. She volunteered to
save the inhabitants of this region, and bewitched the
demon with her beauty at their first meeting. She
agreed to marry him on two conditions — that he stop
eating people and cease plundering their property. The
demon agreed and they were married. The couple had
two children, but the demon's behavior did not improve,
and although he claimed that he had reformed, he kept
on with his evil deeds. The goddess learned the truth,
however, and one day made her husband very drunk
and killed him with her sword. She then mounted a
demonic beast and headed back to the Western Heaven.
The demon in fact had not died, and when he awoke
from his drunken stupor set out in hot pursuit. His first
arrow struck her steed directly, and today the statue of

the horse still bears the scar. The goddess' children, who were following along behind, were struck by his next arrows and transformed into semi-human creatures.

3. The Temple of Universal Peace (Puningsi). The Puningsi, situated on the western bank of the Wulie River, is the most easterly of the northern temples and occupies an area of over 30,000 square meters. It was built in 1755 during the reign of the Qianlong emperor on the model of the Samye Temple, the earliest Buddhist monastery in Tibet.

Inside the first courtyard of the temple is a pavilion containing a stela inscribed with the record of the temple's construction. The text, written in Han, Manchu, Mongolian and Tibetan, was composed by the Qianlong emperor himself. Behind the Mahavira Hall (Daxiongbaodian) on a stone terrace approximately nine meters high, stand a group of halls that comprise the center of the temple. Here in the Hall of the Great Vehicle (Dashengge), a giant statue 22.3 meters tall towers up through the building's five stories. Known as the Goddess of Mercy (Guanyin) with a Thousand Hands and a Thousand Eyes, it measures nearly ten meters around the waist and weighs 110 tons. Each of the fingers on its 42 arms is thicker than an average person's leg. On the head of the statue stands a smaller image, 1.2 meters tall, which according to tradition represents Guanyin's teacher Amitabha. His position on top of Guanyin's head denotes the high esteem in which he was held.

The Hall of the Great Vehicle is surrounded by a number of smaller halls and white terraces which have been arranged in a mandala pattern, which symbolizes the structure of the universe. The hall itself symbolizes

Mount Sumeru, the center of the Buddhist universe, and surrounding it are the "four greater continents" and the "eight lesser continents" which are described in the Chinese classic novel *The Journey to the West* (*Xiyouji*).

4. The Temple of Universal Happiness (Pulesi). This temple is also known as the Round Pavilion and was built in 1766 in honor of the representatives of the Kazak, Kirgiz and other national minorities who came to Chengde for audiences with the Qianlong emperor. The main building, the Pavilion of the Brilliance of the Rising Sun (Xuguangge), is famous for its caisson ceiling and unique wooden mandala, the only one of its kind in China outside Tibet. The temple's outer walls were once topped by eight colorful glazed tile pagodas erected on lotus flower pedestals, but now only one of them remains. Traditionally they are said to represent the lotus flowers that appeared at every step taken by Sakyamuni, the founder of Buddhism, when he was very young.

Of the remaining temples at Chengde, the Temple of the Image of Manjusri (Shuxiangsi) and the Temple of Universal Benevolence (Purensi) are both built in Chinese style. The Temple of Pacifying the Outlying Areas (Anyuanmiao) lies to the north of the Temple of Universal Happiness and was built in 1764 on the model of the Gu'erzha Temple in the Ili Valley. Today only the Hall of Universal Conversion (Pududian) remains intact. Inside this hall is a statue of the Queen of Conversion to Buddhism (Lüdumu). The walls are decorated with murals depicting Buddhist legends.

Eastern Qing Mausoleums (Qingdongling)

The Eastern Qing Mausoleums, located 125 kilometers northeast of Beijing, are among the finest and largest extant mausoleum complexes in China. Like the Western Qing Mausoleums (Qingxiling), the Eastern Qing Mausoleums are the sacred burial grounds of Qing emperors, empresses and imperial concubines. Situated to the west of Malanyu Village in Zunhua County, Hebei Province, the entire complex covers an area of 2,500 square kilometers.

The construction of the tombs was begun in the second year of the reign of Emperor Kangxi (1663). The main mausoleums include those of the following emperors, here listed with their reign periods: Shunzhi (1644-61), Kangxi (1662-1722), Qianlong (1736-96), Xianfeng (1851-61), Tongzhi (1862-75), and the Empress Dowager Cixi (died 1908). In addition, four mausoleums with 14 empress tombs, five mausoleums containing the remains of 136 imperial concubines and one mausoleum for princesses are also located here.

The Jingxing Mountain, which resembles a gigantic inverted bell, serves as a natural barrier for the area to the south. From the top of this mountain, one can look north across the valley of the tombs to the tall central peak of Changrui Mountain and follow its lesser ridges as they slope down gradually to the east and west.

The main entrance to the Eastern Qing Mausoleums is marked by a large white marble archway. Similar in design to traditional wooden memorial archways (*pailou*), its rectangular panels are carved with swirling patterns and other geometrical designs. Paired lions and dragons decorate the bases of the standing columns.

After passing through the marble archway, one comes to the Great Red Gate (Dahongmen), which serves as the formal front gate of the entire mausoleum complex. There is a stela tower containing a large stone tablet mounted on the back of a tortoise-like creature known as a *bixi*. This tablet, decorated at its top with carved dragon and bat designs — dragons symbolizing the emperor; bats *(fu)* as a pun on "good fortune" *(fu)* — is inscribed with the "sacred virtues and merits" of the Shunzhi emperor who is buried here.

Heading north after passing a small hill which acts as a natural protective screen, one comes to a road lined with 18 pairs of stone figures and animals. Somewhat smaller than their counterparts at the Ming tombs, these sculptures include military officers, civil officials as well as lions, camels, elephants and unicorn-like beasts. The road continues through the Dragon and Phoenix Gate and across a seven-arch marble bridge 100 meters long. The longest and finest of nearly 100 arched bridges in the mausoleum complex, it is called the Five-Tone Bridge after a peculiar acoustical phenomenon: by tapping gently on any one of the more than 110 panels between the bridge balustrades, the five tones of the pentatonic scale can be heard.

On the other side of the bridge is the Gate of Eminent Favor (Long'enmen), the entrance to the Shunzhi emperor's Xiaoling. At this point, one has covered a total distance of five kilometers from the white marble archway introduced above. Just north of the Gate of Eminent Favor is the Hall of Eminent Favor (Long'endian). This rectangular building rests on a marble platform which extends to form a terrace in front of the hall, and is surrounded with a marble balustrade. Inside the hall are provisions for storing ancestral tablets and carrying out sacrifices to the ancestors. A stela tower (*minglou*) stands directly behind the hall. The stela it contains is painted over with cinnabar lacquer and inscribed in Han, Manchu and Mongol scripts with the words "Tomb of Emperor Shunzhi." The stela tower is the tallest structure in the entire mausoleum complex and from here one may obtain a panoramic view of the entire area. The underground tomb of the Shunzhi emperor, who reigned as the first emperor of the Qing dynasty, has not yet been excavated.

The mausoleums of the Qianlong emperor, called the Yuling, and the Empress Dowager Cixi, called the Dingdongling, have been renovated and are open to visitors. The Qing dynasty attained its greatest power and prosperity during the reign of Qianlong. He was emperor for 60 years (1736-96), longer than the other nine Qing emperors and for three years served as regent for his son, the Jiaqing emperor. In 1743, after reigning for eight years, Qianlong began directing the construction of his mausoleum at a total cost of 1.8 million taels of silver. The underground palace occupies an area of 327 square meters and consists of three arched chambers. Although it is smaller than the Dingling underground palace at the Ming Tombs, the Yuling tomb houses finer stone engravings and sculptures. A detailed relief of the standing Goddess of Mercy (Guanyin) is carved into each of the eight leaves of the four double doors.

Behind the doors are meticulous carvings of the Four Heavenly Kings in sitting positions, each holding its own characteristic Buddhist icon: pipa (Chinese lute), sword, banner and pagoda. Other bas-reliefs cover the dome and the walls of the mausoleum: the Buddhas of the Five Directions, 24 miscellaneous Buddhas, as well as lotuses and Buddhist scriptures in Sanskrit and Tibetan. These carvings in stone are the finest examples of this genre to be discovered in any tomb to date.

The Dingdongling is located approximately one kilometer west of the Yuling. Entombed here are the two wives of Emperor Xianfeng: the Eastern Empress Dowager Ci'an and the notorious Western Empress Dowager Cixi. The tombs were constructed simultaneously and in the same style. However, Cixi was not satisfied with her "accommodations" and in 1895 her Hall of Eminent Favor and its eastern and western wings were torn down. The mausoleum rebuilt for her at the cost of 4,590 taels of gold is even more spectacular and extravagant than either the tomb of the Eastern Empress Dowager or that of the Qianlong emperor.

Cixi's Hall of Eminent Favor was rebuilt entirely of Phoebe nanmu wood and decorated with gold leaf. Yet since Cixi died before the work was completed, the underground section of the mausoleum remains quite plain compared with the Yuling of Qianlong. This is perhaps compensated for by the fine workmanship displayed in the marble slab set between the staircases in front of the tomb and the balustrades in front of the Hall: intricate carvings of lively dragons emerging from the waves and phoenixes hovering beneath the clouds, traditional symbols of the emperor and his empress.

Today, the Hall of Eminent Favor houses an exhibition of Cixi's clothing, articles of daily use and a number of other burial relics discovered in the underground palace — painting albums, pillows, quilts and her burial garments, including one gown decorated with the word *fu* (good fortune), another of satin embroidered with the word *shou* (longevity) and a dragon robe. The treasured "Dharani" or Sacred Verse quilt woven in pure silk and embroidered with gold thread is also on display. A total of more than 25,000 Chinese characters are embroidered on this 3-meter-wide quilt made in Nanjing.

Thirty-six burial mounds for the concubines of the Qianlong emperor are located in the mausoleum area. The first tomb mound in the second row of tombs to the east of the stela tower is that of Rongfei, who was buried here in 1788. Better known as the "Perfumed Consort" (Xiangfei), she was, as the legend goes, the daughter of a prince from Central Asia. Her burial garments and a fragment of colored satin inscribed in an undeciphered language were found in the tomb. Another magnificent tomb reputed to belong to the same princess was found at Keshi in the Xinjiang Uygur Autonomous Region. It contains a number of burial relics and articles of clothing.

Other minor tombs worth visiting at the Eastern Qing Mausoleums are the Xiaodongling, the tomb of Shunzhi's empress (died 1717); the Changxiling; and the Mudongling. Although these tombs have been excavated in recent years, many artifacts were stolen by Chinese warlords and foreign invaders. For example, in 1928 the warlord Sun Dianying closed the tombs under the pretext of using the grounds for military maneuvers. Actually, he and his troops took this opportunity to open and plunder the tombs of Qianlong and Cixi.

The Zhaoxiling stands alone outside the Great Red Gate. Although Zhaoxi, buried here in 1687, was a mere concubine, she received the title Empress Dowager because she gave birth to the child who later became the Shunzhi emperor. According to the Qing dynastic history, Zhaoxi's political influence in the early Qing period also resulted in the selection of her 8-year-old grandson as heir to the throne some 20 years later. When in 1662 this youngster ascended the dragon throne as the Kangxi emperor, Zhaoxi's title was raised to that of Grand Empress Dowager (Taihuangtaihou).

Western Qing Mausoleums (Qingxiling)

The Western Qing Mausoleums are located at the southern foot of the Yongning Mountains in Yixian, Hebei Province, 125 kilometers southwest of Beijing. The mausoleum area lies in a hilly region of great natural beauty and has a circumference of more than 100 kilometers. It is bordered by the Zijing Pass in the west, the ancient Yi River in the south and the former site of the secondary capital of the Kingdom of Yan in the east. To the southwest of the mausoleums is the Yunwu Mountain, site of the legendary Rainwater Cave. The whole mausoleum complex contains the tombs of four Qing emperors (Yongzheng, Jiaqing, Daoguang and Guangxu), three empresses, seven princes and a number of imperial concubines. The buildings occupy an area of over 500,000 square meters and were constructed over the course of two centuries.

The principal tomb of this imperial burial ground is the Tailing of the Yongzheng emperor (reigned 1723-35). It is often asked why Yongzheng chose to be buried in a new site rather than in the Eastern Qing

Mausoleums. One interpretation is that since Yongzheng ascended the throne in an improper manner, he was reluctant to be buried in the vicinity of the Jingling, the tomb of his father, Kangxi. To consolidate his 13 years' reign, Yongzheng did not shrink from imprisoning and executing his brothers and close ministers. He was highly suspicious and developed a system of spies to watch over the activities of his ministers. Other aspects of his peculiar personality are that he rarely left the Palace for very long, and began to look for a tomb site only six years after his ascension to the throne. At that time, he sent Prince Yunxiang, his most-trusted 13th younger brother, together with the able geomancer Gao Qizhuo, Viceroy of Jiangxi, Jiangsu and Anhui provinces, to the mountainous region. In 1790, the eighth year of Yongzheng's reign, they chose an auspicious plot to the east of Taipingyu. The tombs of the emperors after Yongzheng were distributed alternately between these two royal tomb complexes, in accordance with an edict of Qianlong. Thus the Jiaqing and Daoguang emperors were buried at the Western, while the Xianfeng and Tongzhi emperors were buried at the Eastern Qing Mausoleums.

Built between 1730 and 1737, the Tailing is the largest imperial tomb structure of the entire mausoleum complex and a natural starting point for sightseeing in the area. Along the "Sacred Way" leading to the mausoleums are a series of meticulously arranged buildings. To the right immediately inside the Great Red Gate (Dahongmen) — the main gate to the mausoleums — is the Dressing Hall, where the principal worshipper in the imperial sacrifice would change his robes before performing the rites. To the north of this stands a double-roofed hall, 30 meters tall, in which are found two tablets in commemoration of "holy virtue and merit." Outside the hall is a small open square with four ornamental white marble columns at its corners. Passing over a seven-arch stone bridge, the "Sacred Way" leads northward to a pair of mounting stones and ten pairs of stone sculptures (six of animals and two each of civil and military officials) which line both sides of the way.

Bypassing a naturally formed screen wall called Spider Hill, one arrives at the Dragon and Phoenix Gate (Longfengmen). Heading north one passes a small stela pavilion and three triple-arch stone bridges before coming to a large square, to the east of which are found the sacred kitchen and a well pavilion. On the terrace to the north are the eastern and western waiting rooms and the eastern and western guardhouses.

The Gate of Eminent Favor (Long'enmen) serves as the main entrance to the Tailing. Within the gate are burners for sacrificial offerings of silk and the eastern and western auxiliary halls, the former a storage place for sacrificial papers and the latter a temple where Lamaist priests chanted Buddhist scriptures. Both contain displays of cultural relics.

The Hall of Eminent Favor (Long'endian), the main building in the Tailing complex, was where sacrifices were conducted. Built with a double roof, it houses the thrones of the emperor and empress and a sacrificial altar. Behind the hall are two decorative gates, a set of stone sacrificial vessels and a stela tower (*minglou*) containing a stone stela which stands atop a square rampart. Beneath this rampart is the underground palace of the emperor. The Yongzheng emperor died suddenly in 1735, but it was not until 1737 that he was interred here with Empress Xiaojingxian and his concubine Dunsuhuang, who had predeceased him.

Not far to the west of the Tailing is the Changling of the Jiaqing emperor. The two mausoleum complexes are nearly identical in terms of the number of buildings and style of architecture and decoration. The rear square rampart of the Changling stands slightly higher than that of the Tailing. The floor in the Hall of Eminent Favor was laid with polished granite marked with natural purple patterns.

The Changling was completed in 1803, though Jiaqing was not buried there until March 1821, when the underground palace was sealed. In accordance with Qing dynasty practice, Empress Xiaosurui, who predeceased Jiaqing, was buried in the Changling, but her successsor, who died after the demise of the emperor, was buried separately in a tomb to the west of the Changling.

Five kilometers west of the Changling is the mausoleum of the Daoguang emperor, the Muling, built between 1832 and 1836. Soon after his ascension to the throne in 1820, however, Daoguang began the construction of a mausoleum at the Eastern Qing Mausoleum district, a project which went on for seven years. One year after its completion, however, it was found that the underground palace was flooded. Enraged, Daoguang laid the blame for this on those in charge of the construction work. The matter was settled when fines were imposed on those officials responsible for the site selection and construction.

In 1832, Daoguang went personally to the Western Qing Mausoleum area and selected a new site for himself. Work began that year and was completed in five

years. It was said that Daoguang attributed the flooding
to the fact that the construction work had deprived
serveral dragons of a home, forcing them to burrow
aimlessly for a new place to live. When he ordered
his underground palace built, he had the structures decorated with as many dragons as possible. The Hall
of Eminent Favor in the Muling is unique with its
nanmu wood checkerboard ceiling, each square
of which contains a carved, curled-up dragon, and its
unpainted nanmu beams and brackets carved in the
form of dragons. On entering the hall one notices immediately the scent of nanmu wood and countless
dragon heads with their cheeks expanded as if they
were spitting forth clouds. Although the Muling is
smaller than both the Tailing and Changling and has
no stela pavilion, stone sculptures or stela tower, the
quality of its workmanship surpasses that of the two
other mausoleums.

The site where the nearby Mudongling (Eastern
Muling) stands was originally reserved for the tombs of
the imperial concubines. Its name, however, was introduced for reasons explained above when an empress
of the Daoguang emperor was buried there.

The Chongling of the Guangxu emperor is five kilometers to the east of the Tailing. Built in 1909, it is
the last imperial tomb to be constructed although its
occupant was not the last emperor of China. That honor
belonged to the Xuantong emperor (Aisin-gioro Puyi),
who reigned from 1909 to 1911 and abdicated at the age
of six. Dying as a commoner in 1967, Henry Puyi, as
he was also known, unfortunately had no opportunity
to share the underground splendor enjoyed by his predecessors.

The construction of Guangxu's mausoleum was begun posthumously and left unfinished at the fall of the Qing dynasty in 1911. Funds provided to the former Qing imperial household by the Republican government enabled it to be completed in 1915. Though the Chongling is small in scope, and like the Muling has no stela pavilion, stone sculptures or subsidiary halls, the entire structure is nevertheless quite dignified. The elaborate drainage system still continues to function well.

East of the Chongling stands the mausoleum of Guangxu's concubines. The tombs contain the remains of the famous concubines Zhenfei and her sister Jinfei. Zhenfei became Guangxu's favorite by extending active support to the emperor's program of reforms, but for this she became an object of the Empress Dowager Cixi's enmity. She was subjected to torture, placed in isolation and forbidden any further contact with the emperor. In 1900, the Eight-Power Allied Forces invaded Beijing. As Cixi was fleeing Beijing she ordered her chief eunuch Cui Yugui to dispose of Zhenfei and, as the legend goes, he threw her down a well in the northeast corner of the Palace. Her body was recovered in 1901 and buried in Tiancun, a small village outside of Xizhimen. Her remains were interred at the Western Qing Mausoleums in 1915.

Beidaihe and Shanhaiguan

Beidaihe (Peitaiho) is one of the better known summer resorts on China's east coast.

> *As I approach Jieshi Hill from the west.*
> *The boundless sea extends before me.*

. . .

Above soughs the autumn wind.
The insurmountable waters swell below.

These lines, written by the famous statesman-poet Cao
Cao (155-220) to commemorate his visit to Beidaihe,
testify that the natural beauty of this seaside resort was
appreciated quite early in Chinese history. A number
of the principal scenic spots are described below:

Eagle Promontory (Yingjiaoyan): On a corner of
East Hill is an outcrop of bare rock known as Eagle
Promontory. With its pointed tip jutting out into the
sea, it resembles an eagle standing on one leg. A pavilion built on the highest point of the promontory provides the best spot in the area from which to observe
both the sunrise and the entire panorama along the
coast. A natural stone staircase descends to the beach.
Looking up at the pavilion from there one gets the feeling that this huge pile of stone may fall down at any
moment. A fine view of fishing boats in the misty
distance off Qinhuangdao can also be obtained here.

The Pigeonholes: Twenty or thirty meters from Eagle
Promontory to the right of the pavilion stands a huge
yellowish reef which rises abruptly from the sea and
extends nearly to the shoreline. Countless years of
pounding waves has scored the rock with cracks and
holes which serve pigeons as ideal nesting places. Visitors in the early morning and late afternoon can see the
lively spectacle of the resident birds flying about.

The Tiger Rocks: In the central beach area is a row
of huge rocks near the shore which become visible when
the tide ebbs. From a distance, these rocks look very
much like a group of lively tigers bathing in the sea.

Lianpeng (Lotus) Mountain, also known as Lianfeng Mountain (Mountain of Joined Peaks): The name of this mountain, which stands some 400 meters above sea level, derives from the fact that it consists of an eastern and a western peak. Densely covered with pines and cypresses, it offers a number of interesting vistas. On the western peak is the Conversation Rock, known also as Lion Rock, which is said to resemble a peach or a crouching lion in shape. Nearby is a tomb reputed to contain the remains of a Korean prince who died on the mountain in a battle with the Tatars. One may also visit the Stone Lotus Park, where beneath the shade of pine trees there is a host of rocks which resembles lotus flowers floating on the water. In addition, one may visit Tiger Cave, in which crashing waves can be heard; the Southern Gate of Heaven, a natural rock formation; the Fairy Cave, where female fairies who collect medicinal herbs are believed to spend the night; Tao-yuan (Peach Garden), an imaginary utopia; and Tong-tian (Connected with the Sky) Caves. Nearby Yansai Lake is an ideal place for rowing.

Late in the evening, the pleasant echoes of the bell in the Guanyin Temple (Temple of the Goddess of Mercy) lull visitors to sleep.

The Old Dragon Head (Laolongtou), the easternmost point of the Great Wall, makes a wonderful day trip from Beidaihe. The colorful name of this site is derived from the traditional description of the wall as huge dragon stretching across northern China. With its body winding its way into the Yanshan Mountains in the north and its head jutting into the Bohai Sea, the stony old dragon presents a magnificent sight.

Four kilometers from the Old Dragon Head is the

easternmost pass of the Great Wall, Shanhaiguan (The Pass of Mountains and Sea). Commonly known as the First Pass Under Heaven, it was built more than 600 years ago in the early Ming dynasty to defend the strategic six-kilometer wide coastal plain which lies between the Bohai Sea and the Yanshan Mountains.

Near the pass is the Temple of Menjiangnü, the Mengjiang girl. The touching tale of this woman, known to every Chinese, may be summed up as follows: During the Qin dynasty (221-206 B.C.), Mengjiangnü's husband was conscripted to work on the construction of the Wall. He died during the cold winter and was buried amidst the rubble in the base of the Wall. After many years of separation, Mengjiangnü came to look for him, and, when she arrived at the site where he had been assigned to work, discovered that he had died years before. Her crying was so loud that the section of the Wall where he was buried collapsed.

Convention credits the Englishman Claude William Kinder with the discovery of Beidaihe as an ideal summer resort at the end of the 19th century. But Kinder was hardly the first person to come here. Actually, ships called here as early as the Han dynasty, over 2,000 years ago. The Han Emperor Wu Di is reputed to have enjoyed the seaside beauty here and to have built a special observation platform for this purpose. Cao Cao, whose poem we read above, was another early visitor. Due to the growth of sea transport, the population of the area increased rapidly during the Ming dynasty and Beidaihe became quite prosperous. In 1898, the Qing government officially designated Beidaihe as a summer resort. However, in the following 50 years, the region developed very slowly. Except for foreign establishments such as the American and British government estates, there were few other buildings besides the private villas of Qing bureaucrats and warlords, such as Wu Peifu and Duan Qirui. In November 1948, Beidaihe was liberated. Since then, the People's Government has built highways in both the city proper and along the beach. Besides the restoration and enlargement of five parks, 3,000 new hotels, villas and sanitoriums have been constructed.

From Eagle Promontory in the east to the mouth of the Daihe River in the west, 22 swimming areas have been opened in Beidaihe's ten kilometers of fine sandy beaches. The average annual temperature is approximately ten degrees Centigrade, 26 degrees in summer. Breezes from the southeast cool the region, and even on the hottest summer days, the warm, calm water is ideal for swimming. Travelers from Beijing can reach Beidaihe conveniently by train.

Chapter 10
Famous Beijing Restaurants and
Chinese Regional Cuisine

Beijing Duck

The Quanjude Restaurant, the largest roast duck restaurant in Beijing if not in the world, opened for business in 1979. Located near Hepingmen (Peace Gate), it has a floor space of 15,000 square meters divided into 41 dining halls, including one which can serve 600 customers simultaneously. The dining halls reserved for overseas guests can accommodate a total of 2,000 diners, and include a hall where all-duck banquets in which all the dishes are made from parts of the duck can be served to 600 people. Filled to capacity, Quanjude Restaurant can serve as many as 5,000 meals a day.

The art of roasting ducks evolved from techniques used to prepare suckling pigs. For more than a century, specialized chefs have developed the idea that the skin of the duck should be so soft and crisp that it melts in the mouth. In applying the traditional method of preparation, the chefs at Quanjude pay particular attention to the quality of the duck, the auxiliary ingredients and the type of wood burned in the oven. Plump Beijing ducks weighing an average of 2.5 kilograms each are supplied by special farms. The dark tangy bean sauce

spread on the pancakes is supplied by the two famous
Beijing condiment shops, Liubiju and Tianyuan. The
fragrant sesame oil and refined sugar are also specially
selected. Finally, only the wood of fruit trees such as
date, peach and pear are used in the roasting process to
give the meat its unique fragrance.

The preparation of the dish requires a series of com-
plicated steps, which include inflating the unbroken skin
like a balloon so that it roasts just right. Quanjude
employs chefs who specialize in these techniques, while
other chefs prepare the non-duck dishes. Whereas in
the past the restaurant's staff numbered no more than
40, it has at present grown to over 800. Among them
are chefs and managers with records of 40 or 50
years of faithful service.

The slicing of the meat from the carcass of the duck
is an art in itself. A skilled chef is able to cut between
100 and 120 slices in four or five minutes, each slice with
an equal portion of both skin and meat. Inventiveness
is another quality cultivated at Quanjude. One
seasoned chef has mastered more than 80 dishes made
from the duck's innards, head, wings and webs. A
selection of these dishes, whether hot, cold, boiled, fried,
stewed or pickled, will be the makings of an all-duck
banquet.

The first restaurant to bear the name Quanjude
opened in 1864 during the reign of the Qing Tongzhi
emperor. Due to its high standards, the restaurant's
fame spread rapidly and for many years the supply of
roast ducks could hardly satisfy the demand. For this
reason, the restaurant was rebuilt and expanded in 1948.
In 1954 a branch (known as Hongbinlou) was opened
in West Chang'an Boulevard and another in Wangfujing

newest addition to the Beijing "duck family" at Hepingmen (described above); and the Sick Duck, so called due to its proximity to the Capital Hospital.

Restaurants Featuring Chinese Regional Cuisines

Chinese cuisine is characterized by its long history, distinct regional schools and immense variety. Tourists visiting different parts of China will have ample opportunity to taste local specialties, although many of the better known regional cuisines are available in the restaurants of Beijing.

The Beijing Hotel employs specialized chefs to prepare the famous dishes of Sichuan, Guangdong (Canton), Huaiyang and the Tan Family. Some noted Guangdong dishes are listed below:

(1) Roast sucking pig (*pianpi ruzhu*): Following careful roasting, the meat comes out a deep red color with a thin layer of shining fat. When served, the sliced meat is arranged on the plate in the shape of a pig.

(2) Sweet and sour pork (*gularou*): This famous dish is made of deep-fried cubes of pork coated with a slightly hot, sweet and sour sauce. It is a good stimulant for the appetite.

(3) Honey-coated roast pork (*mizhi chashao*): Marinated pork is hung inside a specially built oven and cooked to perfection. The saltiness of the meat itself is balanced by a thin coating of honey-flavored sauce which is spread on its surface. The lean and fat sections are equally tasty.

(4) Steamed mandarin fish (*qingzheng guiyu*): This
is listed among the ten great seafood dishes of Guangdong cooking. The dish requires careful control of both
the temperature and duration of cooking. The mandarin
fish is renowned for its tender flesh and relative absence
of tiny bones.

(5) Stewed giant salamander (*haigou* or *wawayu*):
From its rather shocking title, it is difficult to gain an
appreciation of this fish. However, it is held in great
repute in its native province. Rich and somewhat glutinous in consistency, the broth is particularly tasty while
the meat melts in your mouth. The dish is usually
served in the winter.

(6) Wrinkle-skinned pigeon eggs (*zhousha baige-
dan*): Set against a background of green vegetables, the
pale yellow eggs make a lovely sight. This dish fulfills
the three ideals of Chinese cooking — color, fragrance
and taste.

(7) Chicken with coconut milk (*yenaiji*): A recent
addition to the repertory, this dish is characterized by its
soft colors and tender textures.

Beijing Hotel also serves the cuisine of Huaiyang (a
region in the general vicinity of Nanjing). Notable
among these are butterfly sea-cucumbers, braised shark's
fin and stewed mixed seafood shreds (*haihui quansi*).

The dishes of the Tan Family (Tanjiacai) originated
from recipes of the family of Tan Zongjun, an official
of the late Qing period. The style is popularly known
as *bangyan*, the title given to the runner-up in the imperial examinations. Tan Zongjun, a native of Guangdong, obtained this title at the age of 27. During his
lifetime, Tan obtained quite a reputation as a gourmet.
His son, Tan Zhuanqing, exceeded his father in this

respect. In order to satisfy their highly refined tastes,
the chefs who worked for the Tan family were required
to come up with countless culinary innovations. With
the downfall of the Qing dynasty, Tan Zhuanqing lost
his official position and opened a family restaurant.

Tan Family dishes show the influence of various regional cuisines, the most obvious being that of Guangdong (Canton). Of one hundred "name" dishes, we
might mention such specialties as braised shark's fins,
Lohan prawns, steamed bear's paws and steamed duck
with ham. The Tan Family cuisine also includes de-
licious vegetarian, sweet, and cold dishes, as well as a
variety of desserts. These dishes have been enjoyed in
Beijing for more than a century.

Noted Sichuan dishes served at the Beijing Hotel
include crispy rice in tomato sauce and camphor-smoked
duck. But for more authentic Sichuan cooking, the
Sichuan Restaurant in Rongxian Hutong near Xidan is
also recommended. The restaurant is set in a former
noble's mansion with several inner courtyards. Its specialties include crispy rice with squid, shredded pork in
hot sauce, chicken and peanuts in hot sauce and fried
fish in hot bean sauce. Glutinous rice balls filled with
sweet sesame paste are a favorite snack.

The Fangshan Restaurant in Beihai Park features
dishes served at the Qing imperial court. To satisfy the
lavish tastes of the imperial family, the Qing court
established a large-scale imperial kitchen, though when
the 1911 Revolution overthrew the Qing dynasty, the
work of the chefs in this kitchen came to an end. When
Beihai Park opened to the public in 1925, Zhao Runzhai,
formerly employed in the imperial kitchen, gathered
some of the former chefs and opened the Fangshan

Restaurant on the very spot where the Empress
Dowager once took her meals. The restaurant faces the
park's lake and is set in the midst of a fine rock garden.
The traditional-style buildings contain 11 dining
halls distributed over three courtyards. In 1980, four
chefs formerly employed in the imperial court kitchen
were still working there.

The dishes at Fangshan are known for their del-
icacy, pleasing appearance and mild flavor. These
virtues are demonstrated in such specialties as sauteed
breast of chicken, braised venison, stuffed mandarin
fish, steamed duck with pigeon eggs, and citron rolls.
Hors d'oeuvres include a pastry made of ground peas,
kidney bean rolls, miniature steamed corn bread and
baked rolls stuffed with minced meat. It might be noted
that some of these dishes originated among the common
people and were "promoted" to a permanent position in
the imperial cuisine.

In recent years, the Fangshan Restaurant has begun
to reproduce the former Manchu-Han Feasts (Manhan-
quanxi) which were held regularly in Qing times. This
bountiful gourmet's marathon is served at six consecutive sittings. The dishes and desserts number nearly
two hundred, including over 130 hot dishes, 48 cold
dishes and a variety of pastries and fresh and dried
fruits.

In the past, the dishes for such feasts were made out
of ingredients received by the imperial court as tribute.
The feasts themselves were held to honor ministers, and
were a means of demonstrating the "might and prosperity of China" under the Qing dynasty.

The Manchu-Han Feast includes all the known and
available delicacies "from land and sea" in one lengthy

menu. The dishes fall into several distinct categories: the Eight Fowl Delicacies include wild goose, "flying dragon" (a species of pheasant from northeastern China), quail and swan; the Eight Marine Delicacies include swallow's nest, shark's fin, sea-cucumber, fish maw, fish tripe and abalone; The Eight Mountain Delicacies include camel's hump, bear's paw, monkey head, gorilla lips, leopard foetus, rhinoceros tail and dear tendons; and the Eight Vegetable Delicacies include monkey-head mushrooms, silver tree-ears fungus and sheep-belly mushrooms.

After more than three decades of inactivity, the Zhimeilou Restaurant reopened on Liangshidian Street near Qianmen in May 1981. The original Zhimeilou was famous in Beijing for serving the cuisine of Jiangsu Province. But in Qing times, many Manchu officials were especially fond of dishes from Shandong, and in 1842 the restaurant engaged a corps of chefs from that province and others from the imperial court kitchen.

Many of the dishes are taken from a precious old menu with a total of 700 dishes which was donated to the restaurant by Ma Dening, a former chef. These "lost masterpieces" include the "Dragon Boat Festival Shad Tribute" — a reminder that this fine fish was delivered from southern China to the Ming imperial court in Beijing; "Five Willows Fish in Vinegar Sauce," favored by the Qianlong emperor; and a seasonal dish known as "Sanniang Jiao Zi" (which may be translated as "Madame Sanniang Instructs Her Son"). The name for this dish is a pun on "Three Ingredients Dumplings" and was an impromptu creation of Empress Dowager Cixi. Another item on the menu is honey-preserved fruit, the recipe for which has been lost.

Zhimeilou serves such typical Shandong dishes as stewed sea-cucumber with scallions, chicken velvet, stewed mullet roe and chicken breast with peas. Some poetically named dishes from the Qing court include: Fried Dragon and Phoenix Shreds (sauteed chicken and carp shreds), Five Scholars Pass Their Examinations (a stew of chicken and duck breasts, pork fillet, prawns and kidneys), Swimming Dragon and Dancing Phoenix (braised cubes of chicken breast and squid), and Chicken Bits with Double Dragons (chicken with sea-cucumbers and eels). Lighter specialties include yam and date puree molded into the shape of peaches, and steamed dumplings filled with sea-cucumber.

In addition to the All-Duck Banquet and Manchu-Han Feast mentioned already, one more Beijing specialty must be mentioned. That is the All-Pork Banquet prepared by the Shaguoju Restaurant located near Xisi. The site of the restaurant was originally the quarters for the watchmen guarding the Mansion of Prince Ding in the Qing dynasty.

Shaguoju was founded in 1741. At that time, entire boiled pigs were used in sacrificial offerings in the Imperial Palace and princely mansions. Knowing that officials were fond of pork cooked in this manner, the watchmen bought a huge casserole dish and went into business. The name Shaguoju, which literally means Residence of the Casserole Dish, became very popular in Beijing, and a number of profit-seeking merchants opened restaurants serving similar dishes. As a testimony to its eminence in the field, the following couplet was hung up outside the original restaurant:

"Our name has prevailed in the capital for three centuries; The fragrance of our pork tops all rivals throughout northern China."

In fact, for several hundred years, Shaguoju has used the same large cauldron, some 1.3 meters wide and one meter deep, to boil its pork. The all-pork banquet consists of cold and hot dishes of deep fried, smoked and boiled pork products. The restaurant is also famous for its casseroles.

"Where do you get the tenderest mutton hotpot in Beijing? Donglaishun, without a doubt!" People well versed in the history of Beijing know that at the turn of the century, Donglaishun was merely a porridge stall at the northern entrance to the Dong'an (Eastern Peace) Bazaar. Three rooms replaced the former stall in 1906 when it began serving mutton hotpot and became the Donglaishun Mutton Restaurant. Its present three-story building dates from 1930.

Mutton hotpot is, of course, the most famous dish on the menu. Only the finest cuts of mutton bred at Jining in Inner Mongolia are used. Diners dip paper-thin mutton slices first into the water boiling in the chafing-dish and then into the prepared sauce before eating. This do-it-yourself cooking method ensures that the meat will be both tender and tasty. The hotpot season generally lasts from October to April. During the rest of the year, one may also sample roast mutton, shashlik, sauteed mutton fillet, stir-fried mutton slices with scallions and fried sheep's tails.

At the Moslem dining hall of the Cultural Palace of the Nationalities, an all-meat decorative cold plate is served, the recipe of which has been handed down through three generations of chefs belonging to the Ruan family. The more than 20 assorted dishes which make up this fine hors d'oeuvre include "The Pine and the Crane Under the Moon," "The Moon Reflected on the Sea," "An Egret Resting on a Lotus," "Three Sheep Ushering in Tranquility" and "The Emergence of the Phoenix."

At the Listening to the Orioles Restaurant (Tingli-guan) in the Summer Palace (Yiheyuan) eight dining rooms are set around two courtyards. Both the table-ware and the dishes here retain the characteristic features of the Qing imperial court. With its proximity to Kunming Lake, the restaurant naturally specializes in fresh-water fish. The menu includes an All-Fish Banquet and dishes and soups cooked with fish netted directly from the lake.

Below some of the other regional cuisines available in Beijing will be mentioned briefly: (1) Shandong dishes at the Fengzeyuan Restaurant at Zhushikou West Street; (2) Shanxi dishes at the Jinyang Restaurant on the same street; (3) Mongolian-style barbecue at the Capital Barbecue Restaurant on the banks of Shichahai Lake at Di'anmen; (4) All-mutton banquet at the Hong-binlou Restaurant on West Chang'an Boulevard; (5) Shandong dishes at the Cuihualou Restaurant in the northern section of Wangfujing Street; (6) Mutton you-eat-with-your-hands and grilled beef at the Qinghai Restaurant on North Dongsi Street; (7) Spicy Hunan dishes at the Chuyuan Restaurant on North Xidan Street; and (8) Kingfisher jade soup from Zhejiang, pork flavored with rice wine lees from Fujian, steamed chicken from Yunnan, and other popular southern-style family dishes at the Kangle Restaurant on Andingmen Street.

Appendix 1

A Brief Chinese Chronology

Xia Dynasty			C. 2100-1600 B.C.
Shang Dynasty			C. 1600-1100 B.C.
Zhou Dynasty	Western Zhou		C. 1100-771 B.C.
	Eastern Zhou		770-256 B.C.
	Spring and Autumn period		770-476 B.C.
	Warring States period		475-221 B.C.
Qin Dynasty			221-207 B.C.
Han Dynasty	Western Han		206 B.C.-24 A.D.
	Eastern Han		25-220
Three Kingdoms	Wei		220-265
	Shu Han		221-263
	Wu		222-280
Jin Dynasty	Western Jin		265-316
	Eastern Jin		317-420
Northern and Southern Dynasties	Southern Dynasties	Song	420-479
		Qi	479-502
		Liang	502-557
		Chen	557-589

Northern and Southern Dynasties	Northern Dynasties	Northern Wei	386-534
		Eastern Wei	534-550
		Northern Qi	550-577
		Western Wei	535-556
		Northern Zhou	557-581
Sui Dynasty			581-618
Tang Dynasty			618-907
Five Dynasties	Later Liang		907-923
	Later Tang		923-936
	Later Jin		936-946
	Later Han		947-950
	Later Zhou		951-960
Song Dynasty	Northern Song Dynasty		960-1127
	Southern Song Dynasty		1127-1279
Liao Dynasty			907-1125
Jin Dynasty			1115-1234
Yuan Dynasty			1206-1368
Ming Dynasty			1368-1644
Qing Dynasty			1644-1911
Republic of China			1912-1949
People's Republic of China			1949-

Appendix 2

Chronological Lists of Ming and Qing Emperors

Ming Dynasty (1368-1644)

Temple Name	Name	Reign	Reign Title
Taizu	Zhu Yuanzhang	1368-1398	Hongwu
Huidi	Zhu Yunwen	1399-1402	Jianwen
Chengzu	Zhu Di	1403-1424	Yongle
Renzong	Zhu Gaochi	1425	Hongxi
Xuanzong	Zhu Zhanji	1426-1435	Xuande
Yingzong	Zhu Qizhen	1436-1449	Zhengtong
Daizong	Zhu Qiyu	1450-1456	Jingtai
Yingzong	Zhu Qizhen	1457-1464	Tianshun
Xianzong	Zhu Jianshen	1465-1487	Chenghua
Xiaozong	Zhu Youcheng	1488-1505	Hongzhi
Wuzong	Zhu Houzhao	1506-1521	Zhengde
Shizong	Zhu Houcong	1522-1566	Jiajing
Muzong	Zhu Zaihou	1567-1572	Longqing
Shenzong	Zhu Yijun	1573-1619	Wanli
Guangzong	Zhu Changluo	1620	Taichang
Xizong	Zhu Youxiao	1621-1627	Tianqi
Sizong	Zhu Youjian	1628-1644	Chongzhen

Qing Dynasty (1644-1911)

Temple Name	Name	Reign	Reign Title
Shizu	Fulin	1644-1661	Shunzhi
Shengzu	Xuanye	1662-1722	Kangxi
Shizong	Yinzhen	1723-1735	Yongzheng
Gaozong	Hongli	1736-1796	Qianlong
Renzong	Yongyan	1796-1820	Jiaqing
Xuanzong	Minning	1821-1850	Daoguang
Wenzong	Yizhu	1851-1861	Xianfeng
Muzong	Zaichun	1862-1874	Tongzhi
Dezong	Zaitian	1875-1908	Guangxu
	Puyi	1909-1911	Xuantong

Appendix 3

GLOSSARY

Bei: A large engraved stone tablet used either as a memorial, to mark an important site or to announce a proclamation.

Bixi: A mythological animal resembling a tortoise. The stone pedestal that supported a stone stela was often sculptured into this form. The creature was reputed to have the strength to support a heavy weight.

Bodhisattva: see *pusa*.

Bu: A unit of length about 1.7 m.

Daxiongbaodian: (The Mahavira Hall or the Precious Hall of the Buddha) the main hall in a Buddhist temple. *Daxiong* is an honorable term for the Buddha signifying that his power is sufficient to subordinate malignant spirits. The hall was used for worship and for presenting offerings.

Devaraja Hall: see *Tianwangdian*.

Dian: In ancient times, a general term for large tall buildings. It was later used in the names of halls where gods and Buddhas were worshipped, or where the emperor held audience and handled state affairs.

Dizang: Sanskrit Ksitigarbha ("womb of the earth"), one of the four major Bodhisattvas of Chinese Buddhism. He is particularly important as a savior who delivers believers from the sufferings of hell. Worshipped at Jiuhuashan in Anhui Province.

Ge: A traditional Chinese building, often square, hexagonal or octagonal. The walls are often latticework panels which may be removed, leaving empty spaces between the supporting columns. It may be surrounded by low wooden balustrades that double as seats. *Ge* were used for admiring scenic views, resting after a stroll, storing books or worshipping the Buddha.

Gong: In ancient times, *gong* meant "residence," but later referred specifically to the residence of a monarch. It also referred to palaces of immortals, such as *Yuegong*, the Palace of the Moon Fairy or religious temples, such as *Yonghegong*. The term is now used to describe a place for cultural activities or an amusement center, such as *Wenhuagong* — Cultural Palace, or *Shaoniangong* — The Children's Palace.

Guan: A Daoist temple.

Guanyin: Sanskrit Avalokitesvara, a Bodhisattva. Also known as *Guanshiyin*, the observer of the world's cries. Originally a male figure, he was attributed with great compassion and mercy. Later he came to be represented as a female — the Goddess of Mercy. One of the four major Bodhisattvas of Chinese Buddhism, *Guanyin* is worshipped at Putuoshan, a small island off the coast of Zhejiang Province, near Ningbo.

Gulou: Drum Tower. The building in an ancient city which held the huge drum used to sound the hours.

Huabiao: An ornamental column usually made of stone, placed before bridges, palaces, city walls and tombs in ancient times. The stem of the pillar is often carved with coiling dragons and other designs, while near the top a sculptured cloud extends horizontally through the center of the column. A carved stone beast squats in a dish at the top. The finest extant *huabiao* are the two pairs to the south and north of Tian'anmen Gate (Gate of Heavenly Peace).

Hutong: A lane or small alley.

Jian: The smallest unit of a building. It can mean a room or the area between adjacent pillars in a large hall.

Jiaye: Another name for Kasyapa, one of the ten great disciples of Sakyamuni. According to tradition, he presided over the first synod and supervised the first compilation of the Buddha's sermons.

Kasyapa: see *Jiaye*.

Ksitigarbha: see *Dizang*.

Ling: The tomb of an emperor, his family and principal concubines. It may also refer to the tomb of important people in general.

Lou: A building of two or more stories.

Luohan: (Sanskrit) Arhat, a saint or perfect man in Hinayana Buddhism; the 16, 18 or 500 famous disciples appointed to bear witness to Buddhist truth and save the world.

Mahavira Hall: see *Daxiongbaodian*.

Maitreya: see *Mi-le*.

Manjusri: see *Wenshu*.

Men: a gate or door.

Miao: A temple for the worship of ancestors, spirits, Buddhas and Bodhisattvas, or famous historical figures.

Mi-le: (Sanskrit) Maitreya, the Laughing Buddha. A Bodhisattva often worshipped in China as a fat, laughing man. In the Five Dynasties period (907-960), a monk named Qi Ci was believed to be the reincarnation of *Mi-le* and his likeness was used as a model for the Laughing Buddha.

Minglou: Tower of Brightness. An open stela tower erected in front of a royal tomb. The stela inside the tower is engraved with the entombed monarch's name, title and accomplishments.

Pailou: A decorative or commemorative archway formerly built in key centers of a city, or in famous scenic or historical spots. It consisted usually of an even number of pillars topped by a series of rooflets.

Piluzhena: (Sanskrit) Vairocana. Literally, the illuminator. Regarded by many Mahayana Buddhist sects as the supreme Buddha. In monuments, he is always represented in the center of the other Buddhas.

Pusa: Bodhisattva, also commonly and indiscriminately used for religious images.

Puxian: (Sanskrit) Samantabhadra. The Bodhisattva of Universal Benevolence, depicted riding an elephant. One of the four great Bodhisattvas of Chinese Buddhism, he is worshipped at Mount Emei in Sichuan Province.

Rulai: (Sanskrit) Tathagata, one of the highest titles of a Buddha, meaning "one who has thus arrived." It was frequently used by the Buddha Guatama to refer to himself and implies one who has experienced enlightenment and will teach others how to achieve it.

Samantabhadra: see *Puxian*.

Shendao: (Sacred Way) A road built of stone slabs leading to a royal tomb for the use and enjoyment of the dead emperor in his afterlife. Bridges across the road were known as Sacred Way Bridges and stela pavilions along the way were known as Sacred Way Stela Pavilions. Stone figures and beasts as well as pine and cypress trees lined the roadside, giving the Sacred Way a solemn, majestic air.

Shijiamoni: (Sanskrit) Sakyamuni, the sage of the Sakyas. This is the most common title of Gautama Buddha, the founder of Buddhism.

Si: A Buddhist temple or monastery.

Ta: Pagoda or stupa. *Ta* is the shortened form of what in ancient times was called *fota* (Buddha pagoda) or *baota* (precious pagoda). Most *ta* are either square or octagonal in shape and were used to store sutra scrolls or Buddhist relics.

Taihu stones: Originally stones used for decorative purposes which were found in Lake Taihu (Jiangsu Province). The term now refers to any curiously pitted rock displayed individually or used in combination with others in the construction of artificial hills and rockeries. Taihu stones are frequently seen in traditional gardens and courtyards.

Tan: An altar used in ancient times as a place for making sacrifices to the gods.

Tang: A hall. In ancient times generally the main hall of a building complex.

Tathagata: see *Rulai.*

Tianwangdian: Hall of the Deva Kings, usually set at the entrance of a Buddhist monastery or temple. The hall usually contains the images of the "four heavenly kings who protect the world," a borrowing from Indian Buddhist mythology. They were the King of the North, Dhanada or Vaisramani, green-skinned and carrying a parasol in the right hand and a snow weasel in the left; the King of the South, Virudhaka, black-skinned and carrying a double-edged sword; the King of the East, Dhrtarastra, white-skinned and playing a pipa; and the King of the West, Virupaksa, red-skinned with a dragon coiling around his hands.

Ting: A small open pavilion generally built of bamboo, wood or stone and sometimes of copper or glazed tile. *Ting* were frequently constructed in parks and gardens or in famous scenic spots.

Vairocana Hall: see *Piluzhena*.

Wangfu: The residences of the highest ranking Manchu princes.

Wenshu: (Sanskrit) Manjusri, one of the four great Bodhisattvas of Chinese Buddhism. His hair is worn in five coils on the top of his head and he carries a double-edged sword to symbolize his wisdom and acuteness. *Wenshu* is generally depicted riding a lion to denote his wisdom and fierce might. Worshipped at Mount Wutai in Shanxi Province.

Xinggong: An imperial traveling lodge, or the government offices or residences where the emperor stayed when traveling away from the capital.

Xuan: A long corridor or small pavilion. *Xuan* was often used in the name of a scholar's private study, or to add refinement to the name of a restaurant or teahouse.

Yuan: 1. A courtyard. 2. The name of an ancient government office.

Yuan: 1. An orchard, flower or vegetable garden. 2. A park or place for amusement, e.g., *gongyuan* (park), *dongwuyuan* (zoo).

Zhai: A poetic name given to scholars' studies, bookshops, antique shops, restaurants and teahouses, etc., e.g., *shuzhai* (a study), *Rongbaozhai* (Studio of Glorious Treasures).

Zhonglou: Bell tower. The building in a city which housed a large bell used to sound the hours.

ISBN 7-80005-040-8

古 今 北 京

周沙尘　著

*

新世界出版社出版（北京）
中国国际图书贸易总公司发行
（中国国际书店）
北京399信箱
1984年第一版
1987年第二次印刷
编号：（英）12223—144
00800
12—E—1905 P